A Year Around the World

A Year
Around the World

A collection of letters by David Olds

Formatted and edited by Hannah Olds

A Year Around the World is a work of nonfiction.
Some names and identifying details have been removed.

ISBN: 978-1-7356147-0-0
eBook ISBN: 978-1-7356147-1-7

At the time of their writing, these letters were not intended to be read by the public. The statements made had not been thoroughly researched and may not be an accurate representation of the mentioned cultures or historical facts. This is a subjective description of a series of unique experiences.

Dedicated to my dad, David Olds.
Thank you for letting me share your story.

Contents

A Year Around the World

To view the photos taken on this trip, go to:

www.ayeararoundtheworld.wixsite.com/photos

Cardiff

Pre-October

November gets nearer with each item bought. The camp stove is the last item to be bought, and all items are stored ready for the off.

Memories of my injections still linger in my mind.

On seeing the doctor for my travel injections he inserted a large needled syringe into one bottle and sucked up the vaccine. He then inserted this syringe into another bottle and started to push the plunger down, at which point the bottle top shot off and squirted vaccine all over the doctor.

Trying again – this time the vaccine went in and mixed together.

"I always have trouble," said the doctor. This made me start to worry.

When the exchanging of vaccine was complete he pulled out the syringe, held it towards the ceiling to squirt some out, and the top shoots off.

PANIC– 'oh my god,' I saw this large needle and started to shake.

What will he do to me, I thought, if he can't get it right out of one.

He approaches, needle heading towards me, oh dear can I go!!!

He now searches for the right place and puts it into my arm and starts talking. I feel myself getting woozy, the room starts to go round. The doctor is still talking but I must do something – "Excuse me," I say, "I feel faint."

"Lay on the floor," says the doctor and continues talking.

When I finally got up and left the doctors my only thought was "oh goodness I've got to go back for the second one!!"

In trepidation I went back the following week. The nurse said the doctor was busy so she would give me the injection... What a relief!!! Any injections after that was child's play, nothing could be as bad.

Well, my injections completed except for hepatitis B, which I could not have until the week before we left, I am now ready to go.

I had bought a backpack for £100 and decided on its contents:

A medicine pack was essential, along with the usual sun tan and insect repellent creams. Then there were 3 T-shirts, 1 trousers, 2 shorts, swim trunks, a towel, wash things, sleeping bag, and maps. The final item a tent which was packed on top, and the whole lot strapped together.

Trial packs were made to decide the weight limit and luckily I got everything in I needed. Passports, insurance, and personal documents were to be carried in a waist belt.

October

It is now October and time to leave my job. I had given in my notice a month before and received many well-wishes from the people I work with. They were interested in what I was doing and wanted postcards sent to be able to follow my journey round. Everyone was very nice, and so with some regret I completed my final day.

I moved my belongings from the house I had been renting into my mini and headed home.

There had been several journeys home over the last few months, taking my music centre, computers, guitars and synthesizers home. So, with the last items including my bike piled into the mini, I was off.

Goodbye Cardiff.

Goodbye house.

Goodbye to a good two years of my life.

Hello World.

Chapter 2.

Home with Mum and Dad will last three weeks before we depart on November 17th.

When home I have friends from schooldays I keep in touch with, so these last weeks were busy ones with visits and 'nights out'.

On deciding to do this tour I wrote to several people in other countries in the hopes of collecting addresses as stopping off points. So while at home I received several letters back from people who were willing to put us up. There is a world of travellers out there, people who have travelled around and are willing to put people up. By talking to these people a lot of information can be gained.

It is our last week in England... The hepatitis B finally placed into my posterior.

I am ready – months of planning and waiting are over.

Sat 16th Nov:

The final pack of my backpack was made. Passport, cheques, tickets- yes all of them there. Banbury station, here I come.

The next train leaving the station is the 3:15 to Paddington.

Goodbye Mum.

Goodbye Dad.

See you in a year.

The train pulls away – Paddington station is very busy and I am due to meet Mark, whose train from Cardiff was the same time as mine. So I look for a bright blue backpack.

Sonesta Beach Resort

Hurghada

Hello,

Well, as you can see, we made it here. Hello Mum, happy birthday for last week, hope you enjoyed it in Tenerife.

O.K. I've got a lot to tell already so I'll try and write as much as I can. Starting at the beginning: Flight to Cairo was good, a nice plane (747) with a lot of empty seats. Landed at 9 p.m. roughly on time – temperature 17°C. Going into the airport we were 'assisted' by a tourist office woman to get through the controls, and then she passed us on to a 'friend' who would sort us out accommodation. In fact, he took us to a little office and tried to flog us tours for £25. We got passed on again and taken to a hotel in Cairo about 12 km away from the airport. £10 a night each we paid. We knew we'd been done. Next day we went into the city to search for accommodation and found a hotel with a double room for less than £3 (£1.50 each). If you're a standard tourist and get nabbed at the airport you don't realize how cheap it is here. That tour for £25 we did for less than £3.

We stayed in Cairo for four days. It's a really chaotic city, the driving is just unbelievable. No use of lanes, horns going every second. There are no breaks in the traffic so you have to stick your neck out to cross the roads. To see the number of people in the city makes London look like Northend, 18 million in the day. To catch a bus the people wait in the road and leap on as it moves past. Sounds easy, but twenty people leap on as twenty people leap off. We took a trip to the sights around Cairo, out to pyramids etc. What is left is pretty awesome, 4 ft high stones in a 500 ft high pyramid. All around is sand, so where they brought them from I don't know. Many pyramids in the desert.

Toured the museum, saw Tutankhamen tomb stuff. So much was crammed into the tomb, all gold covered. The mask and coffins are so detailed. He was covered in gold when wrapped, covered with a gold mask, put in a gold coffin shaped like him with face, hands, etc. which went in a larger version of the same, which went inside a third coffin, which then went inside a series of massive wooden boxes inside one another, all covered in gold and very detailed. Masses of sculptures and mummy cases in the museum.

Walking through the touristy main part of the city is pretty bad, but we walked out of the centre into an older area. There are street stalls, people trading food off the mud on the floor, poverty and disease all around. Either horses or donkeys hanging up in butchers. We think they were donkeys as they still had the tail on, although they had been skinned.

In the tourist area it's probably worse in that we get hassled all the time by shop owners trying to get us in to buy junk. They chat you up in the street, really friendly, and then try and con you. We got wise to that quickly and used them to get info on where things were, etc., before making a sharp exit. Food is cheap, well everything is cheaper than home. We had a kebab from a street stall for 20p, but we didn't ask what the meat was.

We looked around Cairo and went up Cairo Tower to overlook the city – looks a very nice place from up there, with a river through the centre. A few miles away from the Nile is just desert. Temperature in the day is around 25° or more.

Caught a train down from Cairo towards Luxor – cost us £3 each for 400 miles first class – 10 hour trip. Seats good – loads of room. Travelled during the day (Friday 22) so we could see the scenery. Beside the railway was an irrigation channel, so greenery and palms were all around. In the distance was again desert. The country life looks so laid-back compared to the chaos of the city.

Got off before Luxor to head towards Hurghada. Only way there is by taxi. We eventually got a 'special', a large car with eight passengers and all the bags. We headed off away from the Nile into the desert with music blasting. Two and a half hours later we got to the coast, and after another half hour we got to the hotel. For two and a half hours all we saw was desert, well, that was when the driver had his headlights on, which he didn't do much. What a trip. Cost us about £5, and I think we were done! Walked into Sonesta Resort to check in, looking rough and travel worn, had not had a decent wash for a week. Very posh place, if they could have refused us I think they would have.

The apartment is quite nice and the hotel grounds are very well-kept. By Egyptian standards it is very expensive here. In this area are a few resorts such as this one, all self-contained, with their own shops, restaurants, etc. The town is a fair distance away and the area is full of development, half-finished resorts. It'll be nice when it's finished! This resort is the only 5-star place in Hurghada. It is quite quiet here, as it seems to be in the whole area, and it seems Germans are the main visitors, although we have been chatting to a couple here from Rogerstone, S. Wales!

The apartment is quite large, two bedrooms, but being a hotel there are no cooking facilities apart from a small grill/oven thing. The staff do everything for you. It has a nice pool, which is where I am now, soaking up the 30° heat, and a private beach with nice clear water. It's now Monday, and yesterday we went on a snorkelling trip for the day in a boat, from here an hour along the coast. We stopped first a way offshore near some coral reefs. The crew threw bread in the water and masses of fish appeared. The water is so clear and the fish are all shapes and colours. We snorkelled through the coral and hundreds of different fish. Brill! Later we ate on a boat (fish!) and stopped off on a beach nearby. We got away from the Germans we were with and walked up onto a dusty hill to overlook the water. So many different colours of blue. Snorkelling on the beach there were still masses of fish feeding off the sea bed.

We're taking it easy today, as tomorrow we shall leave here. It's early, but we haven't long in Egypt and we want to see Luxor where all the tombs are. It's been nice to have a break here, as although we've only been gone a week we seem to have done loads. This was the easy bit.

After being in Luxor for a few days we will probably get a train to Cairo and fly out to Bombay as planned.

Soon, I will probably be sending a couple of films in the post for you to get developed as it is very expensive to do films here. If you do get them get two sets of each, 7"x 5", matte, by that postal one, costs £6 per film. The first two are of Cairo, pyramids, and a couple here. Cheers.

We are both fine anyway, and as I guess you've worked out, having a good time. I'll phone soon,

David.

PS. I've put in a card of the resort they gave me. It shows reception and shops.

Somewhere in Bombay

1/12/91

Hello all,

Everything is fine. Hope all's well at home. Ok, so on with the info I guess. No time for idle gossip. Last time I wrote I was in Hurghada at the apartment. We left there on Tuesday the 26th and caught a bus (five and a half hours) to Luxor through the desert in the daylight this time. It's just sand and rock, although every so often you'd see a woman walking goats in the middle of nowhere. Met an English couple catching the bus who are doing the same sort of thing. On some flight to Bombay. They were going to Luxor to go back to Cairo. They knew of a hotel in Luxor, so we headed straight there from the bus. Not bad, with a double room costing us nearly LE8 (£1.50) (75p each). Dumped our gear and went out to get train tickets to Cairo. Luxor is a lot quieter and nicer than Cairo, with a few more restaurants it would seem. Had a great meal. They just threw food at us. We had some nice potato things in some sauce as a side dish. Excellent. Soup and chicken, rice, potatoes, salad and bread and drink cost £1. Walked around town, bazaars were now surging into action. Mark and Lisa knew their way around, so we tagged along. Clothes were very cheap. Mark haggled a bloke down from 23 to 7 pound for a T-shirt (£1.20). Town was very lively and there was a good atmosphere in the bazaars and cafes. Had a mint tea and game of cards with the others. Nice to have company, as there have been very few British travellers so far. Our hotel is very popular with tourists/travellers. Owner is a good bloke, called Ali Baba. Mark and Lisa were off the next day so we arranged to meet in Cairo before our flight.

Wednesday – Up early to see the Valley of the Kings, which are the tombs of the dead kings where many of the artefacts were found. It is across the Nile and three miles away, so we hired bikes for LE3 for the day. Good bikes. Got a ferry across the river and cycled to the tombs. Some of the tombs are under people's houses. The whole area is dust and rock, with the possibility of hundreds of tombs remaining unfound under the dust. Valley of the Kings is really lots of holes in the ground. We tagged on to a tour group and got a guided tour of Ramses VI tomb, probably the best that was open there. The detail and amount of work and different colours is unbelievable, and we got to hear what it all meant. It was a passage 200 m long with paintings and inscriptions on the walls and ceiling. The tomb itself was massive with detailed work all over describing how the soul would travel to the underworld and how the sun god blows the sun from east to west (life to death), which is why the dead are buried on the West Bank. Saw a few more tombs, all very detailed. Cycled through the desert and rock and found a temple cut into a rock face. There are holes in the rock faces all around. Valley of the Queens was not so impressive. Hot in the desert.

We ate in the hotel, with special treatment from the owner. Nice, his soup is very good. Cheap again. Could live on £2 a day if you wanted. Still very hot. Thursday we walked to Karnak Temple on the outskirts of Luxor. Biggest place of worship in the world. The Hall of Columns is amazing. 134 pillars 60 ft x 6 ft down, with hieroglyphics all over. Obelisks there are massive, the tallest 30 m high, 320 tons of solid granite. Unfortunately most of the details are crumbling and in 100 years there may not be much left. We tagged on to a tour group again in the temple to get information. We can laugh because we know this mob have paid a packet for their tour! Sculptures etc. massive and impressive.

Sunbathed on the roof of the hotel, 30° again, although they tell us winter is arriving. In summer it's 45-50°. Looking over the rooftops, Luxor looks the pits. It's not too bad on the ground. You get used to it I guess.

While in Luxor we tried the fruit drinks they sell from shops at the roadside. We had a banana drink. Milk, something else, and four liquidized bananas. Really nice and healthy too. Next day had a drink; banana, orange, mango, and strawberry. Nice too. All fruit is squeezed there. Luxor was a nice change from Cairo and the hotel was good, shame to leave. Got a train early Friday to get us to

Cairo for the flight out. We couldn't put back the flight, which we would have liked to do, as there is loads more to see of Egypt that we didn't have time to do. Next time! Train took 11 hours this time, arriving around 6 p.m. The Nile valley away from the towns is very beautiful, with palms and greenery. They grow masses of sugar cane, which they drink at the street fruit stalls (that was the something in our drink!), liquidized of course.

We had no trouble finding Mark and Lisa in Cairo as planned. Trying desperately to spend our remaining money, as it was no good outside (cannot change). Had a Kentucky Fried Chicken meal, one of the few western-style places in Cairo. Large meal for £1 again. Got a taxi to the airport after trying to tell the driver where we wanted to go (did he understand?). No language problems in Egypt overall, English very well spoken by most we met. Lucky really, Arabic is such a hard language, with dots and squiggles for writing, though I did suss out the numbers.

Arrived at the airport about five hours early. Met some travellers (Australian), so we had six of us to check in on the same plane. Together? No chance, spread out all over the place. The flight left 3 a.m. Saturday morning. Five hours in the air. I had been awake 26 hours by the time we landed. Registered and through check-in no problem. We headed for the railway station to sort out our trains. A taxi took us through the city. Very busy, passing streets where people had set up home with sticks and sheets or corrugated iron on the roadside. Beggars came up to the taxi every time we stopped in unmoving traffic. The taxi was a wreck, as are most. Not many other cars, just millions of taxis and three-wheel moped taxis. Overpopulation again. Funnily enough, the area where we have found accommodation is very nice, and today (Sunday) we walked around and it was quiet and quite clean. Staying in a Salvation Army hostel, costing 55 rupees for B&B (£1 to 45 rupees), so very cheap. We arrived very tired after around 30 hours on the go. Had a sleep and then a three-course meal for 22 rupees (50p). I hope it stays this cheap!

Sunday, got up for breakfast which was very good. The Salvation Army place is full of travellers from all over, some of whom have been going years, all with useful info and gossip. Pictures of the queen all around! The tea is really good here too. Took a boat trip to an island just off the coast from Bombay. Old dodgy boat, which took one and a half hours to get 10 km. That was the deluxe one as well. The non-deluxe must be rough. It's ok, we were insured for 0.5 rupees (1p) if it had sunk.

Arrived at the island (very nice place), but the boats didn't moor. The water was disgusting. We had to get off the boat onto an even dodgier boat to be punted ashore. Excellent. Soaking up the culture. It's so easy here, with most people speaking English, even the Indians. With seventeen languages I guess even Indians can't communicate with each other any other way. Not much to see on the island, apart from some caves which were in fact temples cut into solid rock off the hills. Locals seemed to go there for picnics. Being Sunday all the families were out. They play cricket everywhere.

After a trip we braved a curry in a restaurant nearby. Better than at home and still very cheap. From what we have seen so far, although very little, India should be really good, and it's unfortunate we only have a couple of weeks.

So, overall, Egypt was really good. The fact it was cheap made up for it being fairly dirty. The Egyptians are very friendly really, and the culture is wildly different from home. Where we fuss to be comfortable with modern possessions, none of that matters there. Western products haven't got there yet. I don't think we could sell them cheap enough. If you accept it as different it's a place not to be missed.

Now it's Tuesday 3/12. Yesterday we walked around Bombay after talking a couple of hours and sorting out a train out of the city. We leave tonight on a fifteen-hour trip to Ranthambore National Park, where tigers, leopards etc. hang around. Should be good. Then Delhi, Agra, Bharatpur Bird Sanctuary before leaving India. We have a 15 day rail pass, so we will be out by around the 18th. Shame, I'd like to stay a lot longer. Another excellent curry last night for around 50 pence.

OK. Say Happy Christmas and New Year to everyone there. No presents this year (what's new), but you never know, if I see anything worthwhile on my travels you may get a parcel home.

Love,

David

P.S. I've entered info on Egypt I want to keep – cheers.

Info on Egypt

Tourism is obviously Egypt's aim, which is shown by a visit to Hurghada, where 'holiday resort' developments are being thrown up at a rapid rate, with, at the moment it would seem, no hope of filling them. The four-hour trip, by bus or by car only, is well worth it when you reach the different blues of the Red Sea. Snorkelling or diving in its waters reveals hundreds of multicoloured fish of different shapes and sizes in amongst the life of the many coral reefs. Due to its popularity with German tour operators, Hurghada is expensive when compared to other areas of Egypt.

Egypt at present is very cheap. With LE6 to £1, a night's accommodation costs as little as LE4 a night in parts. Food is interesting, with most dishes being chicken or meat, very unnerving when skinned donkeys can be seen hanging in the streets. Food from street stalls is cheap and edible, being kebabs or sort of meat sandwiches in the main. Small shops sell fruit drinks of squeezed orange, mango, banana, or mixtures of all that seem tasty and healthy too. Streets seem to be lined with plenty of shops selling very little in each.

Entertainment for locals is sitting in the streets smoking tobacco? from water pipes. Religion seems to dictate most people's lives, with many mosques and calls to prayer at very unsociable hours.

All together is it very interesting and makes life in Britain seem far too routine.

Without the Nile, Egypt would not and would never have existed. It has brought life to its banks, with the vast fields of sugar cane and palm trees contrasting with the barren desert only two miles from the river. The towns and cities are filthy, with shoddy housing and dusty streets. Even so, with the ancient Egyptian treasures of the pyramids, tombs and museums, the beauty of the Red Sea, and the welcoming people, the country is very worth a visit.

Cairo highlights the problems Egypt has, with, in its centre, large plush hotel blocks on the river bank for the rich tourist. A ride away are the crumbling, half-finished buildings of the poverty-stricken locals, who survive by selling anything they can from the dust and dirt of the roadside. Overpopulation brings the centre of the city to total chaos, with the unending noise of car horns as drivers and pedestrians fight for space. A white face brings cries of 'Welcome to Cairo' round every corner, which is usually intended as an opener to some sales pitch.

Tourism has not yet hit Egypt in a big way, which makes a visit to the pyramids seem quiet compared to Cairo. Even here, though, camel or donkey rides are offered every minute. 'No' is not really understood. The sight of the pyramids, sphinx and other works, along with the hieroglyphs and paintings, and of course Tutankhamen's treasures, makes you wonder how Egypt lost such skills and talent. Today they cannot build anything very well.

On train to Delhi

10/12

Hello,

I'm still fine. Hope everything and everyone there is fine and all set for Christmas. You'll have to tell me what's happening if you write to Kathmandu. We are on schedule and due to be there January 7th to the 14th of January '92.

Where shall I start. Basically having a brilliant time in India. It's just so much better than we were led to believe. Things have been fairly easy up until now. I think I last wrote from Bombay around 3/12. I have to write these letters every week, as so much happens every day that I can't remember all the fine detail if I leave it longer.

On Tuesday 3/12 we left Bombay and the Salvation Army hostel. We spent the day in the museum and walking round the city. The museum had an amazing collection of animals and birds. It showed India is so vast and varied that really every type of animal lives in the country somewhere. We had a 'special lunch' in a small restaurant, which turned out to be a tray with eight small pots of sauces and mixes, some nice and crispy things. We didn't know quite what to do, although the locals made gestures that we should mix them. Mixed up it was so good and very filling, all for 20p.

Walking around the city a local lad came on to us and talked for a half hour. He took us to a place where they cremate people, a little yard with five metal grates, in open air. They fill the grate with wood, put a body on, more wood on the top. Ashes then go in the ocean, which is obviously why the sea was so dirty. Anyway, there was one alight when we saw it. Death is such a strange thing here, and this place was for the poor dead who couldn't afford a proper cremation. Made us think.

Anyway, we caught an overnight train from Bombay to Sawai Madhopur in Rajasthan, leaving at 9:15 p.m. We had a seat in a section with six seats, three facing three, which converted to six bunks. Things were fairly cramped when it came to baggage as well, but we were quite comfortable and slept well. We chatted to an Indian army officer on the train. They are treated very well and respected here. His wife was a dentist or doctor I think, and earned 8,000 Rs a year (£200). We had reserved our places on the train on Monday, with the computer reservation system. The setup is amazing, for so many people using the train. On arrival to get the train they post a list of all the seats and who sits in them, so we checked our names on there. We left at 9:15, and after fifteen and a half hours arrived <u>exactly</u> on time at 12:45 a.m. Wednesday morning.

We left the station after a coffee to find the tourist office in Sawai Madhopur. Wow. The man there sorted us out accommodation at a Rajasthan Tourism Development Corp hotel, in a dormitory for 25 Rs a night (50p), in five minutes. We went straight there. We dropped our bags and in ten minutes we were on a safari straight from the front door of the hotel. At Sawai Madhopur is the Ranthambore National Park. It is an area of around 400 km^2 of protected land with various animals in it. Jeeps run people around, but we got on the RTDC minibus, which was actually a truck with twenty seats in the back, so it was open air. The trip through the park took over three hours, with the scenery just stunning. We started around 3 p.m., seeing monkeys, deer of many types, all sorts of birds, and crocs and driving through dusty tracks through trees, dry river beds, and past large lakes. It started to get dark by 6 p.m. and quite cold too. To cap off our trip we saw one of the 42 tigers in the park. It just padded along casually by the side and across the road. So big and powerful, but stunning. Some people do many trips without seeing anything. The day had just gone so smoothly we couldn't believe it! Perfect way to finish.

The dorm we had was quite large and as it happens there was only us two in a room for six, so that was good. Not many tourists here, which is even better! We are off the Thomas Cook tour route now! Real India. Thursday 5/12 we got up at 6 for the early safari. Sunrise through the park. We saw and heard things come to life in the trees and lakes. We stopped many times on our way round. Only six were on the truck. With the engine off, parked on a cliff top, we had a cracking view and heard only the sounds of countless bird cries. It was such a change from the hassle of the city, and very relaxing. We saw eagles, vultures, more deer and crocs. The scenery looked even better in the morning light. No tiger today.

We sat in the sun in the afternoon. We were quite a highlight for some local kids who were watching us over a hedge. They definitely don't get many tourists here. A walk through the 'town' proved that, with all the signs in Hindi and being given strange looks, but still everyone is friendly. I think once you get away from the tourist traps, where the locals just want money, you see the real people, more of which we experienced in the next two days.

We left Friday for Bharatpur, three hours by train, which has a 30 km² bird sanctuary. We got there and traded to an RTDC hotel there to stay in a dormitory for 20 Rs a night. By this time we had made friends with a girl called Joanne from Wythall, near Birmingham. The dorm had a few other travellers in it. By the time we were in it was around 5, so we went to eat. Six of us, three English, one Israeli girl, a German and a Dutch guy were eating at a real local eating place. No 'tourist' would do this. It was basically a straw roof, with a few pots and stoves under it, and a few benches and chairs out in the open. The locals all got up to let us sit down. It was like a special occasion to have us there. The food was brilliant, a sort of mish-mash of vegetables, potatoes, carrots, other stuff in a spicy sauce. With rice, masses of chapattis, and chai (sweet milky tea). It was nice and really cheap. We stayed after eating and played backgammon. Some locals came over and watched with interest and although they spoke no English and us no Hindi we had a great time trying to communicate, as both they and us didn't stop laughing.

We got up really early on Saturday, and using our rented bicycles we peddled into the sanctuary about 500 m from the hotel. There were now four of us, me, Mark, Joanne and the Israeli, Yofeet. Spent hours cycling around. In the centre were swamp-like lakes with trees in them. These were full of storks and various other nice but unknown birds. I could have done with Chris to tell me what they all were. My camera was not powerful enough to get any good shots, but anyway it was really peaceful and nice to see. The kingfishers we saw were a dazzling bright blue. So many different sorts of birds all mixed together. Around the edges of the park it was dry and dusty, with deer and crocs and other animals. We saw an otter, buzzards, and plenty of other things (showing my animal knowledge here). On cycling round we saw a young calf stuck in the water's edge in the mud. Some Indian children were near so I got two, who were already plastered in mud, to pull the animal out by the ears. The kids were very excited to see us.

We headed straight out of the park and saw some young lads who looked ten years old playing cricket. They shouted to us so we went and joined. I haven't played for ten years, which is just as well really. We were there about an hour and had a great time. I don't think they see many foreigners here.

We ate in the same place as the previous night, this time seven of us. Food was good again. The little lad who served us was really interested in what we did and was very funny. Sat and played cards and backgammon and talked to others for ages, getting more info. All for 50p.

We left there thinking what a great day we had had. We heard some music up the street, so we went for a look. It was a wedding party down the street. There were about 50 men all dancing inside a circle of lights, which was actually a horse and cart with a generator on, and around a dozen children each carrying a box with two of those tube-type strip lights in, all connected together by a ring of wire. This party had a cart at the front with music coming from it and some brass band players in the crowd of people. All this moved slowly down the street. The groom was on a decorated horse, wearing a fancy turban. All his friends drank and danced while he headed to marry a woman he had probably never seen. The party was heading for the bride's house.

We thought we would look and go, but straight away people came over and shook our hands, inviting us to join in. They all seemed honoured we were there. The groom's father shook our hands with excitement. A lad who spoke some English looked after us, telling us about the wedding, etc. The party was wild, so many people talked to us, all very friendly. We were, of course, pushed into dancing and got hugged afterwards. The party continued some hour later at the bride's house, where the groom met the bride. We were invited to the reception tent for coffee and food and then to the ceremony. We felt imposing, mainly because this sort of thing would never happen at home, inviting strangers (who weren't related) to a ceremony. It was interesting to see. They exchanged flower necklaces and that was it. Photos were taken and we left, otherwise we would have been there all night.

Every day we do something we think we can't better, but the next day we do.

We left next (Sunday) morning to get a bus from Bharatpur to Fatehpur, an old city now deserted, about 40 km from Agra. The bus was a wreck with few windows, with bikes and people on the roof. Felt like the lad in the Building Society add – you know, 'stepping in the footsteps of older wiser people' (or something like that).

Fatehpur Sikri was an amazing place. Fatehpur was the holy part of the old city, and in the centre is a marble tomb with very fine detail. We walked through the very quiet 'ghost' town, which was still in good condition, built a few hundred years ago. Mostly temples for the ruler. A local guy befriended us and took us to the 'tomb of the elephant,' a tall tower just out of the town. We sat on the top away from the crowds, overlooking the green fields. So quiet. This was just a day trip on the way to Agra. We caught the train around 5 p.m., arriving in the darkness at Agra. We had a card of a place in Agra from the German in Bharatpur, so we tried to get a rickshaw there. It took ages, as we went up and down the same street trying to find it, for which they wanted more money! No way.

When we arrived at Agra it looked pretty rough in the dark, and there was a power cut. The streets were mad, with hardly any lights on bikes or rickshaws. The "Mumtaz Mahal" was in darkness and we scrabbled around by candlelight. Place was O.K. for 25 Rs, for a double room it's our cheapest yet. Still hadn't shaken off Joanne! We thought that we hadn't been on our own since Hurghada, which was good. Pigged out in the local restaurant for 25 Rs!

Monday 9/12 was Taj Mahal day. The Taj was near the hotel so we walked there. When you walk through the gates it just hits you. The Taj looks beautiful from a distance, with shining white marble, a large dome, four towers, a mosque of red sandstone on each side and a line of trees and pools in front. Not that busy, so we could really appreciate it. Getting closer you realize why it took 20,000 people 22 years to build it. The outside is covered in carvings, but more impressive are the insertions of precious stone, cut and inserted to form flowers and writing. Inside is even more spectacular, with a tomb just plastered with inlayed flower patterns, each leaf a carefully shaped piece of precious stone. Priceless. The inner tomb was surrounded by a decorative marble fence, sculpted from solid marble into a lattice of patterns. Each must have taken five years of work. The sound inside is surrounding, with a cry echoing for ten seconds and a hum all around. The work involved to create this memorial to an emperor's dead wife – Mumtaz – just cannot be imagined.

A walk to Agra Fort followed. This large fort of red sandstone is built next to and along the river from the Taj, giving a good view from the roof. The stonework here was impressive too.

Stuffed ourselves on some good samosas and gulab jamun, some sort of doughy ball in honey syrup. Overheard someone talking of a place called Dayal Bagh Temple, still being built. After the fort we took an auto rickshaw ride through the grubby, ox-filled streets of Agra to the temple. After seeing the Taj Mahal and the work involved there, here we had a half-built temple after 87 years of work, scheduled to take 200 years, with people still working on it. We were taken behind the scenes by a worker there. This is not a tourist place so they seemed to like to see us. We saw how one solid piece of marble is marked and chiselled by hand, with a simple piece taking a month. The inlay work was just amazing, with one piece of hard precious stone of colour cut, ground, and shaped over a period of two or three weeks. There are literally thousands of these!

Old men sanded large columns of marble. To see them still working, and with very little modern help, is amazing. The workers asked that we take their photos and send a copy to them.

As it started to get dull, we went back to the Taj to see the sunset. It was nice to sit and watch it as the marble changed from white to pink to a silhouette as the sun went down. Had some more nice spicy food as Joanne tried to make us think with some of those lateral thinking questions. On the way back from the Taj, Mark had a shave from an old bloke in a shaving shop. He put his thick glasses on as he picked up a nasty looking razor. Not me.

Now on the train to Delhi. We shall be here for a few days before we head to Nepal around the 18th of December. It's Mark's birthday today – although I think we're pushed to do anything special after the last few days!

My hand has worn away now, so have a good Christmas and New Year and I'll think of everyone as we sit up a mountain somewhere. I'm so glad you got the photos. The first couple of films aren't brilliant photos, as it's a bit too typical, but you'll get an idea of what we've seen in terms of 'sights', though unfortunately not the day-to-day things. I hope from my letters you can work out what's what and where. Have fun.

Love,

David

PS. I forgot to say that at the wedding they all told me how I looked like the No. 1 film star in India, Aamir Khan (or something like that). It's funny, in Egypt they said I looked Egyptian.

Also, I've been told to mention how intelligent, witty, charming, and attractive (for a brummie) Joanne thinks she is, but we hope we can dump her in Delhi soon!

Pokhara, Nepal

19/12/91

Be prepared for a novel

Hello everyone,

So, I hope Christmas went well and you didn't miss me too much! If you got this before New Year, have a good one. If not, I hope you had a good one. I think that covers the good wishes, just to add that I hope everyone's keeping well under the winter cold. I'm looking forward to getting to Kathmandu to receive the mail from you (Oh, I hope you did send it there!), as it's tricky to write without knowing what's going on there.

OK, I'll carry on with my adventures. I left off in the last letter heading for Delhi on the train. We arrived at 11 a.m. Stepping out of the railway station we hit the traffic and crowds, and it was complete madness. The streets were solid with auto rickshaws (scooters made into three-wheel taxis), cycle rickshaws, oxcarts, and thousands of people. After a few quiet days this was a shock. Searched around for a place to stay for a while, and in the process had a puncture on our auto rickshaw. They are so badly maintained. There can't be any motor or road laws here. His tyre was down to the cords. The one he replaced it with was no better! Found a cheap hotel. Delhi is more expensive than most other places, being busy and the capitol. 75 rupees a double room. It was in an area not that far from the station, off the main bazaar, a long street of stalls and shops selling nearly everything (all Indian products of course), and very busy. We headed off into the city centre to find the Nepalese Embassy to sort out our visas for the next leg.

It was closed. We went for food and had a great Chinese meal. Back at the Embassy – No they don't do them in the afternoon – come back tomorrow. That's fine, but it was a long way there. We walked around and down to the India Gate – one of our relics, built by the Brits in the 30's to commemorate 90,000 soldiers who died in WWI. It stands, with an eternal flame, at the end of a mile-long straight road that leads to the large official buildings of parliament. This is probably the best road in India, and people obeyed the traffic lights. All along the sides people were setting up rows of seats and stands. We think it must be for the Independence Day (Republic Day) celebrations on January 26th. (They work slowly over here!). As it was about 3 or 4 p.m. now, smog came down over the city making it hard to see the buildings clearly. You could feel the dirt in the air when you breathed. The sun was shining, but blotted out by this cloud. Was around 23°.

Walked back to Connaught Place, a large circle at the centre of the city full of shops, banks, hotels, etc. Traffic was just unbelievable. Being a circular road, there is never a gap in the traffic and it's never stopped by lights or police.

This meant you had to risk it to cross the street. A wide road one way, which meant as many as four or five 'lanes' of rickshaws and scooters (very popular to get through traffic). It took twenty minutes to cross that street, just like that computer game 'Frogger'!

We had a struggle to find a restaurant, but found what was by our standards 'dead posh'. Celebrated Mark's birthday, and the food was very good. Now we know what all the different dishes and things are, easy. In the darkness the smog is very thick, with the vehicle lights, when they use them, being just about visible. I can see how this would be a shock to your system if you flew in here straight from the U.K.

The next day we took our time. Decided it was time for a decent wash, after all the travelling, etc. My hair was all clogged up from the dirt in the air of the city. 3 rupees for a bucket of hot water got me sorted for the day, and washed my clothes too!

Very busy this day (Wednesday 11/12). Went to the Nepalese Embassy and got our visas done, booked ourselves on a city tour for the next day (Thursday), and booked our train ticket out. Already we were looking forward to leaving. Decided to walk to Red Fort around two miles from the railway station. On the way we met a huge procession/carnival that moved slowly, if it moved at all. It was, we discovered later, a Sikh celebration of a 'martyr' day. It took ages to get through the crowds, thousands were involved, and it went on for miles. A whole day's celebration, bringing the city to a dead stop (nothing new there).

Walking through the streets of the city is quite entertaining. Their shopping areas are grouped; one area all the shops sell bathroom fittings, next area they all sell pumps and generators, etc. If you want all sorts of things it's a lot of walking.

The fort was OK, it was red, but nothing special. Heading back to the hotel we got down a wrong road (not lost) which was very muddy and had live chickens in cages, fish stalls, food being cooked in the street. Very interesting to see. Met Joanne (still with us) at Wimpy's, one of the few western things, although prices are extortionate. Had a cheap meal elsewhere and headed back to hotel. The main bazaar had a carnival going down it (now around 8 p.m.). Sat on the roof of the hotel watching the goings-on. Free food was given out, masses and masses of flowers, music, etc. Good atmosphere and the people seemed to be having a great time. It seems hard to imagine in the U.K., but we are now so used to walking down streets past lepers and beggars, avoiding cats and bicycles and scooters, which in turn go round cows or pigs resting in the middle of the filthy, rubbish-filled roads. Cycle rickshaws act as goods carriers, often stacked ten feet high with produce, which are then sold off carts, stalls, or the ground. It also seems hard to believe that people can make a living with such simple 'jobs', so many street sellers selling only bananas, of which you can get a bunch for say 3 Rs. It's just a world apart from the West.

Thursday saw us getting up early for our DTDC morning tour of the city. On the five-hour tour, we saw Jantar Mantar, an observatory (not as we think of one) of stone columns and arches, positioned and marked so the sun would indicate times, latitudes, and astrology. How did they work it out, I wondered. (Built around 1700). Next we saw a Sikh temple. Had to take off our shoes and cover our heads. Interesting to have a Sikh describe his religion, equality for all, etc., and hear the things this very new religion has endured. They look after their own, free food for anyone who goes to the temple. Haven't seen a Sikh beggar yet.

Next we saw a Hindu temple, 1938, but not too impressive, a bit grubby. The symbol everywhere was the swastika, symbol of goodness and purity. The Germans stole this as well then.

We drove on the bus through the slums of the south city, little areas full of canvas shacks that had been thrown up. Just past this we stopped at a large temple, Baha'i, built in 1986. The grounds were beautiful and the building impressive, although you wonder about religion when they spend 100 million Rupees (£2.5 million) while two minutes down the road is in such poverty.

Last stop at Qutab Minar, the 'first city of Delhi' built way back. At the centre a tower 238 ft high. Couldn't do a tour for a whole day, as it began to get tedious, with only twenty minutes at every place. We retreated in the afternoon, waiting for the night train out of Delhi at 9:15 p.m.

When we went to the station it was hard to work out where to go, as the platform was packed. The train was two and a half hours late, and we had a hassle getting our reserved seats. I had seat No. 13 on Friday the 13th! Long trip, although slept OK on the bunk. Arrived in Varanasi, our destination, to the east of Delhi some sixteen hours later at 4 p.m. (Friday). Booked in to the tourist bungalow just five minutes from the station. Beds in a dorm were 20 Rs (40p). By this time we had changed our tagger-on from Joanne to Larry, a middle aged (45) South African, travelling, very cautiously, on his own. He was with us all of the two days here. Interesting to hear about S.A., and now we've got somewhere else to stay on our list. He spoke Hindi as well, so it helped us find our way around the maze of a city.

Varanasi is one of the holiest places for the Hindus of India, with the Ganges being the real heart. The dormitory had a lot of mosquitos and bed bugs, and an unsociable occupant, but we survived.

A walk through the quieter, but still busy, streets; more animals roaming, and going down to the river was a nice change from Delhi. Sitting by the river was just great, watching the goings-on of the people washing themselves, their clothes, and the water buffalo in the river. The river bank has hundreds of 'ghats', or series of steps, down to water.

One of the main reasons for the pilgrimage of the Hindus to Varanasi is to die or be cremated by the banks of the river. A couple of the ghats are burning ghats. Bodies of the dead are brought in, wrapped, and carried on bamboo poles. The cremations are done on the ghat. A pile of wood is built up, a body is put on, a bit more wood, and then blessed. A shaved-headed, cloaked man lights the fire, of which there were around ten on the go while we watched. Sat and watched as more fires were lit and more bodies brought in. The ashes ended up in the river, so the water was stinking. Small bodies, obviously children, were taken out and dropped in the middle of the river. Very interesting, so many watching, fairly unconcerned with the things they saw. Walking back from this area we wandered through a maze of narrow alleys, all full of stalls and people cooking. We booked ourselves on the bus trip (two days) to Pokhara in Nepal for Monday, 175 Rs including a night's accommodation on the border.

Sunday (15/12) we sat out in the sun on the lawn in the hotel grounds. Walked down to the river again in the afternoon. This time we went on a boat along the river. The water really was dirty. Apparently if you have a sick relative you fetch water from here, they drink it (!!) and recover (?). Holy water, you see. In the evening we spoke to a couple who had just come into India from Nepal. They told us how much we would like it.

Monday- Up early at 7 a.m. for our 8:30 a.m. bus towards Nepal. Free breakfast, not much though. The bus was reasonable, as Indian buses go. Argued with some bloke about putting our bags on the roof when the bus was half empty. The trip, which took nine and a half hours, was a bit of a bone-shaker, the Indian roads aren't good. We stopped very often to pick up unofficial passengers. Really though, the scenery meant that the trip wasn't boring, seeing an elephant working, a classroom in a field, and many other interesting goings-on in the countryside. The northern area is a bit greener, with banana plantations and crops growing. In all our travelling in India we haven't seen any rice fields or many fruit trees, so where is the vast amounts they eat or sell on the streets grown? We had a supply of bread and biscuits for the trip.

We arrived at Sunauli on the Indian side of the border at 6:30 p.m. We had our Indian visas checked for departure. An old guy pondered for ages whether I should be allowed out, as someone called Patrick David was on a blacklist and there was a 'David' on my passport. Escaped eventually. We then had to walk 100 yards across the border to Nepal where our visas and forms were checked/stamped OK, and through the non-existent customs. We had a night's free accommodation in the Nepal Guest House, next to the border. A small room, but was quite good, mosquito free and comfortable. It was so strange, but as soon as we crossed the border it just seemed so much more easy-going and friendly.

We ate at the guest house and paid in our few remaining Indian rupees. We had done our stint in India for an unbelievable £100 for two weeks, which for two of us is £25 a week each. We were done to some extent, in that we were misled by Indian Railways into buying a rail pass for fifteen days, costing $65 or £40 each. The actual cost of trips we did on the train would have been £20 without a pass. So overall two weeks cost me £90. (Although should have been £60).

Had a good sleep there, ready for our 8:30 a.m. departure to Pokhara, about nine hours away. The bus for this trip was a bit rough, broken windows etc. Bags went on the roof, later joined by many passengers and the odd goat. The bus was packed all the way, although some Nepalese let us have two seats. We again stopped every five minutes to pick up or put down someone, usually in the middle of nowhere. The first hour of travel into Nepal was flat land. The houses were nice brick ones, all very organized, so different to the mud huts of India. When we reached the mountains the road was just frightening. It wound its way through the fairly small mountains about halfway up, with a river a long way down on one side, up and down for eight hours, like being on a roller coaster with stunning views. As we came nearer Pokhara we saw the snow-capped mountains and then dropped into the Kathmandu valley. Now, in darkness around 6:30 p.m., we saw the lights of the small town and many individual lights of the many hillside houses spread through the mountains.

On arriving in Pokhara we knew we wanted a hotel near the lake, so we went to 'Hotel Florida' in the dam area. The town had many hotels, all spread out along a few streets. The houses, shops, etc. are even better than India again. The hotel is good, very clean and cheap. At £1 to 77 rupees (official rate), we payed 80 Rs for a double room. We settled in, and at 8 p.m. walked across the road to K.C.'s restaurant. The hotel faces one end of the Fewa Lake, by which Pokhara is built, and is on the opposite side of the road. Anyway, at K.C.'s restaurant they had all sorts of good food. After rice and more rice in India, treated myself to steak and chips and salad in some great sauce. It wasn't beef steak, probably buffalo, but still it was the best. Followed by a chocolate cake and coffee, all for only £1.50. After living through virtually vegetarian India this was heaven. The steak etc. was cooked on a cast iron plate, which was then put in a wooden plate to bring to us, still sizzling. The night now began to get quite chilly.

Early morning Wednesday the 18th we woke up and stepped out onto the balcony. The mist rolled across the lake. At the rear balcony of the hotel you could see the snow-capped mountains starting to shine white in the morning. Just brilliant.

We had a lot to do and sort out for our month in this country. We headed for the tourist information office, having a coffee with 'special' milk (goat?) and cakes on the way. A man there told us how he found London great but expensive. Got info on Pokhara.

We wanted to find out about trekking, rafting, and visiting Chitwan National Park. We had heard that to get a trekking permit you have to officially (with a bank) change $20 for every day of your trek. Unfortunately you struggle to spend $5 a day up in the mountains, and you can't take money out of the country and it's hard to change it back. This would mean you'd have to buy loads of stuff you didn't really want. The alternative is to get a black market permit, needing no $20 a day charge.

We walked through the small town, positioned in probably the best scenery we've seen yet. It's very quiet, the season just finishing. That's in our favour as everyone wants our business. Inquiring about rafting and Chitwan, we could get a two-day river raft (white water), camping on the river bank one night, followed straight after by three days (three nights) at Chitwan National Park in a resort there, for only $85 (£50). This includes everything, all the transport, rafting equipment, food, and a whole series of things in the park; elephant rides, canoeing, jungle walks, all organized for us. Brilliant value. They would also take us to Kathmandu after, saving a day's travelling.

We pondered whether to get an official or unofficial trekking permit over lunch. Could we spend $280 in four weeks, of which two would only cost us $80? No. A travel agent offered us both types of permit, the unofficial one and a legal permit, but something underhand meant we didn't need proof of money charge. This would cost us more than the official one, but save us money in the long run. Also, it meant we could change our traveller's cheques on the black market, getting 88 Rs per £1 instead of 77!! so making things cheaper again. So happy with this that we had a beer by the lake's edge, 50p a pint, with sunshine and beautiful scenery and friendly people all around.

In the evening had another brilliant meal, soup, main course, chocolate cake, two coffees – £1 (Jealous?).

Thursday (today) we had a cracking breakfast on the water's edge in a cafe opposite the hotel. Nice views again. Sorted out our trekking permits then hired a boat for four hours and went out on the lake. Peaceful and relaxing just floating along. Got right up to the far end of the lake. On heading back we found a very strong current against us, and for ages we seemed to get nowhere. Hard work to get back in time. Around the lake's edge are hills lined in trees, probably full of wildlife. Treated ourselves to another beer. Walked along the shops on the lakeside, looking for equipment rental and jumper stalls. The shops are, in the main, those types, so it's not hard to haggle prices down. We want to rent jackets and sleeping bags for our trek. Bought a woolly hat and thick wool jumper. So many nice clothes, and wool jumpers are a specialty here. Jumper and hat cost about £5. Should keep me very warm. It's hot in the day, but up the mountains at night at 2,500 m it can get below freezing.

Have just had another nice meal, barbequed chicken, etc., and of course another large slice of creamy cake! The trouble is it's so cheap you can't buy enough. As we'll live on rice for two weeks it's worth pigging out while we can.

Another relaxing day tomorrow before we start our two-week trek on Saturday (21st). We want to be at the popular stop-off point on the trek for Christmas Day on the way up and New Year's Eve on the way down. It's about the only place you can get a decent meal (not dal and rice) on the trek, and has hot springs to bathe in.

Should be back in Pokhara on the 3rd of January '92, ready to start our rafting/jungle trip on the 6th–10th of January. Kathmandu then, until our flight out to Bangkok on the 14th.

O.K. So I know it's long, but when I get writing it's hard to stop. I guess really these letters are for my benefit, so I can remember in detail what we did. Hope you didn't get too bored. It's hard to describe how beautiful it is here and I can't wait to do the adventurous bits.

I'll write again after I've had the letters in Kathmandu, if there are any, and tell you how we survived. So far Nepal is just brilliant, everything you could ask for, and the locals are all so friendly, always smiling and laughing.

Take care, I won't ask how this or that is, as I know you'll tell me when you write. Send any more mail now to Sydney. We'll probably stay in Thailand longer than planned, so getting to Australia mid-February. So any mail after now basically.

Still healthy etc.

Love,

David.

P.S. Can you photocopy this if you can, as Mark will want a copy when we come back. Thanks.

Hotel Florida, Pokhara

Nepal

5/1/92

Hello all,

Hope everyone's OK and had a great Christmas and New Year. I'll tell you about mine in a bit. At the moment I'm sitting by the lakeside in Pokhara in the sun, taking it easy after our two-week trek up the mountains. Can't remember where I got to when I last wrote, probably around the 20th of December, when we hired a boat and went on the lake, sorted out our trekking permits, etc. On the 20th we got up and had the misfortune of bumping into Joanne, who we had left in Delhi about a week earlier, who was by chance staying in the same hotel out of hundreds in Pokhara. As she was looking for a company for a trek we allowed her to come with us, having to sort out our permits that day. We hired down sleeping bags and jackets for the trek as it was said to be cold up in the mountains, costing all of 10p per day per item. Bought an embroidered T-shirt for just over £1 and a thick jumper for about £4. The clothes are all pretty nice and cheap, with loads of little stalls selling all sorts of things. Had yet another steak and large cake that day too, I think.

On the 21st we started our fourteen-day trek up into the Annapurna mountains, heading for Muktinath at 3,700 m. Pokhara is actually at 900 m. The walk up is around 150 km (90 miles) scheduled to take seven or eight days, coming back more or less the same way. I'll explain the trip as a whole before I go into daily detail. I'm sending a map of our trek route and the photos I've taken. I've had four rolls of film developed here, as it is fairly cheap and we wanted to see some. Some are really good. The numbers on the map are photo numbers on back of the photos, so you could see the changing scenery as we went along.

We started off from Pokhara, climbing to around 1,500 m the first day, dropping down to 1,000 m, and climbing again to Hille (1,500 m) the next. Quite a strain to go down and climb up finishing at the same height! We then climbed up into what was by now snow-covered mountains to Ghorepani at 2,800 m. Christmas Eve we dropped to Tatopani at 1,100 m, where we spent Christmas Day. The next few days we climbed back up again finishing at 3,700 m, where the land was barren and snow-covered. We came back the same way, reaching Tatopani for New Year's Eve, arriving here on January 3rd.

The scenery on the trek back was amazing, not so much for mountains, but how the landscape and plant life changed from one day to the next. First a river valley, the next a damp, moss-covered forest coated with snow. Further up we had mountains, dry river beds, sprawling rivers, and pine trees, which the next day became like a desert with rock and little plants, then the next just snow-covered mountains. The changing scenery kept us going, as each day was usually a good seven hours walking which seemed to be mostly uphill. The accommodation at this particular trek was good, little 'guest houses' in every small village. This trek is probably the most popular, with paths well-defined, built for local trade. We timed it well, as it has just passed peak season and so was very quiet. The food in the guest houses in the main was good. There seemed to be a standard menu issued to these places from above, although one place's interpretation of a dish would be very different from another.

Even at 3,700 m you could still get a Coke, which had been carried up by either donkeys or porters, in glass bottles! The food was typically rice or pasta dishes, pizzas, or Chinese, all cooked from fresh, as we were often the only customers. Electricity and hot water don't really exist high up; cooking was done on wood burning brick stoves.

Interesting things to see were the men carrying massive loads up slippery, rocky paths with no shoes, donkeys and a yak or two blocking it often. Very hairy paths, grubby half-dressed children shouting 'namaste' and asking for 'school pen'.

If you look at the photos you'll see that our brilliant planning came off again, having just a brilliant Christmas at Tatopani, which has hot spring pools, and the best place for food on the whole trek. Christmas Day we soaked in the hot pools, next to icy rivers and snow-covered mountains, and had a great meal of chicken, duck, turkey and buffalo steak (all of these) – menu photo (it's not a choice of meats!), with a pint of beer for 50p, and a good crowd of fellow trekkers!

All in all, I think it was hard going in parts, with a few days suffering from dodgy stomach and fatigue, but well worth every step of the 180-mile round trip.

O.K. now for the detail, hey! I'll use the photos to help.

Day 1 – 21/12

Set off from Pokhara about 9 a.m. after a massive breakfast – was this our last decent meal for two weeks? Walked around the lake and started a serious climb from the 900 m above sea level of Pokhara to the 1,500 m to the top of the first hill. It seemed to take ages to get up, and stopping halfway up we hoped it wouldn't be this hard every day. When we reached the top three and a half hours later we fortunately had a fairly flat walk to our first night's stop of Naudanda, arriving around 5:30 p.m. At this height the surrounding views were terraced fields of rice and mustard (photos 1 & 2) with the fairly wide rocky path well inhabited. Naudanda appeared over the hill, along with a road from Pokhara which takes an hour by bus! Stayed in a guest house there for 10p a night and had a disgusting curry, which made us all ill. Views of mountains good (3), perched on a ridge (4 & 5), although quite hazy.

Day 2 – 22/12

Naudanda to Hille.

Followed the road for a while before turning off onto a stony path through Chandra. Dropped down from 1,500 m to around 1,000 m at Banthanti on a river (6, 7). Really nice river valley, river a bright blue. After a lunch stop we had to climb back up a steep hill heading for Tirkedunga (8,9). We had our first rain since we left the UK and had to stop at Hille. Stopped at a small guest house, where we sat in the people's kitchen by the fire to dry. We were the only guests so we were well looked after. Great house – a wooden house with candles.

Day 3 – 23/12

Climbed up from Hille to Ghorepani at 2,800 m, hearing they had snow there. Passed by barefoot porters with large loads strapped to their heads (10). The scenery changed to thick moss-covered forest (11) as we got up into the snow (12 & 13). It was hard work to climb up. Luckily we stopped at a place for lunch with a nice fire so we dried our wet clothes from the day before. Arrived up in the misty mountaintop at Ghorepani (14, 15, 16). Climbed right to the top to stay in a guest house – Super View Lodge. Nice place full of other trekkers of all nationalities (OK, around ten people). Nice fire and very cosy. There was an inch or two of snow so it felt Christmassy. Very misty, so views not all that good (17 & 18).

Day 4 – 24/12 – Christmas Eve

Up early on this crisp morning. Looked good in the snow (19, 20, 21). Better views in the morning (22, 23). Started our easy day descending from 2,800 m to 1,100 m to Tatopani ("Hot water"). Passed a load of donkey trains (24, 25) sometimes having to wait ages for them to pass on the very narrow paths (26). As we descended we had some great views of valleys (27, 28). Scenery was different on the side of the hill, no longer forest but sparse trees and terraced fields. Arrived at Tatopani early in the afternoon. What had taken us around ten hours to climb 2,800 m had taken about five to come down. Checked in to what was recommended as the place to be – Kamala Lodge. Food was excellent. After lunch we went down to the hot spring pools that have been made in the river valley to get a decent wash and clean up (29). Our first for four days. Pools were really hot, but next to the ice-cold river (30, 31). In the evening we had the best meal since we left Pokhara, they serve all kinds of food there, rather than all veggie stuff on the way to here. Good crowd of trekkers there and so we spent the evening celebrating Christmas, singing, and sitting up until midnight to celebrate Christmas Day.

Day 5 – Christmas Day – day off

Spent the morning in the hot spring pool in the river valley (32, 33, 34, 35, 36, 37). I think that was what they call bliss. Really hot. It had snowed in the mountains again. Climate here is good, although we did have a bit of rain. Citrus growing area (38). After our soak, back for the Christmas special menu (39). I bet you wondered what I'd eat. We got all the meat on the menu, a great soup, and a massive cake. The meats were all cooked on steaming cast iron plates (40). The others there were entertaining and so we had a great time, but obviously not as exciting as being at home! The whole meal cost £2.50, which really was quite expensive. Beer was 50p for over a pint bottle, so we made the most of it (44). We were kept going in the afternoon by Ella from Leics, who was like a human dustbin. With the Xmas meal we had hot buttered rum, which was disgusting. She was bet 500 rupees that she could drink it in one, which she did and used the money to buy nine bottles of beer. After eating her second Christmas dinner and a few more beers, she was bet 300 rupees to drink a quarter pint of tomato sauce (43), which of course she did. And guess what, with her winnings she bought another six beers. Within half an hour she was dancing with the rest of us, as a little party began, with no after-effects (44-49). The Nepalese were very entertained by everyone's dancing (48). A great day!

Day 6 – 26/12 – Time to move on unfortunately.

We had brilliant mountain views from our rooms (although doesn't show on 50). We headed up the valley to climb Kalopani (51, 52). We all suffered from overeating, so couldn't walk very far this day, only getting to Ghasa after six hours, and making many toilet stops. We crossed a dodgy suspension bridge (53), and followed a hillside through some stunning mountain scenery. We walked through the deepest gorge in the world, passed some beautiful waterfalls, very different again (54–57). Stayed in Eagle's Nest rest house in Ghasa. Not bad. Joined by Richard from Bristol, who we had met in Tatopani over Christmas. He was to trek with us until Tatopani on the way back.

Day 7 – 27/12 Ghasa to Marpha.

A spectacular day's walk. Headed up to around 2,700 m gradually becoming surrounded by snow-capped mountains (58-62). We climbed to Kalopani from where it levelled out, following a river bed rather than up and down hillside paths (63, 64, 65), although at one point we couldn't get any further. It was someone's bright idea (not mine) to wade across the river which had snow on both sides. Freezing. Got across eventually (66) and discovered we were really cut off so had to wade back again. Climbed up the hillside path to get past the river before going back down to the river bed (67). Some just awesome scenery (68). Landscape more snowy with pine trees, and getting quite barren (69-70). Got to Marpha, staying in Paradise Guest House, with hot water and a shower. We were introduced to under-table heating, with coals under the table. Great. Good food. Marpha is a really nice little place, small stone paved streets.

Day 8 – 28/12. Climb to Jharkot (3,700 m).

Headed along the river bed towards Jomsom, a bit of a dump. Straight through. Ended up on a hillside path which dropped away, so scrabbled along the scree slopes to get down. Very frightening, and thought I'd fall a few times. Stomach still not right.

Reached Kagbeni for lunch before our monster climb to Jharkot (3,700 m). Scenery now really barren, like a desert. Climbing once more into snow and drifts. (71). Halfway up we could see a plateau and amazing views of the valley (although itself 2,700 m) (72-73). Clouds coming in to create amazing effects (74). Climb not so bad when we saw Jharkot in the distance (75). As it got dark clouds came down once more (76) (77). Freezing here, passing an ice fall (78). Stayed in a nice place here, Himali Hotel, although we weren't all that well. Don't think it's the altitude.

Day 9 – 29/12

Walked up to Muktinath (3,800 m) and on to the Buddhist temple, a place of pilgrimage, without our packs, which we collected from Jharkot on the way back down. Some just amazing views, great to be surrounded by snow. Really fresh outside, although didn't seem that cold. Very clear skies (79, 80–83). Took a different route on the way back to Jomsom. We were suffering a little, and arrived in Jomsom virtually unable to take another step, having stopped a number of times on route with stomach trouble and breathing problems. Had an early night (6 instead of 7 p.m. to bed). We were OK in the morning.

Stayed in the Everest Guest House in Jomsom.

Day 10

Jomsom to Kalopani. Put on pace today, having seen this scenery already, aiming for Tatopani for New Year celebrations. Got to Kalopani without much trouble, and had a little snow around 5 p.m. Guest house was OK there. Ate some 'international' food (i.e. pasta dishes) while a couple of American girls scoffed. Should eat 'Dal Bhat' (rice, lentils, curry etc.), they said. "Nothing like it when you're hungry". Half an hour later Mark saw both of them leave the two toilets in the guest house.

Day 11 – to Tatopani 31/12/91

Rushed full speed to Tatopani. Did the trip in five hours, arriving around 2 p.m. Soaked in the hot spring after a good lunch. Heaven. Good tea, too, and celebrated all the New Years, the New Zealand one at about 5:30 p.m., just about staying awake for midnight. Didn't celebrate British New Year (5:45 a.m.) Good night.

Day 12 – 1/1/92

Left Tatopani towards Beni. Didn't fancy the monster climb to Ghorepani, so we followed the river. The walk was fairly easy, though Mark was hobbling. We left Richard in Tatopani. Walked through some really nice woodland and some surprisingly large villages. Beni was not all that nice, and guest house was O.K. Nearing the road they are building up the river valley.

Day 13 – 2/1/92

Carried on down the river towards Kushma, hoping to get a lift when we reached the start of the road. Got to the road around 1 p.m. Waited for a while. Group of fourteen trekkers/porters tried to bargain with a truck driver for a lift, and he wanted to charge us 500 Rs each. Too much.

We didn't go, so we walked on to Kushma. Nice little town. Stayed in a small guest house with a couple from London, Jane and James. People there were really nice and good food.

Day 14 – 3/1/92

Walked for an hour to a place with workers based on road-building. Got on a truck for 20 km to another town. Pretty rough ride. The road was still just a dust track full of holes. Caught a petrol tanker to Pokhara from there, with about ten of us clinging on to the top. Good trip, with the road getting better nearer Pokhara. Arrived at Pokhara in the early afternoon with time to get a large meal and cakes down. A really good trek. Enjoyed it all, especially Tatopani.

OK. The photos aren't all here yet. I've another ten or so on a roll to be developed but I wanted to send these rather than carrying them.

Hope you got my letter that follows on from this and receive my two films (undeveloped) from Delhi. Also enclosed are photos from India (Taj up to Pokhara), written on back. Use the old letters to find out more.

OK, Enough for now, have fun looking at photos etc.

Loads of love,

David

Kathmandu

12/1/92

Hello,

Writing this just after phoning. Nice to hear everything is OK there. I've written a letter about our trek and I'm going to send that with all the photos I've developed here, which have come out well, so I won't say much about it in this letter.

Since we finished the trek on 3/1/92 we've been pretty busy. The trek was really good, loads to see on the way. Had a couple of relaxing days in Pokhara, catching up on our eating, doing all the writing, and looking at all the photos I had done. On the 4th and 5th we didn't do much at all, just taking it easy, getting some sun. Pokhara is just so relaxing, it's a great place. Had some more great food there. Unfortunately not a lot more to say about those two days.

On the 6th we set off for our rafting. We caught a bus, well actually it picked us up from our hotel, at 7 a.m. At 7:30 we were stopped in the bus station with the sound of spanners, welding, and banging from underneath. I went for a look to see they had dismantled the bus's drive shaft – Ahh ?! Would we make it to rafting?

By 8:30 we were moving again. The road out of Pokhara could be compared to Long Lane without tarmac – and this is their main road between the two main cities, amazing.

We arrived in the middle of nowhere around noon, where the three of us who were rafting were dropped off. With us was Richard, who we had just met in Tatopani on Xmas day on the trek, and again in Pokhara. The three of us were on the raft with two Nepalese, one paddling and one guide. We had paddles and life jackets and got changed into shorts and T-shirts. By now it was quite warm and we set off down the river. Our packs had gone off ahead by road and our valuables went in a drum on the raft. Within half an hour we were tackling our first rapids, having mastered the paddling bit. During our first stint of one and a half hours on the river we hit some pretty big rapids, which from a distance never looked to be too bad. We got soaked, but it was great fun, having to use buckets to empty the raft of water after nearly every rapid. Fortunately they were well spread out.

The river was quite fast and rocky, so we didn't need to paddle much. About 2 p.m. we pulled in to a nice sandy beach for lunch, where our two 'staff' unloaded a mountain of bread, cheese, biscuits, jams, fruit, etc., which was all laid out on a sheet for us, while we dried off in the sun. Setting off again for another two hours it started getting colder as the sun dropped behind the hills. We travelled another 10 or 15 km down the river to Mugling, our overnight stop. We hit some even bigger and better rapids this time, finishing on a series of three big ones in succession. The tiny raft was tossed around as we clung on with our feet, while larger rafts with more people cruised over the rough water. I think ours was better!

We pulled onto a beach at 4 p.m., where we found our staff had increased to four, they had put up two tents, started cooking tea, and made us a cuppa. We changed and lazed on the beach as they ran around setting us out food on the little fires they had built. We were the only people on the beach. Eventually they presented us with soup and then pots of rice, noodles, curry, dal and more tea. We could hardly make a dent in it. When we finished eating they built a campfire for us, which we sat by as it grew dark. Great to be by the fire in the dark with the clear and starry sky and the sound of the rushing river.

Two of the lads who looked after us slept out at night under the raft, guarding all the equipment and us as we slept cosily in the tent. Was this exploiting the Nepalese? Call it a Christmas treat!

Next morning, we were woken at 8 by 'staff' with a bucket of hot water outside the tent. Breakfast was cooking away, and in a half hour they presented us with pancakes, eggs, toast, rice pudding, more tea, and coffee. We were amazed at what they had done on a little fire by a rock on a beach. Ate it down in minutes. Around 9 they took down the tents. It was very misty and cold and we weren't all that keen to get moving. We were told we were being joined by three more people, so we hoped they didn't arrive until the sun came up, which luckily they didn't. By 11 it was sunny and fairly warm, and we set off again, with our three Hong Kong lads, all kitted up with goggles and coordination. Within twenty seconds of starting I was soaked by a rapid, sitting at the front this time. This day we hit perhaps bigger rapids, although they were well spread out. I was sent flying a few times, and as well as fending off water I had to cope with flying Hong Kongers. We probably covered another 20 km, getting drenched and using the buckets well. Great experience, although they say this time of year it's pretty smooth. Rough enough for me thanks!

Arrived at the end of rafting after three or four hours on the river where we had another beach lunch. Went down a treat. Changed and got up to the road. Our transport to Chitwan was the next aim, which turned out to be a 45 minute trip on the top of a coal truck. From the top we had great views of the plains we were headed into. A change from the mountains and rivers. Truck took us to Tandi, from where the only transportation to the park was either Jeep or oxcart. A Jeep was waiting to take us to Sauraha on the edge of the park, having to drive along a dust track and across (through) a river to get to the village, consisting of genuine mud huts.

When we arrived at our prearranged accommodation it was full, so we had to go to another lodge about a ten minute walk away. Bumped into Joanne again, can't get away. Had to walk through unlit roads to get to the lodge where the food was laid on. Dal bhat – ahh! Not bad, but rather something else. Went elsewhere then for banana cake. The lodges are little shacks with mud walls and straw roofs. Hot showers are big cans of water heated by wood fires.

On the 8th we started our expeditions. Very misty in the early morning. Had breakfast, managing to get extra porridge and toast. Richard was with us on the same package. At 9 a.m. we left with seven others, of which at least four were Germans, on a 'jungle walk'. We crossed a river by canoe to enter the park. The guide explained how we entered at our own risk and said we should be quiet, which in German means being as noisy as possible so it seems. We followed a large path for a while and then turned off the path, battling through grass 7 ft high, then areas of trees and bushes with carpets of leaves. We climbed a few trees to get a glimpse of a grey blob described as a bit of a rhino. We were unlucky not to see much.

Back to the lodge for 1 p.m. for lunch. We saw a guy was not well so we had his as well, and then someone else's too. Getting our money's worth here. At 2 we set off for a canoe trip up the nearby river. About eight or nine people balanced in this large dug-out canoe, which seemed very unstable and near water level. Of the two guides we were getting on very well with one. We went down the river, not seeing the infamous riverside crocs, although we saw some women wading across the river with bundles of wood on their backs. After three-quarters of an hour on canoe, we got out for a two-hour walk back through the jungle. The afternoon was warm and clear.

On our walk our guide heard a rhino chewing in the tall grass (good hearing). We sneaked up and saw two rhino through the grass and then ran away, with Mark right at the front (of people running away). Later we saw two large clumps of 8 ft high grass moving and heard loud crunching sounds, about 10 m away. These were rhino. The guide threw sticks as we crouched down, and we saw the rear of a rhino as it ran off. Walking back we were directed by one guide from up a tree who had seen a tiger catch a deer. We found the paralyzed deer scrabbling around. We had scared the tiger off – what a shame! If we waited long enough it may return, said the guide with a smile. We left rapidly. Waded across the river to get back for our stunning tea. By this time (that morning) we had moved into the lodge we should have been in.

On the 9th we got up, had breakfast, and were taken for an elephant ride. Some massive elephants. We targeted ourselves for the mean one with big tusks, about 60 years old. Three of us squashed up painfully on its back and we thumped off through the grass and bush, crossing a couple of rivers. At one point the driver pointed to a rhino and then turned and went the other way. It was good to do, but we were glad to get off.

Our guide friend had our day planned, so we joined him in going to Tandi for an Indian movie. Three hours for 10p, just great. Couldn't understand a word, but could follow the story. Great plot, loads of dancing, lightning, gun battles, and humour. Seemed to have it all. In the evening we were taken to a little shack by our friend for buffalo curry and local wine (horrible stuff). Being polite we drank the stuff. After this he took us to a stick dance show, where twelve blokes danced in a circle around two men with drums. They were each armed with meaty looking sticks and didn't hold back as they cracked them into the one in front or behind. Daring stuff. They changed to smaller sticks for the next dance, and then we joined in for the last dance (without sticks luckily). After the official tea we went off to another cafe for chocolate cake, where we sat outside by a large campfire watching the drunken owner and his family dance and beat a drum. Fog was really thick now.

Next day (10th) we left for Kathmandu. We pulled a good one on the package deal, getting a day more than everyone else for the same price, otherwise it wouldn't have been value for money. We got the bus at 11:45 and headed off along the 'MI', dust road, passing huge drops as we followed the hillside and Trishuli River. A few coaches lay at the bottom of the valley, having tumbled off the windy road. Terrified? – not me. Bus was probably one of the best we've had, although after four hours there was a massive twang from the rear axle. I daren't look at what they did when we stopped, in case I could tell it would take hours to fix. Half an hour later we were off again. By 6:30 we climbed up a hillside as it grew dark before our drop into Kathmandu. The road was full of buses and trucks now. We arrived in the Thamel area of Kathmandu around 7 p.m., which is where all the accommodation is, so in ten minutes we had a nice place (Nepal Rest House) to stay. The price of a room was reduced from $5 to $2 a night for a double room just to persuade us to stay there. We were right opposite K.C.'s restaurant again, so ate there. Quite expensive compared to what we had been paying. Met June and James, who we had met on the trek. So many people we have seen in Kathmandu we have met elsewhere on our travels. Food was OK. Beds comfy, thick quilts, very nice.

On the 11th, had a hot, hot shower. Luxury. Got some drugs for my still troublesome stomach. Feel OK, but can't shake it off. Still eating OK though. We walked through the cold, misty city, which wasn't as busy as we imagined, although being Saturday everything (most things) was closed. Had breakfast on a now-sunny morning at a rooftop restaurant. Afterwards we walked to Durbar Square, about twenty minutes away. This square was stuffed full of shrines and temples, of which most were used to sell fruit and veg off or advertise 'vote for sun'. Really interesting to see the styles and the way the people just forget they are there. In this area food and accommodation places are a lot cheaper. It started to rain heavily, so we headed back to Thamel area. Got soaked. Stopped off in Kathmandu Guest House where they had a log fire, papers, and TV. Caught up with the world news. Had a nice meal in the restaurant across from the hotel. Lay in bed at 10 listening to live football coverage on World Service (around 4 in the UK).

On the 12th we had a lay in. The mist means it's not worth going out early. Collected my mail OK, although Mark's mother forgot to put his name on his letters! Been away too long, I guess. Had a nice breakfast nearby and have spent all afternoon writing. Been sat in this restaurant for six hours, and have just been brought a free drink. I guess I'll eat here now!

OK, that's enough. I've enclosed a couple of photos you can give to Chris and Grandma. I'll send the other hundred soon with all the info. Glad everything's OK, and dad enjoyed his course!

As I say, we had a good Xmas and New Year. Hope you all enjoyed yours. Nice to speak on the phone. I'll obviously write and will phone from Thailand when we settle on the beaches, if they have a phone. Apart from Pokhara and Kathmandu it's fairly undeveloped here, with little communication, poor roads, etc. We were saying that once you're stranded in the middle of nowhere there's nothing you can do but wait for something to happen.

It's been good to take it easy today, maybe sightseeing tomorrow, and we fly out on the 14th. We hope to change our February 3rd flight to Australia by a couple of weeks, as Thailand sounds so good.

OK, food's coming so I best finish. Chicken, steak, veg, and chips for 70p.

Take care, and expect some large parcels soon. Oh. I did think of sending a few jumpers and T-shirts back, but I don't think I'll bother now.

Hope the phone call wasn't too much. I wanted three minutes, but got cut off after I'd given you the number.

Loads of love,

David .

Bangkok 19/1/92

+ Koh Phi Phi 21/1/92

Hello all,

Me again. Another letter already, just to get all my activities down on paper. So much to say, and we have done so much since we arrived in Bangkok.

Firstly though, I need a job doing. I can't remember how we controlled my money, but basically it's time to make some payments. We've changed our flight out of Singapore to the 17th of February – same time of departure, etc. from the 3rd of February. We've been sorting out our finances here so that hopefully I won't need to use my funds up for Australia. This resulted in Mark using his plastic for the both of us, with me now owing him £600. So what I need is you to send a cheque to Mark's mum for Mark for £600. I guess you can use the money I left in your account and I hope you don't mind doing this, however you work it out. OK, don't worry, we're still on budget, it's just this expenditure now could save us expense later on, perhaps in a big way.

OK, now for more stories. Last letter I was in Kathmandu, probably 12/1. On the 13th it was another cold, misty morning, so not really any good for sightseeing. We started off the day with a steak breakfast. (Keep your eye on my day's food here). Very nice – steak, eggs, potatoes, and fruit salad (?!) (that's what they gave me). Walked around town carrying those green jeans, which I wanted cut to shorts. Instead I was approached many times by people wanting to buy them and my denim jacket. I was offered a pair of trousers for £1.50 at one place. Held on to them for later.

Went to G.P.O. where we mailed the letters and cards. We got some photos developed only 7"x 5". Make them jealous at home! Left a letter at G.P.O for Mark and Lisa, who we had met in Egypt. They arrive in Nepal, at Kathmandu first, a little later. A bit of advice and what we did, etc. Hope they get it OK. They do expect it. We couldn't find any letter from Andy (who is now home – oh!) who had supposedly left us a letter there.

Walked back to the Thamel area for coffee and chocolate cake (excellent) for lunch at Helena's restaurant. When we travelled into Nepal on the bus we were lent a book by a lad we got to know, who then got off without it. So, I sold that in one of the many bookshops – well I don't want to carry it around!, and that pays for a meal!!

Strolled around the town area of Thamel looking at the amazing embroidery they will do on T-shirts etc. If only I had more time and money. Went into the more upmarket Kathmandu Guest House to look at the papers. They have the international Herald (U.S.A), but it had British football results and interesting world news – Bush sick in Tokyo, etc.

Time for our last tea in Nepal. Tried the recommended Hems Restaurant. Opened the meal with a beautiful lasagne with a massive salad. The cheese here is so good. Followed that with sizzling steak, with chips and veg on the steaming cast iron plate again. The steak was three-quarters of an inch thick. Amazing. Finished off with rum and raisin cheesecake (specialty) and cappuccino coffee. Wow, and all for less than £2. One of the best meals I've had here. Eating is all part of the visit to Nepal, as you've probably noticed.

On the 14th we packed all our gear up, paid for our room, etc. We've also been getting our laundry done in Nepal, all my old clothes are very clean, or were, as the laundry service is very cheap. We were to fly at 1 so we went for a steak breakfast at 9 a.m. Met a couple of lads we'd met in Agra, who were going on the same flight. We met them later and got a taxi together to the airport. The airport was really new and clean – very impressed. It was foggy, so the morning planes were delayed, although we checked in and boarded only a half hour late. Plane was a brand new 757 – really smart. I worked out that if we got a left hand side window seat we should see the mountains – I've got these things well sussed. Sure enough, when we took off we had a great view of Everest, etc. Flight was three hours and really good. Service and food couldn't fault – although they couldn't get me in the cockpit, which I asked for. Maybe on my next flight. Flew over India,

Burma and Thailand, arriving around 6 p.m. local time (+7 GMT). The land around this area was dead flat, the horizon just a straight line. Strange after all the mountains. There was a massive flat area just covered in sprawling rivers which looked uninhabitable – I bet there are thousands living there that get washed away every year!

As we approached Bangkok some really nice apartment-type developments appeared – similar to what you'd see in Tenerife. When we landed at 6 p.m. it was 30°C. The four of us got a taxi to the touristy accommodation area of Khao San Road, which is luckily at the centre of most of the things to see in the city. Heading into the city was just amazing. It was so different again to anywhere else we've seen. After the slow pace of Nepal and dusty city life elsewhere, Bangkok was a spotless, modern, busy city. The airport was massive, modern, and really well organized, we were through in half an hour. Sent the package of photos of our trek from the airport. The roads in the city are large to cope with the vast amounts of shiny Japanese cars and buses. Big boards showed pictures of planned developments of large tower blocks and complexes, to go alongside the mirror glass multinational office blocks of the likes of Nissan, IBM, Sanyo, etc.

Neon signs all around flashed with the names of Japanese or American electronics, car, or bank companies. On the taxi radio was English music with an English D.J. Traffic flowed, although sometimes slowly, controlled by traffic lights and a lot of traffic police. All the vehicles were in good condition, the auto rickshaws (tuk tuk's) were sparkling, with padded seats and coloured lights. Organization and planning seemed to be the most impressive thing, which as we saw over the next week makes the city seem probably further advanced than anything we have.

We arrived at Khao San Road around 7 p.m., taking an hour to cover the 26 km from the airport. This street is where the cheaper hotels and restaurants are, and was jam packed with tourists. It took a while to find a place, eventually getting a hotel away from Khao San Road, a little quieter. ฿120 a double room. Exchange rate now £1 to ฿45. Khao San Road is the place to be if you want beer, videos in bars, western music, and toned-down, westernized food. Personally, I preferred to be away from this street, although down the pavements are stalls with cheap clothes, music tapes etc. Tapes (pre-recorded) are only 60 pence here (£6 in the U.K.). I shall be buying.

On the 15th we headed for tourist information to get info and a city map. Walking round the city wasn't too bad, wide roads and paths, not all that busy. We had a long walk to the Garuda Airway office on Rama IV Road. We managed to change our flight date in ten minutes, no problem, to give us longer in Thailand. Rama IV Road is full of big, big company offices and shopping centres. The shopping centres are spotless and all plush. We walked a bit further, coming to one of the many parks built into the city, with green lawns and lakes. A lot of people picnicked here. The sun blazed down as we got used to the heat again.

Next to the park was the Red Cross hospital, where they do work on serum against snake bites. They kept a lot of the poison from the snakes there to do their anti-venom research from, milking poison from the snakes every couple of weeks. It's known as the snake farm, and puts on shows a couple of times a day. They had a slide show telling of the dangerous snakes in Thailand, and how they develop serum by 'milking' the poison and injecting it into horses. After a while they inject more, then remove half the horse's blood and remove the antibodies that fight the poison. Felt a bit dodgy after hearing all this. Then we went to the snake pit, where they brought out all the different kinds of poisonous snakes they had to show us. Out came cobras and vipers, while the handlers prodded them to get them annoyed. They milked poison from a viper and force-fed a python with chicken legs. Quite entertaining.

Walking back we stopped at one of the many fresh fruit barrows on the streets where you can buy bags of fresh fruit for around 10p. Pineapples were very tasty. We were chatted to by a local Thai businessman, who had stopped for fruit after work. He gave us a lift in his new-looking Toyota. He earns ฿8,000 a month in computers, although ฿15,000 after overtime (£300). Walked back towards Khao

San Road, passing street food places on the way. We ate in one later. They know what to do with their food here.

By the roadside they have all sorts of different things, in this case it was a spread of pork in various forms (crispy, honey-coated, sliced), masses of different types of fish and seafood, and a trolley full of vegetables of all types, along with noodles, bean sprouts, rice, etc. I just went over and said some of this, some of that, some veg, rice. They chop up the meats or fish, put it with the selection of veg and throw it in a large wok. Two minutes later you have a meal. Sauces added in as they fry gave the meal a brilliant flavour. The veg was really good and fresh and crispy. You have to take a chance when you order, as English is not too hot here. Mark pointed to one thing to see what it was and ended up being served it, with no veg and being very hot. Mine was excellent.

On the streets they sell all ranges of foods, mostly as rice or bean sprout dishes, or as a soup. It's amazing to see all the ways they serve up the things, every seller or restaurant has a different approach. As well as meats on sticks (like small kababs). It's just hard to describe all the different things. It's also hard to walk along the street without wanting to try it all! Food on the streets away from Khao San Road is cheaper, too. Most of the food we've had so far on the streets has been really tasty, with the great sauces and spices. By the way, as well as being lined with these food sellers, the pavements are lined with tables and chairs! I keep saying that Bangkok has been mental torture for me, walking down the streets past all sorts of foods, past cheap tapes, past really cheap clothes, and past stunning Thai women. Levi's (probably fakes) are £4. The food is the hardest bit! As I said, the food is all part of the trip – different lifestyles and foods.

OK. The rooms at the hotel are alright, but you need the fan on full blast to keep you cool. It's so hot and sticky at night. Next morning (16/1) we planned to go to the National Museum. After sausage, eggs, and toast for breakfast we walked the twenty-minute walk there for 9:30. On a Thursday they have a free tour in English. We went on this for its two hours, with a very well-learned lady showing us the large collection of Buddha statues, and explaining about Buddha, Buddhism, Hindu, and its origins, etc. Really interesting to hear it all and learn how all the shapes and styles of carvings relate to the religion and history. The museum itself is housed in a building that was once the deputy ruler's place, with the very common, beautifully shaped roof and ornamental work.

After the museum we grabbed a bowl of noodle soup with some sort of fishy things in – very tasty. It's hard to know what you're getting when they don't speak a word you do.

At 1 p.m. the Grand Palace opened and we went for a look around. This one was once the home of the royalty, with some amazing temples and buildings inside the grounds. All around the surrounding walls was a really finely detailed painting telling of the story of Buddha's life. One of the main temples houses an 'emerald' Buddha perched high on a massive gold coloured altar, made of one piece of stone. There are around twenty separate buildings inside the grounds, each with decorative roofs or gold coloured coatings. Really impressive.

Left there around 3 p.m., grabbing a small meal on the way to the Ratchadamnoen Boxing Stadium, about twenty minutes from our hotel. Tonight was Thai boxing night. There were nine fights, each of five three-minute rounds. The boxers were all about 110 lbs, with the biggest only 126 lbs. They could basically do what they wanted; kicking, punching, elbowing, and a favourite with the crowd – knee to the stomach – to which they all chanted "knee" (sounded like it) and cheered. The crowd was wild, although the small, circular stadium was only half full (200 or 300 people). Betting was going on frantically, although we couldn't work out what they were doing. We couldn't work out the scoring, either, with our winners often called as losers. We didn't see any knockouts, although one lad did take a serious beating you wouldn't have seen in 'normal' boxing. Very entertaining both in and out of the ring. Before each bout the boxers perform a little dance ritual, and when fighting they are accompanied by Thai instruments: flute, cymbals, and drums. Some nice street food outside the stadium.

On the 17th we had a busy day planned. We were joined by Chris and Paul from London, doing the same thing as us. Caught an express boat up the river taking about three-quarters of an hour. From the river you could see the riverside houses on poles and the new tower blocks being built. Quite a nice trip. From our drop-off point we hired a river taxi after some haggling. This small boat just took four of us, and was equipped with a large, powerful engine with a 4 ft long propeller shaft. The engine was mounted on pivots so it could be tipped to raise the propeller out of the water. Some of the larger boats that carry 40 people have massive six-cylinder engines and speed up and down the river. We hired the taxi to take us down a side canal back to where we started. We sped off down the canal, with the driver leaning the long, narrow boat over, probably getting up to 60 or 70 mph. Pretty exciting stuff. We sped down these canals past the Thai canal houses, palms, and canal-side temples. Very scenic and peaceful off the main river. At one point we met a school of very large fish leaping out of the water. They don't eat these, so they were safe. After half an hour we were back, wondering how much it would cost to buy one of these great little boats. Tried a duck, rice, and black sauce dish for lunch – best yet.

In the afternoon we planned to do some clothes shopping, as stuff here is so cheap. There was an area near Siam Square that sells silks and suits. We priced suits – tailor made, we could get two suits, four shirts, and four ties for

£130. Not bad, but we were sure they should be cheaper. Some nice materials. Silk shirts were around £7 or £8.

Walked around in search of some markets, finding them a good while later. Clothes, mainly shirts and jeans, were no cheaper than on Khao San Rd. Next on the schedule around 6 p.m., we caught a bus to Patpong Rd – the supposedly sleazy area of the city. Getting a bus there is so easy, with streams of buses passing the stopping point.

Patpong wasn't at all as bad as we'd thought. The dirtiest things were the thousands of birds flying along the street messing on everyone's heads (we all got hit). Patpong Rd was full of market stalls down the centre, selling clothes and tapes. The sides were lined with bars. Chris was very worried about going in the bars, having heard stories of people being drugged or robbed inside. There were three types of bars really: open-to-street bars, bars with dancing girls in with the doors open, and then upstairs or closed-door bars with supposedly dirty shows. We were sure we'd be safe in the open bars, which was OK. We had a few cheap drinks in a couple, not being hassled at all. In the bars with dancing girls, they had numbers on, so I guess you could pick which one you wanted. Not very outrageous really. It was quite a respectable area, really, not sure what all the fuss is about.

On the 18th I collected some photos I had developed. These were of our trek, rafting, Chitwan, and Kathmandu. Some great ones again. These will be on their way very shortly (along with another set of all the things I've mentioned we did in Bangkok). When you get them, read this and the previous letter again to work out what they are. We walked to some of the wats, or temples, scattered around the city – one of which, the Golden Mount, rises above the otherwise completely flat city, giving some nice views of the old and new buildings mixed in with all the temples.

Chatted to by so many Thai people, all giving us advice on what to do, where to go, and what to buy. Spent the evening with two other lads down in Chinatown when we found it. Really buzzing down there. We headed back to the hotel for 9:30 because, if we'd worked it right, 2:30 in the UK was the first rugby internationals, although we didn't know who was playing. In fact, England vs Scotland had already started, so we spent hours listening to World Service coverage of England stuffing Scotland, Wales scraping a win, Oldham vs Liverpool, and all the day's results.

Sunday the 19th we had some sorting to do. Read this bit carefully. We changed our plans a little, so instead of travelling around over land from South Thailand to Singapore through Malaysia, we go down south, come back up to Bangkok, and fly to Singapore directly. It's not much more expensive, costing about £50 each to fly and only takes two hours instead of two days. I've paid for this on the Visa, so this will come up to be paid soon. Let me know how they charge me, on this end I was charged in local currency and I'd like to know what ridiculous conversions and charge they use. Also, we've used up nearly all our traveller's cheques (on schedule) and so I've got cash with the plastic too (£100), finding it hard to buy traveller's cheques as I had wanted. Should be OK in Australia. So, an extra flight, another chance to get in the cockpit. We are flying in the day, great views, and a Royal Nepal 757 again.

Also, I bought a fake Student ID card for a couple pounds which should save me a packet in Australia and the USA, and a collection of good tapes for a couple pounds. Bargain!

Sunday night we caught an overnight bus out of Bangkok to the southern island of Koh Phi Phi. Left at 6 p.m., arrived at Krabi at 8 a.m. to catch the 9:30 ferry. Good trip, although we didn't really sleep. Thailand is so flat, and the roads are straight and pretty good, so we really tanked along, with some fairly daring overtaking too. Coach was excellent; air conditioned, reclining seats, blankets. It was a full moon so we could see a lot on the way. Masses of petrol stations, every half mile it seemed, all big and brightly lit, open 24 hours, and mostly Esso or Shell.

20/1/92, 3 p.m.

I'm on the island now actually. It takes a long time to get one of these letters out. We arrived here around 12 p.m., a three-hour boat trip. It's really boiling. We have a beachside bungalow on the small island, and it's just paradise. Nice, clean, sandy beaches with clear waters. I was just snorkelling, feeding bits of bread to the many beautiful coloured fish eating from my hand. I think we'll be here a week or so, before trying some other beaches, Koh Samui on the east side is said to be good. We get back to Bangkok around 10/2/92 (hopefully) to fly on Wednesday the 12th at 2:30 p.m. local. We'll stay in Singapore for our flight to Sydney on 17/2/92.

OK, so I hope you followed all my wheeler dealing and can control my funds OK. I may write soon, although there is not much to repeat about laying on golden beaches. As I said, we're sending a pack of developed photos (see mail this time) soon, but they may take a while to get there. Hope you've received the ones of the trek I sent from Bangkok on 14/1. Also, the reels I sent from Delhi in December.

I'm out of paper, so hope everything's OK there, and that I haven't bored you, telling you what I eat every day! If everything goes as planned, when I get to Sydney I may even phone!

Loads of love,

David.

P.S. Can you photocopy these letters, as I can't see this thin paper lasting very long.

Koh Phi Phi

Thailand

31/1/92

Hello again,

So, as you can see, I'm still on the Phi Phi islands in South Thailand. I think I'd just arrived when I last wrote. Well, I've been very busy since then, lazing in the sun, snorkelling, trying to decide what to eat. I've made a little constructive use of the time by writing a lot of letters to Australia, USA, and various people in the UK. I wrote to Peggy in Australia, too. More than that, though, we stayed here an extra five or six days to do a four-day scuba diving course!!! I finished it yesterday – all the detail in a bit, just to say that after four days training with a few open water dives we are both now certified international scuba divers! After sitting around on the beach for a week we felt we should do something, and this is one of the best and probably cheapest places to learn to dive. Impressed? I know I am.

First of all, finances. As I said in my last letter I've finished my traveller's cheques and am having (will have) to get cash on the Visa until we reach Australia. I paid for both our diving courses on my Visa. Unfortunately Mark told his mother to expect money from me (cheque for £600), but really it was unnecessary to do that, as soon it'll balance out, with money having to come back to me somehow. Anyway, the course was £130, but the total bill on the Visa will be 13,000 baht (£300). Also I'll be changing £250 cash from the Visa. That'll be a total of £750 so far. The bills will probably take a while to get there, so it may be easier if you could just write a cheque to Visa for say £1,000 when the next bill arrives. This should prevent any future charges and all these bills coming together and stopping my use of the card. OK. Hope that's clear.

OK, I'll carry on from where I was in the last letter (still here). From the 20th to the 26th we've just been taking it easy really. The beach where we are staying seems to be the best on the island for both peace and quiet and snorkelling. It's been up around 100°F every day, having clear nights and the full moon. On our first full day here we took a walk along the coastline (no proper path) to the 'village', the main area of development on the small island. The little village is surprisingly commercialized, with plenty of shops, restaurants and beach bungalow resorts (no big developments (tower blocks etc)). The island is really beautiful, later we walked up to a 'viewpoint' to look down over the beaches of the island. From there you couldn't see the resorts for all the palms – looked unspoilt. The two main beaches are nearly back-to-back in the centre of the island, both beaches are in bays. One side is deep enough for boats, the other side shallow, quieter, and lined with palms.

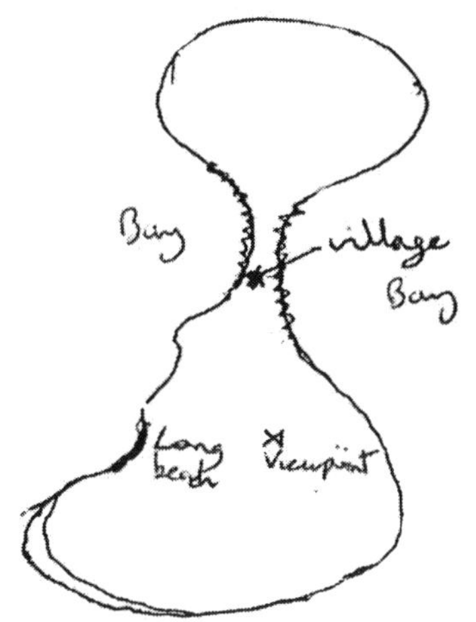

Walking back through the village early in the evening the restaurants were laying out their spreads of seafood. Outside each place are trays full of ice on which they display their selection of fish, squid, crab, prawns, etc., fish of all shapes and sizes. In the resort next to us on Long Beach, "Paradise Pearl," is a nice restaurant, having their display of seafood. One of the items was shark, so we had a chunk of shark with garlic and tomato sauce. It wasn't bad, but had no real taste of its own. They were only small shark. While I've been here I've made a point of eating fish, seafood, etc. as there is so much. Have had some small tuna, unknown fish dishes and coconut milk curries – all very tasty. Fruit is plentiful, pineapple and bananas everywhere, pancakes full of fruit a favourite. Coconuts are everywhere in restaurants and lying around. Had a go at cracking one open one morning – not easy, but good sitting on a beach scraping out the fresh coconut.

In the main the water has been very clear, so spent plenty of time swimming above corals though all the different shapes and colours of fish. Amazing.

After eating one night in the next resort, I read the Bangkok Post paper. It was full of jobs for engineering in electronics and automotive, all requiring English speakers, sounding very interesting. I'll bear it in mind!

Saturday the 25th of course we listened to live football coverage of the FA cup on World Service. Nice to hear so many matches frozen off! Too hot to sleep. The evenings on the island are probably the best time of day; it starts cooling down, gets fairly quiet, and we watch the sun drop over the bay and behind the island, glowing red, very scenic.

On the 27th we started our PADI diving course, having had the course books a couple of days earlier to flick through. The course was at the Phi Phi Scuba Diving Centre in the centre of the village, one of many. Over the four days we would have two days of theory and beach training in shallow water, then two days of open water diving.

The first morning we signed our lives away and began the theory. All very important, but pretty straightforward.

Learnt about the effects of water pressure at depth, air volumes, the underwater world, and so on. The equipment and how it operates, fits together, and is checked was all explained. A few quizzes made sure we followed it OK. The first afternoon we had our 'confined water training' on the beach. First we rigged up all the equipment, tanks, BCD, regulator, mask, and fins, then learnt how to assemble and check everything. We put on wetsuits and went to the beach. There we put all the gear on and sat on our knees under the water.

The first few minutes is very odd, being able to breathe normally. Once you can forget about taking breaths and it becomes like breathing normally it is very relaxing. We had to cover a series of skills while sitting on the bottom, in probably 10 ft of water. Just so you understand a little about what I'll write, when kitted up you have weight belts on to balance out your tendency to float, a tank of air compressed to 3,000 psi, strapped to what is in effect an inflatable jacket (BCD) which fastens around the body, and then all the pipes for breathing (regulator). The jacket is linked to the air tank and can be inflated or deflated to allow you to float, sink, or hover in mid-water, like being weightless. The regulator cuts down pressure from 3,000 psi to a pressure relative to the depth you are at, to allow you to breathe normally.

There are two mouthpieces, one for yourself and one for use of another diver if they run out of air themselves or the first fails. In the shallow water training on the afternoon of both the first and second day we went through skills that are essentially only required if there are problems rather than for normal diving. These included losing/locating and replacing the regulator, replacing and swimming without a mask, signals, and what to do if you run out of air! When you dive you should dive with someone else – a 'buddy' (course from the USA!).

If you're out of air you signal your buddy and take his second regulator to breathe. This was easy, but when Mark and I practiced this with my supply, both of us using mine, we did actually run out of air. Being in shallow water it wasn't too bad, but a bit nerve-wracking. Doing other skills, like removing and replacing all our equipment under water made me more confident, as when you have a few problems the secret is not to panic, relax, control your mind, breathe normally. Removing my weight belt under water was interesting, as being light I couldn't hold myself down. Got the hang of it in the end!

After the first day I was really drained, both mentally and physically. I think the stress was the killer. The second day I felt a lot more relaxed. There were five on the course, with a Swedish instructor, Jürgen, who taught the class of us, a Swede, and two Dutch in English.

The second morning we had more theory, learning about diving procedures, decompression sickness and other problems, and dive planning using tables. You have to be careful how many dives of certain lengths and depths you make in close succession because of absorption of nitrogen into the bloodstream. We finished our theory with an easy test (48/50!), needing 38 to pass. Mark got 38. The second afternoon, as I said, more beach training with emergency procedures, learning to control our buoyancy under water, etc.

The third day (29th) was our open water diving. We sorted out all our equipment and loaded it onto a long-tail boat around 9 a.m. We headed away from Phi Phi Don island to the smaller island by the side, Phi Phi Lee. As we were on a small boat, we had to rig up and inflate our equipment, throw it in the water, jump in, and put it on. We all felt a bit seasick as the small boat bobbed up and down, trying to fit our equipment together. Dropped down cautiously to 8 metres to do some more skills. We had stopped in a little bay, where the bottom was covered in all sorts of corals and sea life, although we had a sandy patch to kneel on for our skills. We practiced 'buddy breathing' – two of us breathing alternately from one mouthpiece, not as hard as it sounds – and emergency ascents.

There's a lot to remember, confidence and relaxing being more important. The more you're stressed the more air you use, and the more likely you are to make a mistake. As I learned from my experience trekking I'm mentally very strong now. The skills are now fairly easy, so we swam to see some life. Unfortunately as I swam up off the bottom I hit a sea urchin that was near me where I knelt. I didn't feel it right away, until I moved my legs and the needles from it were dragged by the wetsuit. I had to stop as the instructor pulled the spines out of my leg. Still very relaxed – very pleased with my control! I had to return to the boat so I missed the best bit, but it wasn't serious. The needles left a few marks of poison in my leg, but it wasn't very painful.

After our swim at 8 m for 40 minutes we got back in the boat and went to a nearby bay for lunch. The bay was very shallow, with light blue water and a nice beach. A couple of hours later we were back with fresh air tanks, ready for our afternoon dive in the bay we had stopped in. This dive was about 8 or 9 m for about 30 minutes, doing a few skills and then swimming around, looking at all the different fish and coral. Surrounded by many little fish. Fairly cloudy because of the sandy bottom. Supposed to be keeping together in our 'buddy' teams, but Mark had a few problems so that wasn't too easy, meaning his mind was distracted from his surroundings.

The next and last day's diving we did another two dives, this time going to 40 ft and over 50 ft deep. Mark had a panic when we got in for our first dive, so he paired with the instructor. I paired with the Swedish lad, Frederick, who was fine. These two dives I found very relaxing. The morning dive we did a few skills, 'buddy breathing' and ascent at depth, etc., and had a fun swim, this being out further at Bida Island. We came back to the location of our first dive for the afternoon, after a 'surface interval' of two hours on the beach again. This last dive was the best, doing skills for say ten minutes and swimming along the bottom for twenty minutes. The forms of coral were amazing, fish ate and lay on the bed. We swam round the edge of the rock, the walls lined with fan corals and masses of small coloured fish, through a gulley.

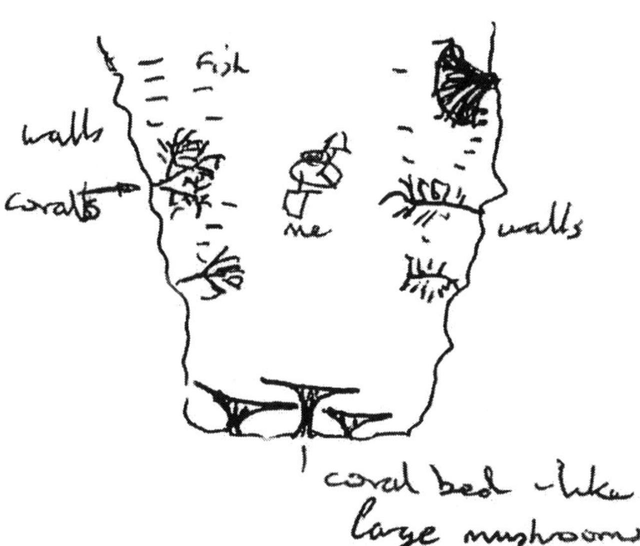

Concentrating less on myself now and more on my surroundings, which was great. Maintaining a stable position (neutral buoyancy) in water will come with practice – really enjoyed this dive. Before we surfaced we swam past a large band of small stationary fish, so many. Didn't see a shark until we were back on the boat!

On our return to Phi Phi we were certified divers!! Meaning we could go out on our own to 60 ft, hire equipment, buy equipment, and go on the scuba diving trips that are run. So, we'd done it! The achievement is probably more than the doing. Can't wait to do some more now – Barrier Reef, California, NZ, plenty more, although the UK doesn't appeal to me.

Anyway, I hope you're impressed with my achievement. If I'd told you before that I was going to do it I think you'd have been scared stiff. Not to worry, 'cause it's done! That was all finished yesterday, so today I'm taking it easy on Long Beach again. It's fairly tiring doing the diving, not to mention a strange feeling, floating around 50 ft under. I think my body still doesn't know what hit it. Anyway, I've got to keep up diving now, to ensure that I don't forget all I've learnt.

Tomorrow (1st Feb) we'll probably leave to go to 'the most beautiful bay in Thailand' Phranang Bay not that far from here, on the mainland. On the 4th we'll travel across to the east side to Koh Samui, another island – a little more commercialized though. On the 9th we'll have to go back to Bangkok, flying to Singapore on the 12th.

So, I hope everything's still OK there, and you should have received my trek photos by now. This letter is fairly brief by my standards, but as I say, I've been lazing around really, soaking up the sun and the beauty of the island. Of course, if you're now a bit sick of hearing me talk about these islands then don't worry because I may be able to sort out a visit for you here, but more about that later!

I'll be in touch again soon, probably with more photos. For now I'll do a few scribbles on the back of here to give you an idea.

Loads of love,

David.

P.S. They'll be sending me a certificate license for my diving (PADI) there, so I'll have to let you know where to send it to me, as I've got a temporary 90 day one at the moment, which may not last until any dive in Australia.

David Olds

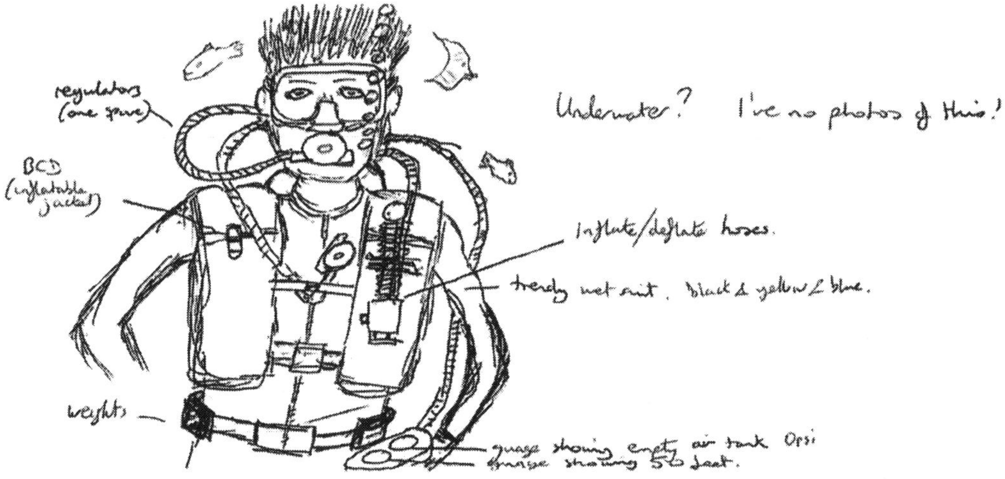
regulators (one spare)
BCD (inflatable jacket)
weights
Underwater? I've no photos of this!
Inflate/deflate hoses.
trendy wet suit. black & yellow & blue.
guage showing empty air tank 0psi
guage showing 50 feet.

Palms
white beach
Straw Beach huts
clear water
coral
Fish
View out from where I am :-
Phi Phi Ley Island
Clear Sky
Sun Sets Back here
Trees
Calm water
dark blue
light blue
Light blue
Beach (empty)
Table I'm on
Needs colour really

Koh Samui

Southeast Thailand

8/2/92

Hello,

OK. Time for another letter. It's been a week since the last, where I was having my last day on the Phi Phi Islands. (31/1). It was time to move on then, as we'd been there nearly two weeks. Finished the day there sitting on the beach (for a change!) having a coconut curry and of course pineapple fritters for tea (Hmmm!). It was a great place to go; relaxing, hot, and very beautiful. Saying that, it was still sad to see the signs of spoiling. Behind our, and most other, resort piles of rubbish were building up, mainly beer bottles it seemed. Coke is OK as they use bottles and these are returned, but beer bottles just seem to be tossed to the back. The bottle tops lie in the sand around the restaurants and have begun to spread to the beach.

Every morning we were woken by all sorts of strange bird sounds (and cockerels crowing), and in the evenings the generator that supplies electricity for our room for lights runs noisily from 6-12 p.m. OK, so it's not quite paradise, but almost! I hope they don't waste it! Long Beach, where we stayed, was away from the village, so quieter, but 'Paradise Pearl,' as I mentioned before, next to us, was commercial. Most people there, generally young, seemed to be on holiday rather than passing through like us, so would happily pay for the more expensive rooms and even buy beer! The place showed videos in the evenings, a trend all the restaurants in the village follow, so it's not really untouched! We also kept ourselves entertained in the night by tuning in to 89 FM radio station, broadcast from the very developed resorts on Phuket, the biggest island not far from Phi Phi. Between 6 and 12 they broadcast English music, between masses of adverts for restaurants in Phuket!

So, have you recovered from the shock news of our scuba diving exploits? Hope so. My leg's OK now, although still is marked.

Right. On the 1st we moved on from Phi Phi Island. Hope you got my postcard I sent that day. I forgot to say about photocopying my certificate in the letter. I probably won't need it, but if I get an opportunity for a job it may help a little! Also, as I said, send me a fax number and I can keep in touch that way too.

Our next destination, Phra Nang Bay, was reached by getting a boat back to the mainland (one and a half hour trip) and a long-tailed boat out to Phra Nang Bay (45 minutes along the coast). Oh, while in Krabi (mainland) I changed 11,000 baht (£250) on the Visa, so yet another bill, as I said I would in the last letter. The trip along the coast was nice, passing so many beaches, mostly deserted. Arrived at Phra Nang around 12 p.m., pulling in to a beach which from a distance had no sign of development, due to all the palms along the beach. The quarter-mile-long beach did have plenty of resorts on it and so we checked them out. Quite expensive, all about 300 baht (£7 or 8) for a bungalow with a shower and toilet. Found one place, "Ya Ya", behind this beach, on a beach on the other side of the isthmus, for only ฿100 (£2). In fact this accommodation was good, not a beach bungalow this time, but the bottom room in a three- or four-level treehouse! There was a group of half a dozen little tree homes, creating a nice sheltered area in the middle. Very nice. This place was only five minutes from all the beaches on the isthmus.

Railay West was most developed, three or four resorts in between palms. The Sunrise Bay side was not really a beach for swimming, as there are trees and roots in the water's edge. Interesting though. Phra Nang Beach is the best. The resort here is closed, so it's quiet. These beaches are even nicer than Phi Phi. The sand is finer and firmer, not so gritty and the ends of the beaches have amazing rocks with dangling formations in the limestone. The water is warm and clear, although there's not much to see in it here. We got our bearings the first day, checking out the beaches and surrounding scenery. This place is even more laid back than Phi Phi, less development, no little shopping street, etc., not many people. Just great. Being Saturday the 1st, we made sure we were tuned in at 9:30

for the rugby. England rolling on! Another grand slam?! Wales – never mind.

Spent the Sunday (2nd) on the beach (Phra Nang). Very hot, so we tried not to overdo it. Had a haircut in the morning – daring, as I didn't know if the girl had a clue what I wanted. Thai haircuts are all the same, and I didn't fancy one like that. Laying on the beach just in the water's edge is great, cooled by the water (although the water is not cold) and looking at the blue sea and the islands in the distance. From this beach you can see plenty of other small islands. Refreshed ourselves every so often with pineapples sold on the beach by Thai women and children.

Stayed on the beach until around 6:30 to watch the sun setting over the water and islands straight in front of us. By now maybe twenty people on the beach. Sunset just... can't think of another one of those words, I've used them all so often. Stunning will do. It dropped and turned to orange over the islands. After it had quickly disappeared the sky gradually changed to red and orange, making the water seem pink. [The next day we watched the sunset again from Railay Beach]. Yet another leisurely evening – can I get any more laid-back than this? Strolled through the little resorts of small bungalows spaced out between the palm trees. Some of the 'resorts' are so nice, although I guess you'd call them basic compared to European concrete 'resorts'.

Even the restaurants etc. are bamboo and straw huts, some great food. The coffees are getting bigger, a massive mug helps to get us going in the morning. We thought of going on a day tour around some of the sights in the area (Phang Nga Bay), but they were expensive and difficult, so we gave it a miss. Tried to find the lagoon that was near, but that involved mountain climbing to get to it, the path turning into a rope and a cliff face, so obviously didn't go there! Spent a little more time on the beach. No hassles of crowds, frisbees, dogs, music, rubbish, etc. Perfect. So scenic.

Continued my healthy diet with a prawn salad for lunch. I didn't think I could ever eat half the stuff I have, but prawns are quite nice. Psychological victory! I think I spent the rest of the afternoon in the shade for a change, wouldn't want to be sunburnt. We are still speculating most of the time as to how Andy had such a bad time, and also wondering what's in store for us. We still have no definite plans for Australia. It's just turn up and see what happens.

On Tuesday the 4th we planned to move on. Phra Nang Bay was well worth the visit and didn't disappoint me, having had such a good reputation. Our next stop was Koh Samui on the east coast. First we had to get a boat back to Krabi down the coast around 9 a.m. We had an air-conditioned bus trip across to Surat Thani, taking around three hours.

The scenery on the way across was fairly consistent – palms, flat land and the occasional wooden house. We had an hour at Surat Thani before getting a bus to the ferry at Don Sak. While in the town we had duck and rice (great sauce), the first duck we'd seen since Bangkok, where it's everywhere. I must find out what's in it or how to make the sauce! The ferry we got to Koh Samui has become quite developed. (No cars on Phi Phi or Phra Nang). Very slow boat, taking one and a half hours to travel the 38 km to the island. Not really much to see from the ferry. We had heard about how Koh Samui was very commercialized, very busy and so on, so I had an idea of what it may be like; lively, hard to find accommodation, expensive. In fact, it was completely wrong! What I know as busy and what the Thai people think of as busy is very different. When on the ferry we were approached several times by different people shouting at us to stay in some accommodation. One bloke showed us a leaflet of a very nice looking place in the area we'd targeted on the island – Lamai Beach. How much? ฿150 or ฿350! Too much. OK. ฿60. Also, he'd take us there when we arrived. Sorted.

Got off the ferry and went to a really plush minibus with the resort name on it! Very surprised. By the time we reached the resort it was 7, so dark. It was right at what happened to be the best end of the beach (beach maybe two miles long) and quite posh. We had the cheapo triangular 'bungalow', but this resort had brick apartments – very nice. Guess what – it was called Nice Resort 2. The restaurant was good too, coffees now half-pint glasses for the same price (฿10 – 20p). First impressions of the area in the dark was that it was a lot of smaller 'resorts' spread out along the beach. I had expected lines of resorts, bars, music, shops, etc.

The next morning we walked down to and along the beach. Great spot. If we hadn't been spoilt by Phi Phi and Phra Nang I'd have been really impressed with the beach! We found the small local town of Lamai, but there wasn't much around. On the way back we stumbled across exactly what I'd expected all the time, a street between the main road and the beach, lined with bars, restaurants, a few shops, etc., but it was surprisingly empty. The beach is nice, although the sand is strange, the sea is wavy and quite rough and drops away sharply – too rough to see anything in the water. A change, I guess. This side of the mainland it's just as hot, but a close, sticky heat. Hard work to do anything! In the early evening around 6 we sat in the restaurant having a coffee and it spat with rain for five minutes, so we ran out to cool off. We went back to the Lamai tourist area, about ten minutes' walk from the resort. Expected a lively evening, maybe even to have a beer! Turned out to be so quiet, though we did have a great meal. I think it's healthy living, eating loads of fried veg, meat, fruit, seafood, rice, and noodles (which you can't avoid really). Waited for something to happen, but it didn't really.

There are so many bars here, most of which show videos, but walking around you could see maybe a couple of people in each. A small beer is around £1 (half-pint bottle). There are nearly as many 'bar for sale' signs as bars, and you can pick up a bar here for ฿40,000 (£1,000). So, is this as busy as it gets? Apparently so. It's funny to see the 'tourists', either young travellers or older men escorted by Thai girls, whose age could be as low as fifteen at a guess. Sad really. It's very confusing to see the place so quiet. It's as though a lot of people thought, yes we can make money from tourists, etc., and too many have set up bars, so no one actually makes any money. Like a modern gold rush. Can't decide if the bars outnumber the resorts or there just aren't as many tourists as they really need. Most of the resorts seem only half-full, if that. Needless to say, we didn't stay there for a wild night!

Koh Samui was said to be a beautiful island, 20 km x 25 km, with so many great beaches around it and nice scenery inland. So, with that in mind we priced tours and decided to instead hire a motorbike for the day. We rented the small Yamaha Mate 100 for ฿150 (£3) and it transported the two of us pretty well, burning along the reasonably-good roads at 40 km/hr. The bike wasn't bad and it was an automatic clutch type, having four gears on the left pedal but no clutch lever. Easy, no worries about going up or down more than one gear at a time, although occasionally you could hear the engine revs compensating for my inaccurate gear choice. It's too easy to rent a bike; no license check, no helmets, and a lot of bikes on the road. There's really only one road around the island, and it wasn't busy luckily. So the bike was rented. I made sure I did the riding, as having seen Mark's car driving and knowing his coordination I didn't fancy letting him loose until I got used to it first. The island road is about 50 km all the way round, so there was no need to rush.

First stop was Hin Lat Falls, waterfalls inland. The roads are pretty much the same all the way through the island, with palms on both sides. The island is just palms! Both this and the other falls were very nice, having to walk into the woodland past the 'Look out for snakes' sign to reach the second. We stopped briefly in Na Thon, the arrival/departure town, which is all it was, before riding up along the very nice north coast. Up here, Mark wanted a go riding, so he did. I was surprisingly calm, after I'd shown him what to do, as I sat on back, although after a couple minutes I thought about braking and asked him if he knew how to brake – Ahh! I think I was calm because I knew he would be able to cope with the complexities of gear changing, even without a clutch, and I'd be back riding within ten minutes – which is what happened. [If there'd been a clutch I don't think he'd have got near it!] If you hadn't guessed already, Mark is one of the people who fits into the 'completely useless with anything that requires coordination, practical skills, or thinking without making a list' category, but don't worry, he'd agree. Enough of this, on with the tour.

Back in the driving seat we headed to Big Buddha – which, believe it or not, is a great big Buddha – gold painted, probably 30 ft high. Beaches round here are nice, but dirty with seaweed. Stopped at a few other spots on the way round, at one finding a massive resort of wooden 'bungalows' in a nice bay, completely deserted. Looked very expensive. What a waste.

Heading down to Chaweng, the most popular beach on the island, we came across a lot of very upmarket resorts, with pricey menus, smart accommodation, and some even with pools. These were reasonably busy (not full) with I think German and European holidaymakers. At the top end of the beach (with posh resorts) the sea was calm, the waves breaking over coral away from the beach. Down the cheap end the water was very choppy as waves broke on the beach. Still nice, palm-lined. In Chaweng town we found the bar-lined road empty. Plenty on the beach, although still not enough to fill bars.

Confused. It seems that in the same town there are posh resorts, with older people and bar-lined streets, perhaps hoping to cater to alcoholics (they'd have to be to keep the number of bars going). Two things at odds – posh resorts not having your 'Spanish' type holidaymakers. We thought perhaps they targeted the middle-aged well-off men who come to go to bars to find a Thai woman, but there aren't enough of them. One will have to give; at the moment it's the bars, selling up left, right, and centre. Maybe in five years the resorts will go down market, getting your Majorca crowd, and so filling bars, etc. Can't tell what will happen.

Back safely to our resort early. Too risky in the dark, seen too many tourists with bandages on for my liking. Anyway, yes, it is a nice island. Think we were lucky to be where we are staying.

On Friday the 7th we had booked a day trip to the Ang Thong Marine Park, a group of islands between Koh Samui and the mainland. This started from Na Thon at 8:30 a.m. We got a taxi there, which was in fact a truck with two benches sideways on in the back, picking up anyone along the way between Lamai and Na Thon. Good idea. School kids and locals jumped in and out along the way. About 200 km to Na Thon. Nice day, sea was very calm, although a little cloudy in the pictures. The Marine Park was about two hours from Samui. The boat we had was a fair size, holding about say 100 people, perhaps 70 on our trip. Sailed to the islands and pulled in to the largest. To get onto the island we had to get onto a smaller boat and be ferried to the nice beach. Here was a viewpoint, a 30 minute climb up a hillside. From the top the view was spectacular, seeing all the small tree-lined uninhabited islands making up the park.

On the way to the islands we saw dolphins jumping and little fish skimming along the water by their tails. Very odd.

After admiring the views and nice beach we had lunch back on the boat, moving to another island stop after touring through the cluster. This stop, again shuttled to shore, was to see a lake in the centre of the island, higher than the sea, lighter blue in colour and 250 x 350 m in size, 7 m deep. More words are needed to describe it. Sat on top of a hill overlooking the lake and many of the other islands for some time. Set off back to Samui, sitting on the boat in a spot where spray from waves soaked us every few minutes. Arrived in Na Thon around 5 p.m., so stayed here for another sunset, being on the west coast of the island. Sunset over the sea, again a glowing red and orange, changing continuously. Nice with the silhouettes of boats, etc.

A nice trip, although with those views you can't fail really.

Bangkok 11/2

OK, now we've moved on, I'll come to that in a bit. The trip on the bike around the island was really good, a great way to travel. Got me back to thinking what I said I'd do for years, get a bike, pass my test, and then tour round somewhere later on with a bigger one, just as I'd seen so many people doing on my trips to Canada and Europe. I said I'd do it (get a smaller bike) last year, but didn't, so maybe when I get back. So many bikes here, it's the easiest way to travel through the city traffic.

After our Ang Thong Island tour we had a quiet day at Lamai. I took my time and had a walk into the tourist village, which was of course deserted even though it was lunch time. Still incredibly hot, sweating away, just moving slowly through the shaded street. Tackled the heat with some muesli, fruit, and yogurt dish for lunch and some nice chocolate ice cream (nice cones). Spent the evening, after writing the first half of this letter all afternoon, watching videos in the next-door resort restaurant, 'Nice Resort 1'. Robin Hood (Kevin Costner) – pretty poor film. Had a nice fish coconut curry though! Being Saturday we again tuned in to the World Service broadcast of Radio 5's sports coverage. Fell asleep when football came on. That reminds me, the Cricket World Cup starts in Australia and NZ on February 22nd, so with any luck we will be able to cheer on our lads in person!

On Sunday the 9th we had finished our islands/beaches/sun part of our trip; time to head back to Bangkok. We had to catch the ferry from the island at Na Thon Pier at 2:45 p.m. We spent the morning sorting out a few things, generally not doing much, before getting to the town by taxi. The boat (smallish) was packed and quite fast, taking two and a half hours for an 80 km trip. Sat on the top side of the boat, falling asleep in the afternoon sun. A bus took us from the arrival pier on the mainland at 5 p.m. to Surat Thani nearby. From there we had to catch the 7:30 coach to Bangkok for the overnight trip. The bus was very spacious and air-conditioned.

Had a video on for a while, showing great crashes (made us feel good!) from car and bike racing. When you see the way these drivers drive these coaches these videos look fairly harmless. They belt along the roads, which are only single-file roads, overtaking all the trucks and other coaches that fill the road in the night. Arrived safely and on time 6 a.m. of the 10th, having slept most of the way not too comfortably.

So, back in Bangkok. Still very busy, having to stay in a bit of a pit of a place, though no problem, and more expensive than the place before (฿150 for a double). Had plenty to sort out; airline tickets for Singapore, more photos to get done, and things to shop for. Got some Levi's for £4 (501's, so they say). Walking around the area looking at all the masses of clothes for sale on the stalls of the streets (it's like a market every day here) we found a shopping centre, nine levels, selling all sorts. It had a food centre on a couple of floors, with all round views over the city, selling so many different types of dishes of food – if only we knew what half of them were. On the top floor was even a couple of cinemas, bumper cars, and fair-type rides and stands. One thing about the Thais, they don't do anything by halves.

Photos: today I'm sending a parcel with more photos in (letter explaining inside) and various other bits and pieces.

Nice to be back to Bangkok street food. Today we've got the photos of Phi Phi, etc. They're really good, nice fish ones. Also got some copies of the workmen in India and sending them to a guy there! Nice touch!

This is my last sheet for now, as we're just waiting now before flying to Singapore. It's quite expensive compared to here, so many camp! Still, we shall see. I'll be in touch soon. Everyone take care in that cold weather!

Love

David.

PS. Can you photocopy this before it falls apart. Thanks.

17/2/92

Jakarta Airport

Indonesia

OK,

Hello, got an hour wait here so I thought I'd write about Singapore, having just left there. Last letter I was in Bangkok sorting everything out to go to Singapore. Sent off a parcel home with photos of Phi Phi, as I said before, should take a month, aiming around mid-March hopefully. Not easy getting a parcel off from Bangkok, having to box up, queue, fill in forms, queue, get value, get stamp, queue. Took an hour or so. After that we calculated our money and decided we had enough spare for a drink, which was the first for a few weeks. Found a dirt cheap place to eat, they had to put chairs out specially when we arrived.

On the 12th, flight day, we got a muesli/fruit breakfast in, probably our last for a while, and sorted our stuff out before getting a minibus to the airport. The minibus was badly driven and had a pretty knackered engine I think. Checked in, waited, went through another non-existent customs, boarded the plane on time, so it's easy. The plane was a 757 again, very posh, Royal Nepal – good service and food again. Only a 'light meal' on our three-hour flight. Leaving at 14:40 it was very clear, although we flew over the water all the way until Singapore. Got into the cockpit! Very tiny—the two pilots had their feet up on the control panels and were reading the papers. 'Hey, this is easy'. The control panels and screens weren't doing anything at all as we cruised smoothly along. An all-round view of nothing but blue, sky and sea. Inside the cockpit was only big enough for three people; above was a large bank of fuses, in front were the round gauges and a computer graphics screen. Plane was three years old. Left them to analyse their share values and sat back in my seat, hoping they put the papers down soon. The flight was really good. Very dull skies over Singapore.

As we flew in we saw so many large ships waiting away from the city on the water, busiest port in the world, not much space between them. The island that makes up Singapore is quite small really, only 600 square km. Skyscrapers and tower blocks sprouted up from the land, although this area was 25 km from the 'city'. Landed at 6 p.m. local time – 30°C again! Walked out of the plane through the spotless airport, the floors shining new. It was a sign of things to come. Our bags were there already. We picked them up and went through a non-existent customs. That easy. No hassles, no fighting. Massive airport, well organized. For ten minutes it rained very heavily while we were in the airport. Picked up information provided free by the airport. Excellent maps and info. Studied that and headed off in search of our bus 390 to city. It was there waiting for us.

Between the airport and the city centre we followed the east coast, passing water parks, big restaurants, tower blocks. Getting into the city at around 7:30 p.m. it was getting dark, and it looked like the Manhattan skyline as we went over flyover after flyover. Loads of tall skyscrapers and smaller hotels. One hotel was 66 floors, one of the tallest. Building more towers and developing and redeveloping everywhere. Dropped off by Raffles City, one area of skyscrapers which was posh hotels and a shopping centre. Walked to Bencoolen Street where cheaper accommodation was to be found. We stopped to check our guide book to find we had stopped right outside one place, Bencoolen House, next to the Strand Hotel! Went in and found a 7th floor of a nine-story block had dorm beds for $6 (£2). (Exchange rate is $3 to £1). Cheaper than we were expecting (a single room (double bed) costs $30). So we couldn't believe it again, another smooth arrival, straight into a place. In a city of 77% Chinese celebrating Chinese New Year this week it seemed good going. Had a look out into the city. Roads were good, wide, one-way systems, so seemed quiet and orderly, even had green men crossings (instead of run-and-hope!). Still really hot and sticky.

Singapore streets are very safe, big fines for littering, city is spotless and built up high with areas of green, and you can drink the tap water. We had heard Singapore was the 'food capitol' of Southeast Asia, so we went in search of this. We found what are all over the city – food centres – basically areas full of tables and stools surrounded by 'hawker' stalls, little stalls that cook up all sorts of different things, so from one you can get duck and rice, another say an Indian dish, another a Chinese, and so on. Great stuff, very cheap and the place is usually buzzing, with people eating and drinking as the hawkers dash around. Over the few days here we found so many of these places, a lot very similar, (down market and cheap) and others more organized with fixed seats and food counters, like you find in shopping centres in the UK I guess (and higher priced), still so much cheaper than restaurants. We had some great food, and it cost around two or three dollars a meal (main dish).

Studied the info on Singapore – seemed such an interesting city, masses to do and see – and other areas on the island. Only four days to do as much as we could. We didn't really know much about Singapore before the trip, but seeing it, the developments, the plans, the lifestyles, and the future in the things we did and visited it was clear that it's lucky we don't know about it in the UK, as it puts us to shame. Admittedly there are only around three million on the island, but their organization makes the UK look years behind. More of the reasons for this thinking as I go along.

------- Writing from Sydney 21/2/92 --------

On our first full day there (13th) we went out in search of breakfast, and found a hotel that had self-service coffee and toast breakfast for $2, so we took advantage of this, as we did every day we were in Singapore. A bargain really, one coffee usually costs $1 and we were having three coffees and ten pieces of toast and jam. Some days we even sneaked a few jam sandwiches we made out to eat for lunch. Anyway, we worked out the things to see and our plan. Decided that this day we would look around the shopping areas, and a few other city areas to see. Orchard Road about twenty minutes away was the large shopping centre area. At the end of Orchard Road was the 'Comcentre', a massive tower block with aerials and dishes on the top. This was the telecommunications centre, and we'd read of an exhibition of high-tech communication equipment. Spent hours in there playing with the things; with videophone, video conference, other equipment to send pictures, info, etc. over the phone, some system like teletext, allowing you to do home shopping (The fashion screens even produced colour pictures of the articles for sale). Some amazing stuff there; our first sign of Singapore's technology.

We spent the rest of the afternoon walking around the bewildering number of shopping complexes. There were so many complexes lining Oxford Street, from the massive hotel shopping centres with top name expensive shops, to the tatty ones with the bargain shops. In the cheaper shops there aren't often prices, so you have to ask and then you can haggle. So much electronic equipment at unreal prices. Some shops were lined with hundreds of models of cameras, Walkmans, watches. Prices are so low. Mark got a camera eventually for only £100, an excellent one, variable zoom 35-80 mm, all automatic with a little gimmicky remote control for a self-timer, Japanese made. It would cost at least £200 in the UK I'm sure. (Canon Sure Shot only £50, mine cost £100 on sale). Music centres are cheap too. Sony systems are only £250. I know that's around £600 at home. I liked the camera, but resisted and stuck with mine. Maybe next time I pass through here!

It chucked it down for ten minutes around 5 p.m. after being boiling and sunny all morning. Does this happen every day?

After our shopping we walked to Raffles Hotel, near Raffles City (66-story hotel and posh shopping centre). Raffles was the guy who found Singapore for the Brits (Sir Stanford Raffles, actually), so everything seemed to be called Raffles. Anyway, this was a mega posh hotel, having had a $160 million refurbishment. Went in (shorts and T-shirt of course) and into the courtyards full of nice plants, fountains, and tables. Building was shiny white and very nice; I can see how expensive it must be to stay there. Peeked through the window of the restaurant at the evening food on offer – same as we have been eating, only a little more pricey. I don't give these rich people the respect they obviously deserve!

Our info told us to go to Bugis Street one night, which was near Raffles, a street full of food sellers, market stalls, and street entertainment. Actually, it was very busy, but was a tiny street with only a few market stalls. The food was quite pricey, and there was no street entertainment to mention. Went back to the food centre of the previous night, though not many stalls were open.

On Friday the 14th, more coffee and toast, and caught a bus to the south of the city to the World Trade Centre. Bus services are so easy, efficient, and cheap. Don't have to wait long for the buses, which are in good condition and clean. Max fares to anywhere on the island is only 90c (30p). Another very hot, clear, sticky day. WTC quite small for such a big trading city (no resources of its own), but next to the massive docks area. The reason we went there was to get a cable car ride up to Mt. Faber, starting on level 13 of a tower block. It was pretty spectacular, seeing the skyscrapers, docks, and hundreds of ships. The view from Mt. Faber over the city showed how many tower blocks are on the island, stretching away as far as we could see.

We took a ride in the cable car, probably a few hundred feet up, down to Sentosa Island, an island of 'entertainment,' only a narrow lane of water from the main city island. Interesting place. On the island it's basically man-made attractions, even the palms on the 'beaches' are put there. Nice peaceful place with nice gardens, museums, and beaches. It's quite a small island, with a memorial running around it. Nice for city dwellers to get away from the place, although, as I say, it's not unbearably busy and it's clean and safe.

Left the island and got a bus back to the city in about one minute. Out for food as it got dark, another hawker food centre under a shipping centre. Duck and rice for only $2! A bit further down the street we saw loads of lights; Chinatown was all lit for New Year, with loads of red and gold banners everywhere. Very busy, the shopping centres still open at 9 p.m., with even more food centres and the herbal medicine shops (selling all sorts of strange things), although this was the commercial shopping centre of Chinatown, 'People's Park Complex' for one. Saw all the romantic couples in the McDonalds! The city is really not too big, not taking long to walk from one end to the other, although to be honest the whole island is built up and could be called city too. Nice relaxed atmosphere at night – still hot!

On Saturday, we decided to go to Chinatown as they were celebrating Lunar New Year. Walking there we passed the Singapore River (tiny) and all the tall, tall office blocks of the 'colonial' area. No manufacturing industry to mention I guess. Reaching Chinatown we heard some drum banging and checked it out. In a food centre, basically a massive area under a corrugated sheet roof, some guys were banging drums while a dragon thing moved around a little in front of one of the food stalls, and after ten minutes produced a fruit salad from its mouth. Yes. Not really too exciting and very loud. Food here was very cheap. Went to Tanjong Pagar, an area of 'old style' Chinese shops that had been tarted up a little, making it completely characterless and very pricey, and with that deserted. The other streets of Chinatown weren't much better, shops just selling tacky souvenir-type stuff, little Chinese hats with pig tails on, etc. Not as busy as we'd hoped and no celebrations to be seen. The new shopping centres were busier, full of people eating or shopping (as usual), as that's all they seem to do! Found a real market full of stacks of veg and live fish and other seafood. In the evening we tuned in to World Service again – England massacre of France!

Sunday the 16th we spent the day at the Singapore Science Centre quite a way from the city, in the west of the island. To get there and back we used the 'Mass Rapid Transit' system, their version of the metro or tubes. Unbelievably shining and clean, modern and easy to use, although there are only two lines in two directions. Not very busy, but even 'small' stations are large and spotless. Part underground and part further from the centre above ground, raised up on a pillar-supported track. For the twenty minute trip we passed nonstop tower blocks. They call it 'productivity of land'; why put 30 people in one area when you can put 300? (Learned that in the science centre under the section on productivity). We arrived at the science centre just before 12 p.m., allowing us to get in to the first show of the 'OMNI Theatre'. This was a five story high 'cinema' which was dome shaped so that the screen wrapped around you. Film and projection meant you felt 'there' when they showed the film, wanting to lean in to any motions that appeared, like flying or roller coasters (confuses the brain!). The film on show was 'Ring of Fire', a movie about volcanoes around the Pacific. Brilliantly filmed, with excellent computer graphics showing all volcanoes located around a big rotating globe. 'Flew' over San Francisco with earthquake devastation, to Tokyo and areas in Japan with volcanoes erupting, and to Mt. St. Helens in the USA. Very interesting, seeing how people live in danger areas and think nothing of it. SF, Indonesia, etc.

Spent the next four hours wandering around the 600 or so exhibits in the centre, which are all 'practical' ones, getting to play with everything. Although nothing was new to me it was great to see how they had tried to explain sometimes quite complex principles with very simple demos. They covered so much, even stuff I didn't do til university. This is another reason I could see the UK slipping, the place was full of kids playing and learning such stuff.

Enjoyed the 'OMNI movie', so went to the planetarium show in the same theatre. Learnt about the sun, moon, and

Earth. Only five billion years before we're engulfed by an expanding sun! Oh no!

Rode on MRT back to the city for more food centre stuff; 'satay,' like little meat kebabs. Hot and sweaty at night, as usual.

Monday the 17th we were off out of Singapore. It seemed hard to believe we were off again already, and heading to Australia. Got the bus to the airport from our street, getting there about three and a half hours before our flight, which was then put back half an hour. Checked in OK. Spent more than every penny of Singapore money we had on coffee and cakes. The plane, Garuda Airlines of Indonesia, was quite large; eight seats across, an airbus something. Half empty. This was only a short 1 hour 20 minute flight to Jakarta, Indonesia. It rained as we left Singapore and was very choppy as we took off and for the first ten minutes – pilots turning pages of their papers too quickly. Just enough time for the crew to get a good meal down us. Landed in Jakarta around 16:15 after going back an hour (confused). Had a two and a half hour wait there, in the small departure area, nothing like airports of Singapore or Bangkok.

The next flight was on a similar plane, again reasonably new, with video and music for the long flight. 1 hour 20 minutes to Denpasar in Bali, Indonesia where we were to stop and pick up passengers to slightly increase the again half full plane. They got another meal down us before arriving there, where we landed OK and waited one and a half hours on the plane. Cleaning crews worked frantically around us in that time. Took off for the next six-hour flight to Sydney. Music channel was no good, so I tried to sleep. At some time very early (2 a.m. on my watch – don't know how it translated to ground time) they woke us for breakfast. Sun was rising ahead of us, very striking, a band of all the colours along the horizon. As it got lighter you could see Australia below. Flat and barren and empty. As we headed to NSW to Sydney the land gradually became a patchwork of fields, then a few hills and trees (Great Dividing Range? Not very great!) getting to a rugged coastline near Sydney. Couldn't see the city as we flew in to land at 8 a.m. local time, 21°C, (eleven hours ahead of the UK), three hours ahead of Singapore.

Getting off the plane the airport was more the rough sort, having to wait for bags and not sure where they should be. Got through immigration, but got stopped at customs. They emptied out my rucksack and didn't find anything except for the dirt on my boots, which is an illegal import! I think he let me off. Lucky. They have fun in their jobs, I suppose.

Went to a tourist place there, but it wasn't helpful as they were the sort who wanted to get people into hotels, etc. Maps and info not too good, although some good backpacker's stuff. Caught a bus to the cheap accommodation area of the city, 'Kings Cross'. The bus driver spoke to me, but I couldn't understand a word he said – I thought they spoke English (sort of) here?! Went through the city, past Harbour Bridge and the Opera House to Kings Cross. There's loads of 'backpackers' places here, and we got a place no trouble. What we got was pretty good; a flat for four people, two rooms of two bunks, with a kitchen and bathroom. It cost $75 a week each. Exchange rate now is £1 to $2.2, so that's around £34. Expensive, but cheapish for Sydney, and with a kitchen we can do our own food. We're not missing anything by not eating out, as it's all standard food and expensive. Very nice place; good view of the city, and in a small apartment block. It was still very early in the day that had been going on for ages. My times were all messed up by now.

A lad that was in the flat already took us into the city centre, around twenty minutes' walk. Very hot and sweaty, although most people are very pale, obviously avoiding the deadly sun. We went and collected our mail. Got a load of your letters. Good to hear all's well again. I'll say more in a bit about those as soon as I've got all this novel stuff out the way.

Got our bearings as we wandered around the city. We opened bank accounts, which was so easy, so we can handle our money easier. Went straight away to do the most important job: purchasing a ticket for Australia vs England World Cup Cricket here in Sydney on March 5th. $25 for a day/night match, starts at 2:30 p.m. and goes until 10:15 p.m. Should be a great day – when we beat them, too! After looking round, heading back to Kings Cross we did some grocery shopping for the first time in ages! Prices about the same as in the UK. Still early. Studied all the letters and piles of info we collected in and on the city. Slept and slept and slept. Very warm in the night.

Doing our own shopping I've now had stuff like cornflakes and baked beans that I haven't had for ages. For our first full day here on Wednesday the 19th we had a massive list of things to do, which meant we spent this day, and the Thursday too, walking round and round the city and planning things in the flat. We thought we would work here, as we went to the CEs (job centre) and inquired about some jobs. Actually we were offered a job the first we tried: collecting for charity, getting 30% commission. They also had jobs where you go out into the 'country' for four weeks doing the same with free accommodation where we could earn $400 a week. With the tax rate of 50% for us, having to claim back 20% later, we analysed the jobs on offer, what we could earn and our overall plans and decided it wasn't worth working. It would be different if we were here for months, but to slog it out for a month in the middle of nowhere earning enough to stay another couple weeks after losing half on tax didn't seem worthwhile. Would take a lot of time and money to get a decent well-paid job in the city, time we may not have. We decided not to bother chasing work unless something comes to us, and so we could work out our tour plan. We managed to get a real bargain tour ticket in a 'backpacker's' travel shop on Bus Australia, a twelve month valid ticket on the coach on a set route (list below), we can stop anywhere for any length, cost us only £175 ($387) – a bargain for 12,000 km travelling!

Food-wise, in some magazines we found a voucher for Big Macs, buy one ($2.50) get one for 50 cents, so we've collected a lot of vouchers. It's a good deal, as a meal in a restaurant starts at $5, and we can get two Big Macs and two drinks for that.

So, after two days of serious planning and organizing (a lot wasted job-wise initially) we now know where we stand and how we're getting around. You can buy cheap cars, etc., but that's a bit risky. Imagine breaking down in the outback. Can't call home for help then!

Thursday night we did go out and have a couple of drinks as things are very social around here, full of travellers. You get a 'schooner' (3/4 pint) for about £1. Reasonable I guess. Sat in the bar listening to Kylie with my schooner of Fosters!

Friday, today, we arranged to meet Michelle. It was drizzling all day, so sightseeing was out really, as all best things are outside; opera house, bridge, harbour. Met Michelle at 12:30 in the city. She also had a Scottish lad, Gordon, with her who had got in touch with her like us and was in Sydney. We had a good day, going round the quite posh shopping area of Darling Harbour and sitting in McDonald's, a pub, and a cafe out of the drizzle. Nice to have some time off from planning things, just chatting to the other two. They were both very nice, and Michelle is funny. She brought us info, too. Unfortunately there wasn't much we could do that we hadn't done or wasn't spoilt by weather, although we had a trip on the monorail around the harbour and a ride on the harbour ferry. We were invited for a real Aussie meal (maybe a barbie!) at her house, about a half hour by train from the city, so I guess we'll go over.

OK. So now the information you've been waiting for. Our plan goes something like this: We'll be in Sydney til Tuesday the 25th, going to Blue Mountains and Marley and Bondi Beach in the following week, returning for the cricket on March 5th. Probably leave Sydney around March 8th, so you can send any mail here up until say March 1st, although if it's not urgent don't bother. On March 8th we will go to the Canberra area, going to some of the national parks between there and Melbourne. We should be in Melbourne say March 15th for a week or so. I'll call in on Peggy. Adelaide next. We calculate that the earliest we can possibly leave Adelaide is March 20th, although it'll probably be a lot later. Any mail you want to send up to March 13th send to Adelaide:

American Express International Inc.,
13 Grenfell St,
Adelaide, South Australia

I'll let you know our plan after this later. Basically though it's Adelaide → Ayers Rock → Townsville → Cairns (Barrier Reef), down the coast beaching and island hopping → Brisbane → Sydney.

If we don't work and keep our time scales as hoped we could be back in Sydney by early May. At the moment we are due to leave on May 20th to get to NZ, then arrive in LA on June 19th. That would only give us two weeks to get into Canada, which isn't enough with all of California to see. We think if we leave Australia in early May, we can get to LA by June 8th, say, having four weeks to get to Canada for July. I need to know which weeks or dates you will be in or can get to Canada. If it's the 6th of July for two weeks then I'll have to get to NZ in early May. If it's possible to go early August then my plans would be different. I think it's possible for us to get there for the first two weeks in July (6th).

So that's the plan. I've a few more things to say, a few more things for you to do for me! Thanks for the certificate and sorting our money and photos, etc. I've got some more money off the Visa paid into my bank account here, only £200, and I should be OK with money now for a month or two (I hope!).

About the letters and photos. Hope you've had the photo (rolls) from Delhi. There's not much we can do otherwise, just wait. I also sent a letter from there; I can't work out if you've had that.

I don't know if it's possible, but if you could try and photocopy the Egypt photos and send a few, or all, if it's not too expensive (the photocopies) to mail. I guess I could wait, but it would be good to see them! Pick out some good ones if not and send photocopies in next letter. Doesn't matter if you can't.

I'll be phoning in the next day or two so maybe I'll have said most of this to you. Still, write and let me know the dates of Canada, as I think it's easier for me to work round your dates than you round mine, as ours will change continually, I think. Hope everything is fine there, weather's better, car's OK, and the rest. I don't think there's much more to say, although I'll probably have masses to write again in another week, other than to say all's well. Oh, I didn't say much about Sydney. Seems a lively city, the centre is full of skyscrapers and tall towers, fairly standard. When we were in the National Library (very nice place) we saw the Queen's hat go down the street (she was obviously standing in a vehicle) over the crowds, I guess she was under it by the cheers. She followed us over! And, yes, it's true, Aussies have no culture at all! I thought we were bad!

Loads of love

David

Bondi Beach

Sydney, Australia

1/3/92

& Canberra 11/3/92

Hello there,

Oh, not another beach you're probably saying.

Anyway, it was another week since I was in touch last, phoning you. Glad to hear everything's OK and looking forward to some more mail when I get back to Sydney. I'll carry on then with more of my tales about what time I got up, what I ate, and all of that!

After the pretty miserable day weather-wise we had with Michelle on the Friday, the Saturday was really nice; a few light clouds, but sunny and hot. This was our chance to do the sights and get all our photos. We'd been waiting so long we knew exactly where to go and when. We started off walking out from Kings Cross to the botanical gardens. From there, at a spot full of Japanese (of which there are thousands here!), is a good point for – guess what – yes, taking photos of the opera house and bridge. By this time we had picked up a South African girl who was wanting to do the sights in a few hours between flights to and from Sydney, looking lost.

Our walk from the viewpoint 'Mrs Macquarie's Seat' took us through the trees, ponds, and flowers of the nicely laid out gardens, along the harbourfront to Sydney Opera House (not much up close, although interesting building style) and a circular quay where the ferries roll in and out every few minutes. In the area next to the quay the city has done a lot of development, tarting up old buildings – the 'rocks' area. Very nice, buskers all along the front, a few markets, and another good spot for viewing the opera house, as it is directly opposite the bit of land that sticks out into the harbour with the opera house on. Along from the rocks is the Harbour Bridge, a monster construction of English steel joints and rivets, built in 1930. Tourists can climb up inside the pillar at one end of the bridge. It's a big stone tower, so not very daring really. From the top there's a great view of the harbour area.

Being sunny and Saturday the harbour waters were stuffed full of yachts. Calling it a harbour probably makes it sound just like some sort of bay, but actually it's more like a large river with rough edges stretching both directions from the city for miles. The entrance to the 'harbour' is about seven miles away! Climbing up the steps to the top was hard in the heat. After this view over the water, opera house, quay, etc., we climbed down heading for an even bigger view. Another bargain Big Mac later we'd used our forged Student IDs (Bangkok) to get a cheaper ride up to Sydney Tower, a 300 m pole with a restaurant and view platform on the top. I can't be bothered to think up a new word for the view, just to say it was better than good. You could see 22 km, we were informed by a digital display. It was just unbelievable what detail you could make out from 900 ft up, being so bright and clear. You could really tell what the people were eating as they sat round the pool on the rooftop of the Hilton hotel, some 500 ft below. They probably paid too much for it, whatever it was! You could see the planes crossing each other at the airport, the people crossing the streets, and all the city 'sights'. From there we could see even more yachts even further away. Looking straight down, which you could do from the angled window, was a bit frightening but interesting. The city itself stretches out in all directions, with occasional patches of green; 'Hyde Park', the botanical gardens, Centennial Park, etc. So much water. While we all battled for good viewpoints to get photos, Japanese people were behind us taking photos of an English woman's baby!

Walking back a different way to Kings Cross we hoped a bar would be showing Australia vs NZ cricket. I assumed Aussies would be boozing on a Saturday afternoon watching their team. No, we never found anything. With that plan ruined we spent some time in the flat cooking our tea, more pasta and sauce, before going out to sample the nightlife. The pub we went in, O'Malley's, was fairly busy, although got busier by 11 p.m., staying open very late. It could have been anywhere; it was just like home. A mix of travellers and drunk Australians made me realize that this kind of thing, that I had done every week while in the UK, wasn't really missed. They did show the highlights of the cricket, as news had (very quietly) broken that NZ had won. Australia's live coverage is pretty awful, the same commentators as the UK, but ads thrown in between every over and every wicket, and not smoothly either. I think it was after I left the still lively pub at 2 a.m. that I phoned you.

Sunday (23rd) started quite nice, so we went, as planned, to Manly, a beach resort seven miles up the harbour from the city. This involved getting down the quay and catching one of the half hour ferries. We missed one as it pulled out as we arrived. The ferries are large, but rocked pretty badly as we headed up the harbour towards the sea. When we arrived the sky had become black. Everyone piled rapidly off the ferry at the 'wharf' there into the shopping centre in case it rained. This was one of those new look centres, shiny floors, steel tubing everywhere, prices still too much. "Before it starts to rain," we dashed to the beach to have a look. The beach was smaller than expected, although the waves were as big as expected. It was still busy, the streets between the wharf and beach full of tacky holiday resort shops and takeaways. People sat along the front with bags of chips, the sky was black, wind was building up. If the beach hadn't been clean and full it could have been at home. On the beach a surfer's lifesaving competition was going on, with teams full of lifeguards in little hats and zinc covered noses, swimming, surfing, and rafting in and out of the water. The rafting lifesaving was impressive, as they speedily started their rubber raft with the propeller engine on the back, raced out over the breaking waves, flying high into the air, picking up the victim in one move without stopping and racing back to shore. These were the people I had expected to see down the beach – remember Paul Hogan's lifeguard.

A few minutes later it (the sky) let rip, everyone on the beach staying there, everyone else going for cover. Luckily, part of our visit plan was the oceanarium or aquarium. This is one on the Sydney hitlist. In here, as well as the few tanks of multicoloured fish, coral life, and other sea life, they had a real show and most importantly an underwater tunnel; an acrylic clear tube running in a circle through a very large tank of large, dull-looking fish, large sharks, and large stingrays. They also had a moving walkway running around the tunnel, although this made things harder rather than easier. The clear tubes meant you could see the sharks and rays right up close without being had. Pretty good, although the circular tank could have done with some plant life. Scuba divers got in at one stage, to be mobbed by hungry fish and sharks. You can arrange to dive in there if you're certified (certified mad more like). This time I was quite happy to be the other side of the plastic as the shark took whole fish out the hands of the divers.

Out in the dry part of the world (above the surface) it was probably wetter, as the rain got heavier. We got the ferry back to the city and rather than our usual walk home we caught the city train. It's a little like the underground, only, you guessed it, a bit better. Actually the compartments are double-deckers, with a lot of seats and carpets and head room. You can also flip the backs of the seats around by a clever series of hinges, so you can face whichever direction you want. The train was clean, big fines for littering or feet on the seats. No class system on the trains, just smoking and non-smoking cars. The coaches look like shiny silver tubes, with corrugated metal exteriors and yellow tinted windows. Not all that cheap.

To occupy the wet evening I watched some Australian TV. Every night they seem to show a good film in amongst the mix of soaps and American rubbish on one of the half a dozen channels. Fish Called Wanda was on, which was interrupted frequently with ads without warning. If you blinked you may be confused how the story had changed from John Cleese in court to an animated chicken puppet crossing the street. The ads are all as bad as the ones you see on those 'let's take the mickey out of foreign ads' shows. Couldn't help laughing. Before we complain about BBC or ITV you should see the TV here.

The next day (Monday) it was unfortunately wet again. We hadn't any plans left for Sydney. We had paid for our accommodation for the week ($75) so we weren't leaving until the next day. Without going into detail we spent most of the day studying info on Australia and NZ in the flat and the local library, and playing cards with Nick, the other lad staying in the same flat. More bad Australian TV – interesting to see their current affairs stuff, learning about how their lives are basically the same as ours in the UK. The weather is seriously messed up here. In February so far they've had 300 mm of rain (summer?), normally the average is 116 mm. In Queensland they are flooded out after having the worst drought for years and years. The world's in a bit of a state it seems, with the Middle East buried in snow, too. The sun will be shining in the UK next!

Tuesday the 25th we left the fast pace of the city for the peace of the countryside. This day was fairly good, a little cloudy, but the clouds were moving very quickly so it was mainly sunny. We packed up and left Kings Cross, getting a train from there to Katoomba, a smallish town in the 'Blue Mountains'. It was supposed to be direct, but because of line work it involved getting off halfway, getting a bus from there to a station further along the line and another train the rest of the way. Took about two hours to get there. There are 'day trips' to the mountains from Sydney, but something like this can't be rushed, and you couldn't fall back into the slow pace of life if you rush in and out.

We planned to have a couple of days here. They call them the 'Blue Mountains' because the valleys are filled with eucalyptus trees that give off a blue haze. It's true too. The trip on the train was good, it must have taken three-quarters of an hour at a reasonable speed to escape the city and suburbs. The houses on the outskirts are all bungalows, some quite nice. The terraced houses of the city are different to ours, having little balconies. The bungalows all have pillars or 'lace' type ironwork on the front and plenty of room around them. Space wasn't really a problem here I guess. As we entered the Blue Mountain National Park, a vast area of trees, valleys, hills, and cliffs stretching out as far as you could see in all directions, signs of life disappeared. Not hard to see now how such a tame-looking set of hills when seen from the plane could actually be called the Great Dividing Range. If you were in amongst all those trees you would have trouble finding your way.

Anyway, we got there sort of in the middle of the day, the sun shining. Katoomba is a really nice place, a good spot for 'bush' walks, and has some of the attractions of the mountains nearby. We left the station in search of a backpacker's place, and got a room in the first we found. $12 a night, and the place was really nice. We had two bunks in a room for three, a nice shared kitchen with a microwave (!), a great lounge with a TV, log fire, and piano, and it was really nicely located on the hillside. Oh, and free coffee too! The place was obviously originally a plain hotel, with carpets, pictures, the log fires, but must have had to make some backpacker accommodation to get the large amount of business. Backpacker accommodation here means cheaper and sharing things, but it's not that different really.

Studying our information, we decided that as it was dry and clear and still early afternoon we should do the walk and sights around the hills by the town. A half hour walk out of the town was Echo Point, a point on the edge of the plateau the town is on, with a very large drop into the tree-lined valley. Spectacular views, unlike anything we had seen on our travels. One of the 'sights' was a rock formation called the Three Sisters, three clumps of rock at the edge of the cliff. I thought the overall view of the endless valley was more impressive. There was a path down the cliffside, the Giant Stairway, but we didn't find it. A few light showers blew over. The large amount of rain that had fallen had washed some of the walking paths away in places, so restricting where we could go. In this area there is a 'scenic railway', a railway that runs straight up and down the cliff face to the valley. It is said to be the steepest in the world at 52°, and it felt steep as we went down, hanging on tightly. It didn't go down to the valley, only halfway.

We walked through the wet woodland paths, all properly set up by the National Park, as far as we could. If you're into trees and plants then there's plenty of variety down there to keep you interested. Braved the trip back up to the railway. It wasn't busy, and so walking back to the town along the deserted streets with masses of different bird sounds and brightly coloured flowers on the roadside was a million miles from the city. We tried to do some shopping for food, but ended up in a supermarket that was closed, so we couldn't buy much. Made the most of the free coffee as we spent the evening in the room with the T.V. and log fire. It's a little colder than down in Sydney.

The next day we planned a day trip to Wentworth Falls, another spot to be visited, only a ten-minute train ride from Katoomba. A nice day luckily. Wentworth Falls has an even smaller town, the reason for the visit was more the walks, cliffs, trees, and a very impressive waterfall. The fall itself was quite a way from the town. As most of the day trips would have done this first (nearest Sydney), there were not many people around. The land at town-level dropped down about 300 ft as sheer cliffs when we reached the falls. The falls were in two 150 ft steps, both with a thin veil of water. A path went down the cliffside across the top of the falls, down some steep steps to the halfway step of the falls. Where the path was cut into the cliff with rocks and plants hanging and dripping over our heads, looking out over the valley at the other cliffs was pretty shaky stuff. Getting safely back to the top and sitting on a cliff edge overlooking all this amazing scenery, watching the trees and hills changing from dark to light as the clouds moved under the bright sun, made all the walking worth it. Some of the path walks are pretty wild, although probably not a patch on what's in the bottom of the valley.

Having taken all that in, we got back to town and fulfilled one of my long-waited aims - having a bacon sandwich and chips! The town was quite nice, but not much to see, so we headed back to Katoomba on the train, which due to works happened to be a bus! We got out at Leura on the way, a small village with supposedly old-style shops. When they say old they're not really, one was dated 1913 another 1988. The style is square stepped fronts and awnings with signs hanging from them.

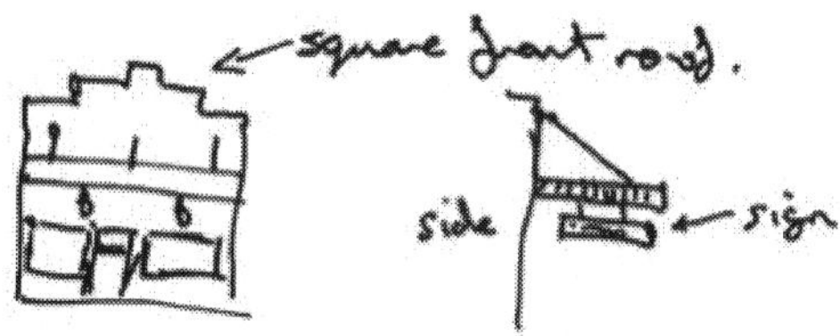

Shops were nice and the village very pleasant. Obviously nothing more than 200 years old. We got back to Katoomba in time to do some shopping, having some more food we hadn't had for ages – jacket potatoes and meat pies.

In the hotel, 'Mountain View Hotel,' they had a games room, so we played table tennis for a while. We hadn't played for years; I think youth club was the last time. Chatted to an old Australian guy who told me about bush fires, frozen railways, and the tough life in the mountains.

We knew Australia had played South Africa the day before, so we listened to the radio in the morning for more news – none. Had they lost? Yes, we discovered later. 'Stuffed' I think is the word. As we've discovered, when they lose they don't say anything here, like yesterday Australia played Germany at hockey in India. Australian radio said nothing, we heard on BBC World Service they'd lost. They were very quiet about Jeff Fenech being dumped on his pants, too, after an incredible amount of hype before the fight. All they said on the radio was the fight had ended in the 8th. Proud perhaps.

On the Thursday we headed back to the big city on the train/bus/train getting straight out to the famous Bondi Beach. We took a while to find a place, but eventually got a place in Lampock Hostel for $60 for the week each. The room we had was in a house being redecorated. It was a bit of a mess really, although being here already a few days it's good enough. A grubby kitchen, with grubby pots and pans, etc. meant the pans we carried all this way were to be used at last!

It was hot and sunny. Bondi Beach wasn't exactly what I expected; about half a mile long, big rolling waves, an area of grass between the beach and front. The front had no tacky shops, mainly restaurants, takeaways, and a few hotels. A pavilion was down on the edge of the beach. The Bondi Hotel, where it all happens, was quite nice. We did our shopping for the week then headed down to the hotel where we watched England walk it over West Indies with my schooner of Toohey's. As we headed back around 10 p.m. things seemed to be getting busier. I sampled Australia's only contribution to world cuisine: charcoal chicken (barbequed), from a takeaway. I don't think they've got anything special to offer, so we're happy to stick to our own concoctions.

Being here in Bondi, at the main surf spot for Sydney, we had to have a shot at surfing. We hired a board Friday morning and went out to 'rip it,' or whatever those surfers do. With the board attached to my ankle by a cord I hit the surf. After a while I could see what I needed to do and did catch a few good waves, lying flat on the board. To get good ones you had to go out beyond the breakers. To get out there, although it was shallow, was so hard, being hit by big waves – two steps forward, two steps back. The strength of the waves can force you under if you don't ride it properly. I managed to get on my knees at one or two points. Good fun, but hard work too. It took a half hour to get out, and ten seconds to get carried back. Even though we hadn't been sunbathing, after a few hours both of us were red and getting sore form the intense sunshine. They really do have problems here. You could feel it burning into your skin, unlike any other sun we've had (and we've had plenty!). Not too bad in the evening as it cools.

In the evening we went to the Bondi Hotel for their special steak. They give you a piece of raw steak, which you cook yourself on the electric/gas barbeque. With a salad and chips it's a bargain meal at $4.80 (£2.20, say). When you see fish and chips at $4 or ice-creams at $3 you can see this is good value. Eating out is really expensive – I suppose no more so than in the UK though.

After eating we went to the Bondi Digger's Club; a working men's (diggers) come social club, where beer is cheap and the locals go. Quite a large place overlooking the beach. One thing they like here, which isn't allowed in the UK, is gambling in the bars, with machines and horse racing, etc. Not too lively really. The disco in Bondi Hotel, although free, was pretty dull. The music was the same old throbbing rubbish, couldn't stand too much of that, though it was interesting to see the Japanese attempting to create some sort of movement to match it.

Saturday started with clouds and showers, so we sat near the beach reading the paper, seeing how the Aussies are having a go at the Brits, as our papers have a go at their PM. I bet the papers there don't say much about the big plans the PM's got to stop the recession. I'd like to see our brave PM announce such major steps (not a pun). Watched a bit more cricket as NZ eased home over SA. Sun started shining in the early afternoon, so we went down to the beach, where a volleyball competition was going on. The beach was busy, but not overcrowded. Always something going on.

Saturday night we'd read in the paper and heard on the radio about a Mardi Gras parade in Sydney, so we took a trip into the city to see it, along with the other 400,000 people squashed along the roadsides. It was very entertaining to see all the floats and costumes, but the nature of it was a bit out of the ordinary. It was in fact a, how shall I put this, a massive 'poofters' parade, as they call them here. I don't know if they were all genuine, but there were a lot of them, both men and women. We just had to laugh at the old bearded men all dressed up in outrageous costumes or dodgy-looking gear. Luckily the crowd seemed pretty friendly in the main, although still a lot of weirdly dressed or sounding people around. Apparently there's quite a concentration of them in Sydney. The city joined in the carnival though, the streets full of people probably all night. Never seen so many people in one place, and never seen so many 'unique' ones either!

Sunday (1/3) we spent the morning on the beach, a sunny day. We'd invested now in factor-twelve sunscreen, taking no chances here, and plastered with that we braved most of the day. The clocks went back an hour, so making it ten hours ahead of the UK, with five time zones in Australia now. On March 21st, when you go forward, we'll be only nine hours ahead, then when we get to Adelaide only eight and a half hours. Their times and time zones are all very odd.

In the evening we were given a few glasses of wine by a couple of young Aussie girls who were hiding out in the house we were in, not paying. They'd basically run away from home, and it was funny to listen to their stories and plans, with everything so definite – you know – 'Oh we're going to Melbourne to work in a hotel.' In the future they were going to England to work as nannies with good pay and cars, etc. I think 'naïve' is the word. Still, can't complain at the free wine.

Monday was more adventurous; we went to the next beach along the coast! Tamarama Bay, a nice little beach with some really strong waves. If you stood in the centre a few metres out into the water waves would come from in front, behind, and the sides all at the same time. Read a Clive James book about his arrival in London; very appropriate reading, I thought, having arrived in his hometown. Funny guy.

Oh, Sunday we watched the Aussies cheat their way into a win over India. It seemed unfair, India had three overs less to get one run less than Australia, and lost by one run. England lost to weather, getting Pakistan out for 74. The rain delayed restart and calculations meant that instead of 74 off 50 overs to win, they needed 64 off 16! Crazy.

Tuesday, with only a couple of days left on Bondi Beach, we hired a board again for more surfing, getting more aches and bruises and battering. It was a little calmer, but still hard work overcoming the waves. Did get on my feet on the board for about, oh, one second once. It's good stuff. Although I think I could get the hang of it with practice, I won't be doing too much more. Another thing on my list I've tried! Spending time in the water means that when you're out you get pretty sore with sun and salt combining as a fryer.

A new lad, Paul, from Leeds arrived in the flat, so we spent ages talking, and ended up going out in the evening to the digger's club for cheap drinks and the pool table. Chatted to a bloke there who was from Aberdare and had been living over here for years, although he didn't sound as though he thought of himself as a local. Plenty of Yugoslavians (I think) In Bondi.

Wednesday was a little cloudy, and we spent the morning in our room. Paul and another guy we'd met, Richard from London (bit of a toff!), were both going to the cricket match so we decided to stay in Bondi until Friday. We took a trip to Bondi Junction looking around the shops etc. Nothing unusual. We hired an icebox, or "esky" as they call them, and bought some drinks to go in it, as it would probably be expensive in the ground. Although beer isn't cheap, cans aren't too badly priced. Because we've been cooking our own food, when we move on we usually eat what we've got left, so having such combinations as on this day: boiled potatoes, bananas, strawberry jam, and toast. Very nice mixed together! Mind you, being our last night in Bondi we treated ourselves to another steak D.I.Y. meal. Pool is popular here, and so we spent another night having a few games with Rich and Paul, with us two winning of course. The drinks we had while in the hotel playing were smuggled in, as it was too expensive to buy there, so we got them from the bottle shop along the street. We save money any way we can (although not drinking may be cheaper!!). Saw karaoke in the club there, none of us were brave enough to have a go. Today though there were surprisingly no Japanese in there.

Thursday the 5th was the BIG DAY! ENGLAND! The tension was building in the flat as we all woke early, on edge, because they said it may rain. That was our biggest worry. In fact it was a nice day in the morning – would it hold out all day? We made up our packed lunches, packed the drinks into our cooler and headed off about 11 a.m. to the ground. The game started at 2:30 p.m., so we would be in nice and early. We were worried for a while that we wouldn't get our esky in, whether you could take your own drink in, etc. I got the job of carrying it through the gate, and got it through no problem. I must have an innocent look!

Plenty of English support was already in, so we settled down near a crowd of Brits, which later turned out to be smack in the centre of the 'mob' of football-style English support. This meant that we had to stand up a lot to see and avoid all the drunken ones as they dropped as quickly as the Aussie wickets. A good atmosphere though, an amazing support, so many British it could have been at home. The national anthem was sung frequently, as well as the other abuse style songs, which was very appropriate at the time with the Aussie/Brit/queen business. The Australian support was not so vocal.

As for the match, well, it was brilliant. Botham was amazing. Australia were maybe reasonable, 140 for 3 I think, then Botham struck and again 4 wickets in 7 balls I think. Turned it around, getting them out easily for only 171 on a (what looked) good batting wicket. The crowd went wild. (If you taped highlights we're in the mob under the guys with the YORK Union Jack). When we batted they got a battering, Botham smashing them around, getting 53 in 60 odd balls. After six overs we'd scored 37 runs. Cruised in for a classic win. As a victory was looking inevitable, a Mexican wave broke out. All but the member's stand of the 38,000 crowd did the wave for maybe twenty minutes, amazing volume, with a hail of paper and plastic cups as the wave passed over.

Oh, I should mention that after achieving the entry of our "esky", we were spotted drinking some cans by the police and it was confiscated until the end of the game. No trouble, the policeman was OK, but we were not allowed to drink cans in ground, mainly for fear of them being used as missiles. Nothing to do with drinking, as seeing the state of the guys buying $3 beers in ground made me wonder why they turn up, as they would never remember the game, if they stayed conscious long enough to see the end.

So many flags and banners, although we never had one ourselves. After the great win we collected the rest of our drinks and sat outside the ground in a small park. The game finished at around 9:30 p.m. and the night was clear. As we sat there a possum ran around us. Bats, big ones, flew around, diving down onto the surface of the pond there with the lit up city in the background. Hard to believe we were still in the city, as all the crowds had gone and the night was quiet again. We got back to Bondi just in time to catch the highlights on the TV.

In the morning (Friday) the papers said 'HUMILIATED', which is the word I used in a letter to Michelle about this game before I left the UK! Good time to be English and be here! I'll try and get to the final! We headed off from Bondi to go back to Kings Cross. We stayed there before in a flat and decided to cheat and book in only one of us. No problem, saving us $12, although one of us would be on the floor (Mark, after we tossed a coin).

The flat we got this time had a cracking view, being on a hillside. From the window as wide as the flat we could see the city centre, bridge and opera house, which when night came looked very good. Didn't do much, except talk to some other blokes in the flat, one guy from England who'd travelled a bit, one being Colonel Gaddafi's dentist! We went into the city and collected the mail. Thanks for the letter, Dad. Had a letter from Mike, so replied to him.

Friday night meant a few standard-looking (dress-wise; suits and awful ties) people were out on the town, although it was quieter than we thought it would be. Kings Cross at night is a bit seedy, seeing a few 'interesting' fights on the way back.

Saturday the 7th we checked out at 10 a.m. and had to fill out time as we had arranged to go to Michelle's home in Parramatta, on the west of Sydney, at about 4 p.m. We filled timed in the park, library, and McDonalds in Kings Cross. We found ourselves in a 'sportsman's' bar, watching the cricket on TV. We started chatting to a couple of blokes (around 45 I guess) and they were really friendly, telling us of some of their travels and places to go, as well as supplying us with some drinks. People here are very friendly if nothing else. It was very funny, but unfortunately we had to leave (now late) to get the train for Michelle's.

We arrived at 4:30 and Michelle collected us from the station as their house, a nice bungalow (surprise), was about ten minutes away. Her parents were very nice, the house was nice, full of the usual bits and pieces you'd see in any house in the UK. They talked of their trip to Europe and the UK, and Gordon, the Scottish lad who also visited, kept us entertained. They provided us with a decent meal: barbequed sausages and chopped salad, potatoes, and a glass of wine! Nice to be reminded of the comforts of home! Quite a pleasant evening, although Michelle humiliated us at Monopoly (with London street names). We had arranged to stay over and catch the coach from there to Canberra in the morning, so we could save money and also watch the England vs Wales rugby match live on TV at 12 a.m. We played well, but should have scored more! We had the BBC transmission, with Ed Butler saying how good Wales were in defence every time we didn't score. Saw highlights of other matches too! Brill.

We slept on the floor, but had a good breakfast done for us in the morning. Very good of them to put us up. May have to return the favour one day. We were given a lift to our coach, nearly missing it as Mark forgot his glasses and traffic problems held us up. The coach trip to Canberra took three and a half hours (250 km) with no spectacular scenery, a lot of trees and greenery. Coach seemed slow, as it travelled at the 100 km/hr speed limit. Coach was pretty good, and they'll all be like this on our grand circuit.

Heading for Canberra, Mark had arranged for some contacts there to expect us, and we didn't know what to expect. We were met at the dropping point at 3:30 on Sunday afternoon, in the city centre.

OK, I'm going to have to send this letter, otherwise I'll be miles behind. We're having a great time here and being well looked after by all the family. Nice to phone, even though it got me out of bed! Looking at our plan now, we'll be here in Canberra until the 19th or 20th, so getting to Peggy about then. I'll phone her before we leave here and let them know. We're hoping to either get tickets or be in Melbourne for the 25th of March for the cricket final. Now we've spent plenty of time here in the south we will have to do the east coast reasonably quickly, having about five weeks. If you can get to Canada for August that's better for me, but we could make July at a push. Anyway, when I get to Peggy's I'll give you a call to say I'm there.

I'll have to carry on with the details of the previous week in another letter. Don't end up not going to Canada because of worrying about which date to go. If you can, sort something and we can make it definite when we talk on the phone next, as my plans will have to be really well defined to make sure I can get there when you do.

At the moment we should be in Adelaide until about the 30th of March. I don't know from there exactly what dates I'll be where. I'll have to let you know when we know the Canada dates. Between now and then we've got four weeks of travel in NZ, and would like as much as possible (say four weeks) to do California and the west coast of America, so you can see why I need to sort it out now.

OK, that'll do for this one. Hope everything's still good and there are no problems. I'll be in touch from Peggy's, and no doubt write another long letter too!

Love

David.

P.S. I've just bought tickets to the cricket final at MCG on my Mastercard, so watch for that on my bills. I just hope England gets there now.

Melbourne

20/3/92

Another dull letter
I'm afraid.

Hello, or is it g'day sports,

Time to write again. Now I'm in Melbourne, arriving yesterday (14th). Since the last letter up to arriving in Canberra, that's where we've been for eleven days. As I said, we were met by a contact that some relatives of Mark had. We were put up by them in their house in one of the suburbs of Canberra, Belconnen, and treated like members of the family. The family, being the parents Pat and Hugh (originally from S. Wales), the two daughters Lisa and Francesca who lived there, and the two married sons Andrew and Anthony, all went out of their way to keep us entertained. A room had been sorted out for us and they had made plans already. The house was unusually a two-floored one, nice and typical. Canberra was a nice city, unlike other cities in that it was a planned city and so it had loads of open space. It is split into suburbs, each with their own shopping centres. Because of this it is very spread out. It's located in a valley around a few lakes, beautiful setting, only a short walk or drive to get into the 'countryside'. I can save a load of writing by saying that while we were staying with the family we were really looked after, being really well fed with some good, healthy meals. Lisa's fiancé even let us use his car for the week, even though it was a real wreck of a Datsun with virtually no electrics bar the fuel gauge working. Lisa is getting married on the 11th of April, and so it was very busy for them with all the planning, etc. We were told that we had to stay until the Saturday, as Steve (Lisa's fiancé) was having his 'bucks' night. We had also timed it right as it was Canberra's festival week. The weather in Canberra was really hot and clear, the sky blue and cloudless on most days.

On our first day we mainly talked to the family, with Pat keen to talk to Mark about Wales. We had a look around the local 'mall' and in the evening were taken to watch Lisa play netball, which was an indoor mixed game, very popular here apparently, although not physically demanding. Lisa and Steve then took us out for some drinks.

The next day we had the car so we planned to sightsee, and managed to leave the house by noon. The area they live in is about 10 km from the city centre. In the centre is mainly offices and official buildings on one side of the lake and the national buildings on the other side (parliament, library, gallery, science centre etc.), so no real residential or shopping areas here. Lake Burley Griffin looks nice, the streets wide and clean, but fairly quiet as most people obviously stay in the suburbs to shop, etc. This city is the country's capitol, but only 300,000 people live in it. We then drove to the Black Mountains, which are near the city centre, a large hill covered in trees with the telecom tower at the top. Going up the tower of 160 m, which is then 860 m above sea level, gave a great view of the city and area. In places, the city was so spaced out with so many hills and trees you couldn't really tell that it is such a big city. The whole area is surrounded by hills, with snowy mountains on one side. So much open space around and in the city. In the suburbs like Belconnen there are nice bungalows, each with space. Could live here quite easily.

That evening we were taken out, this time by Andrew, to another bar where they were having a pool contest. First prize was £150. There were only 24 contestants, but we still lost in the first round.

Wednesday, the 11th, we were taken out for the day by Pat, Hugh, and Andrew. We headed out into the blazing sun to Tidbinbilla, about forty minutes' drive. We stopped first at the NASA tracking station where Hugh shift works. Interesting. Four big dishes track satellites (such as Voyager or the shuttle) and study deep space, and receive information from satellites as much as eight billion kilometres away. The surrounding countryside is very open and dry with a few spindly trees (but green). The next stop was Tidbinbilla Nature Park. Before walking around we tucked into the packed lunch they had made. In the park were enclosures of koalas, kangaroos and birds, all open not like a zoo. The koala area was full of tall peeling gum trees. Saw a koala at the top of one tree, not doing much. Apparently you're lucky to see them in the wild as they're so lifeless.

Walking through the other enclosures we got close to groups of kangaroos. Strange looking animals. They're not as stupid as they look, as we found them all (eventually) in a shaded, cool area as it was blazing hot. These were only about 4 ft tall, but can be much bigger. On leaving the park we saw emus, ugly scraggy birds with evil eyes. So I'd seen some original Aussie animals all in one day. I didn't want to have to go to a zoo, as you could be anywhere for that, so it was good to see them sort of in the wild. After another good tea we were taken out boozing again by Lisa and Steve to the local soccer club. Talking to the young Aussies, they all want to see an English soccer match, but talk of our hooliganism. We do have a bad reputation and they don't understand why it happens – attitude's different here.

The next day we set off on our own in the car to sightsee. Being a planned city, all the attractions have free car parks so it was really easy. The morning was spent at the War Memorial. Very impressive. As well as the depressing roll of honour of dead soldiers along the walks, there are galleries containing details, models, etc. of all their wars. Some models showed battle scenes with six-inch lead figures.

The First World War was bad for Aussies, showing mud and despair. Found out where Gallipoli is, or was. Had a tour, so learnt a lot about wars. Didn't realize how much of Southeast Asia Japan had in WWII. Had planes in the museum too. Well-organized place.

In the evening we were taken out by Pat and Hugh for a meal in the soccer club, joined by Andrew's wife, Debbie. The steak, $8, was the same price as chicken or fish! England had an amazing win over SA. I thought I had better get finals tickets, which I did do the next morning.

The Friday we visited Parliament first, getting on another tour. Impressive building inside, although outside it is built into a hill in the centre of a massive 'roundabout'. The stainless steel flagpole cost millions of dollars. The House of Representatives and the Senate are very well decorated in green for one and red for the other. The system is a carbon copy of ours (fools!), even having Black Rod and a Mace, although it was better laid out and there were less MPs, one for every 70,000 people. Outside there's a good view of old Parliament, the lake, ANZAC parade, and the war memorial.

The mint was supposed to be worth a visit to see production. A walkway went above the shop floor, but there was very little going on, although you could see the capacity for high volume production in there. Recession? We travelled out of the city to 'Cockington Green', a place with some art and craft shops in 'original' houses, and a typical English pub (well nearly), all out in the middle of nowhere.

The evening entertainment was Trivial Pursuit, although the questions were more Australian in nature, but that meant I had an excuse for not knowing this time!

As part of Canberra Festival they held a rugby sevens tournament in Bruce Stadium on the Saturday. This was an all-day event, starting at 9:30 a.m., til 5 p.m., with eight teams; Australian teams, state teams, and Fiji. Obviously Fiji won, throwing the ball around very quickly. The matches were seven minutes each way, and ten minutes for the final. The hardest part of the day was suffering the blazing sun, as we were on a grass bank at one end of the only slightly full stadium. I had a red nose after all that, having to dive for shade at the end.

The night was Steve's bucks night, a month before the wedding as he was scared his friends would ship him to Perth. It started in the bar where he works. I think he got off lightly, from some of the things that were said may happen, as, apart from a kissogram, he was attached to various things through the night; a glass, a jug, a chair, a gas bottle, but he was still in Canberra when we left him at 5 a.m., having by then moved to Pandora's in the city centre.

Bright and early at 9 a.m. on Sunday we had to be up, as Lisa and Debbie were taking us to the coast for Sunday/Monday. Monday was Canberra Day, so they had the day off, whereas people in NSW at the coast would be working. Headed off for the two-hour drive southeast of Canberra to Batemans Bay. They think nothing of driving that far. As we neared the coast we dropped down a mountain through more trees. Another really hot, sunny day. We stopped in the town to buy a wad of food, as the girls informed us we were having a barbeque. We then went to a caravan park and rented a caravan for the night. $50 (£22) for a small but tidy caravan; six berth, a cooker, etc., but no shower or toilet (in a block). The site had a barbeque area and swimming pool. Outdoor life – they know what to do! They took us to a beach along the coast, the coast being full of bays and beaches, and the beach was long and empty. Some really nice big houses on the coast roads.

Back at the caravan site we played cards until it was time to start the barbeque. In the BBQ area, there were piles of wood and a couple BBQs with thick metal plates rather than grills. This meant we could do sliced potatoes and onions without it all falling into the ash! The wood threw out masses of heat, singeing my legs as I cooked the sausages and steaks. This is the way to live (although I must admit it did drizzle for a half hour before we started). We were under a shelter, it was now dark, but with the spotlights on we could cook the steaks to perfection. With that food and a few 'stubbies' (bottles of beer to us) we were quite content. Just as we finished that, Reggie and his ice-cream van pulled up outside our caravan (why?), so we had some chocolate sundaes too! High life, hey?

I was woken around 8 a.m. Monday in the caravan by the sound of Lisa sorting out breakfast – ~~bak~~ bacon (it's been so long, I can't spell it), eggs, orange juice, toast. Wow. Checking out by 10 a.m. we went north to Ulladulla, a small town with a fishing background and a beach. It was a dullish day and we found ourselves in 'Finland' playing on some stupid machines. After a couple hours we'd done enough to win each of the girls a cuddly toy. I was good at a game that involved rolling balls into marked holes. Talented. We had a pub lunch, mine had masses of roast beef, more than you'd get in UK ones. It got quite sunny as we headed back to Canberra, where another big meal was waiting.

Tuesday, the two of us made an early start to drive ourselves down to the snowy mountains, about 100 km south of Canberra. The car was going well as we cruised down the nearly deserted roads to Cooma, a small town at the side of the Snowies. We stopped for info there at an info centre, and ended up watching a video on the hydroelectric stations there. There are seven in the mountains, generating masses of electric, built in the 50's and 60's by thousands of imported immigrant workers. Big project. Also controls the water supply to the plains below the Great Dividing Range. From Cooma we drove to Jindabyne on the edge of one of the created lakes, and on into Kosciuszko National

Park. Here is Mt. Kosciuszko, the highest mountain in Australia at 2,228 m (call that high!) and in the winter is a big skiing area. As it is summer/autumn and there isn't any snow, the whole area was deserted. The drive up and through the rough tree-lined mountains and scenery that looked like the dales and moors of the UK was good, seeing no other cars in 30 km, although we did pick up a Czech hitchhiker who had come to see the snow (obviously not used to getting out of Czech). Didn't really stop anywhere long, apart from a few short walks and a picnic, but driving was very good. Some landscapes were amazing, one area was an open plain with big rocks, some round, scattered over it. The plain was grassy and probably had sheep on it. How did they get there, we asked. Good day's driving, there and back was around 450 km (270 miles) with great views along the way as we went up and down hills.

We had booked our seat out of Canberra for Melbourne for the 19th, so on the Wednesday we didn't do that much, spending some time looking around the local shopping mall. We also took a trip out to Lisa's house, which is being built ready (hopefully) for after their wedding. They got some land and had it built (a bungalow, naturally) with the format they wanted. Big place for their first house. The area is out of the city in a new suburb full of new and half-built houses. They're in the painting and decorating stage now, so may get finished in time. It's not that expensive to do it this way, as there is so much land.

Yesterday we said our goodbyes and got the coach for the eight and a half hour trip here (650 km). On the way we passed through maybe six towns. Victoria is a green 'garden' state, so mainly flat grassy fields of trees. Some scenery reminded me of ours there, rolling hills and grass. Trees here are spread around, not all in lines making hedges, so it looks more unspoilt, which I suppose it is. When we arrived, after watching two videos, at 9 p.m., we were offered accommodation for $8 and taken there by minibus. Nice and easy after a long trip. Reasonable place in the right (backpacker's) area, so can't complain. Can't comprehend the distances really, 650 km trip, then a ten-hour trip to Adelaide to come. (Ten hours in the UK is Cardiff to Edinburgh). On the bus I tried to convince myself I won't be living in the UK in the future, and wondered what will happen on April 9th. By the way, I can't vote because I don't know where I'm registered as I tried to avoid poll tax, so have one on me.

Today (20th) we spent the day looking around Melbourne. It's a nice city, although there's not much in the way of sights. It's again a bundle of tower blocks on a river in the centre and then rest areas of bungalow suburbs around it. We walked around, rode on the good tram setup they have, took a look in the old gaol where Ned Kelly was hanged, saw Captain Cook's cottage (bought and moved from the UK). Some good parks here. Collected the tickets for the MCG cricket on the 25th.

I phoned Peggy and she's expecting us on Sunday, so that's good. By the time you get this I'll have spoken to you, so we should be nearer a date for Canada. As you can see, all's well, and hope it still is there. I'll probably write after my phone conversation, so I'll end this one here save starting another page.

Love

David .

1/4/92

Adelaide

Hello again,

Hope all's well there. Still is here. I'm glad you've managed to get a flight to Canada, as you shouldn't miss the chance to go there. We're thinking that we can make it there when you are, more of which I will say at the end of the letter.

OK, by popular demand, I'll carry on with my travelling tales. Where did I leave off before, Melbourne? Yes, must have been around the 20th of March. I think I stated what we did in the city that day. Melbourne is a pleasant city, fairly open and on a river, but there's not a great deal of interest. We can only look at so many shops and shopping centres in the cities we go through.

On the Saturday we took a trip by tram to the zoo. Melbourne Zoo was supposed to be very well laid out. I expected to see plenty of animals in large enclosures from what I'd read, but no, still in tiny cages. Plenty of variety of animals, including all the odd Aussie sorts, although the platypus was hiding. The day was cool to start, but the animals all seemed fairly inactive. It was a nicely laid out place though, the highlights being the lions, butterfly house (where they flew around the people inside landing on heads and hands), and getting in cheap with our fake

Student IDs. Even though it was a Saturday it wasn't too busy there. The zoo is said to have 350 types of animals in 22 hectares, although most varieties seemed to be variations on a theme, about fifty different types of cats (big cats that is), fifty types of monkeys, etc., all subtly different. Quite impressive. I guess.

Going back through the city on the way to St. Kilda, we passed a bar showing Pakistan vs NZ cricket, so stopped to watch the last hour of play. I thought Pakistan deserved to win, as NZ threw the last game [Little did I know what I'd let myself in for]. Back at St. Kilda we went down to the back there, St. Kilda is about 3 km from the city centre, the city being in off the coast, and St. Kilda the first beach. Quite nice on the front, with park and grass behind sandy beach. A cold wind was blowing by this time, around 5 p.m. There was a small harbour there, and from the pier you could see the skyscrapers of the city (good postcard-style photo!).

That evening we went out in search of life, with a couple of lads from the hotel (English and Swiss), but didn't find much, apart from an esplanade hotel by the beach, which was a place full of scruffier people than us. A couple of bands were playing so we stayed there, the first being OK, good musicians but poor songs, the second being a good reason to leave. I was quite interested in a little synth the girl singer (red hair and black outfit of leather and lace) was using to make the awful screeching noises that went with the Sisters-of-Mercy-sounding music (?). Time for bed.

I'd phoned Peggy on Friday, telling her we were on our way Sunday. We had checked out by 10 a.m. Sunday, so we decided that we may as well go straight there. The train takes an hour, Melbourne to Carrum, and is very regular. I phoned from the station and got directions to their house, only about a ten-minute walk, if that. It was a nice sunny day and we watched the surroundings as we headed down on the train, through all the suburbs of the metropolitan, even though some are 30 miles from the centre. As we approached Carrum we could see the beach only 100 yards from the railway line. Found our way to the house no problem, 'look out for the caravan and cactus in the front garden', arriving around noon, though I didn't feel like going in when two big dogs rushed up behind the posh door on the front (no problem with them really, just very noisy when someone comes to the door). We had a room set aside for us, Kevin's room, as he's away in Queensland.

Over the afternoon, as well as Peggy and George, Simon, his woman Linda, daughter Kiley, Ian and his wife and kids, Bonnie, Rachael and Jason, Melvyn and his wife Leoni and kids all turned up. It was interesting to guess who was with who, etc., although I got it in the end. The afternoon was spent sitting around the kitchen table with about eight big bottles of beer between us, followed by a barbeque with chops, steaks, sausage, all the trimmings, then loads of cake and pies and ice cream. Peggy likes to cook and her pies, etc., were great. The whole family liked their food, and while we stayed there we were very well fed!

Obviously, normally only Peggy and George and Anthony live in the house, and the rest of the mob all disappeared before the end of the night and it was quiet all of a sudden. They (the sons and families) all seem nice and most live in the area. The house is a bungalow (although a 'bungalow' in Australian is something at the bottom of the garden), and they're adding on a couple of rooms at the back and expanding rooms at the front. It's easy to do here as most of the structure is wood and glass. There's a medium-sized garden at the back, which once had a pool, but now has a flagpole (Aussie flag?!) and orange, grapefruit, apple, and pear trees, as well as an aviary of budgies and, of course, the barbeque area. Peggy showed us all her collections of things on the walls and cabinets and windowsills, and tapestries she did herself.

Oh, I thought I'd mention this, I'm writing this sitting under the shade of some big trees, out of the scorching sun, by the bank of the river in one of the parks in Adelaide.

All in all, it's quite a big house. After all the mob had left I watched England sneak into the final (what rain?). My mate Ritchie said we deserved it and I agree, although Monday's papers were all whingeing about it (and they say it's the poms!).

On Monday we decided to have a look around the area. Walking out the house onto Tennyson Street, a smallish dead-end side street, (the dead end is actually a river) around 100 m away is the river. The river is pretty wide and just a little further upstream is the spot people can launch their boats. Walking up the bank past the odd fisherperson and on to the marina, we passed houses, each with pools and BBQs in their gardens along with the odd boat. Really nice spot to live, very quiet. Heading back down to where the river joins the sea and beach, it's about a five-minute walk from Peggy's street to the beach. On the beach, which is wide and sandy and, oh, probably fifteen miles long, you could make out the silhouettes of the Melbourne skyscrapers (of which there are only around twenty).

I said St. Kilda was probably the start of the beach, but it looked as though the beach came all the way from there and carried on another five miles or more the other way (St. Kilda to Carrum around 30 km). It was a really clear, calm, boiling hot day. Carrum itself was only a tiny place, the different suburbs blending in to each other along the beach for a couple of hours. Getting to Frankston, the central town, or 'city' as they called it, for this stretch of coast, was five miles from Carrum. Being in a large bay, the water was quite calm, the beach wide and flat, with small sand breaks along the water's edge in places. In this five-mile walk there were only half a dozen people on the beach, which was backed for most of the way with dunes. The water was clear and clean and not too cold. We chatted to an old bloke going for a swim who said the small sand bank helped keep the sharks from the beach. Frankston itself wasn't much of a city, with a couple of shopping centres and a pier, so after a brief look round it was back, on the train this time, to Carrum.

Peggy prepared us another massive meal; pork, chicken, and nearly every vegetable that exists. By the way, Peggy and George both look well (although I can't remember how they looked before) and by the sound of it have made the most of their time here, and still do, with trips here and there. Chatted to Peggy about family places, etc., and I don't think she misses the UK, and I know for sure George doesn't.

On the Tuesday it was quite overcast, although warm, so we didn't go out in the morning. Anthony works early morning, 5 a.m. til 10 a.m., so after lunch he drove us along the coast. He's a 'P' driver, having to show that for three years after his test, which he passed twelve months ago. We went along the coast as far as 'Arthurs Seat', a big lookout from which you would have been able to see most of the coastline if it had been clearer. The countryside around is green and reasonably flat.

After another big tea Anthony took us to the RSL club across the road. This is like a social club, retired servicemen I think. We had a few games of snooker, playing badly. Anthony spends most of his time involved with the clubs, playing darts, fishing, or golfing for them.

Wednesday was of course the big day. It started off warm and with clear skies. Peggy sorted us out a bag of sandwiches, cakes, etc. to last us the day, if I could have squashed any more in from two days of solid overeating. We caught the train up to the city that stopped outside the MCG. We arrived at 11:30, just as they opened the gates, the crowds still small at this time. We had seats in the new stand they've spent millions just building, and wanted to sit in the shade but couldn't see the scoreboard, so we had to sit in the sun. Really hot now.

The MCG is a big ground, virtually all the way round is tiered up. On the day, well by the end, 87,162 people had showed up. I tried to avoid sitting in the English mob again, sitting in a mixed-looking crowd, who toward the evening had showed themselves to be Australians supporting Pakistan, or was it Australians <u>not</u> supporting the English. Even so, there was a good English support. We did get off to what looked like a promising start, two early wickets and pegged them back during the middle of the innings. I guess the last ten or fifteen overs was quite entertaining for any non-English spectator, with Imran Khan, ul-Haq, and Akram smacking the ball all over the ground. After the interval, with skydivers and pipe bands, England needed 250 to win. This task wasn't helped by Botham being given out (?) for 0, which made the 80,160 "convicts" go wild, especially after he'd walked out of some show the night before, which they'd made a big deal of in the press. I thought there was still a chance right up until our last wicket. Oh well. I suppose they played best on the day. If it had been any other day we would have won. Still, I was here when we lost, that's the main thing!

The trouble was they kept on about it for a couple of days after in the papers and TV, calling it "the Paki's glorious win over the poms," like they'd done the Aussies a favour! It was a good day, looking back, and I was glad when the sun went down as it was getting unbearable for a while. On the way back to Carrum so many people got on the train it packed up halfway there. It was an electric one, so sparks flashed and all the lights went out, which went down quite well with a big cheer. We got back no problem on the next one.

Thursday we had originally planned to head off to Adelaide, but the bus was booked full so we had to book for Friday night. Thursday morning came and went, it was quite cloudy again, but warm. Midday T.V. is the same interview-type stuff they show in the U.K. After lunch I went to the beach and sat there being sandblasted. It was nice enough really, and very quiet, watching the rays of sunlight moving across the water where it broke through the clouds.

My hand's aching, so I'll do a map:

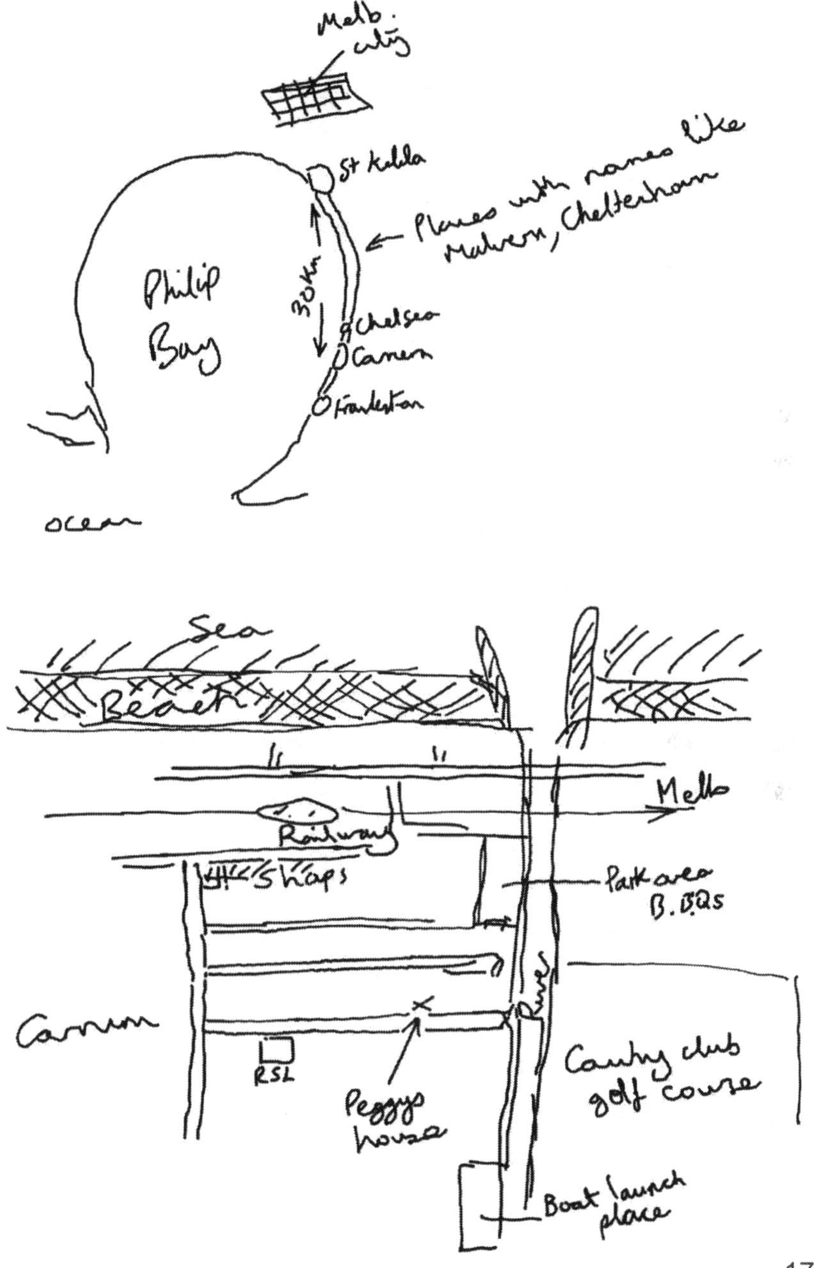
Melb. city
St Kilda
Places with names like Malvern, Cheltenham
30km
Philip Bay
Chelsea
Camen
Frankston
ocean
Sea
Beach
Melb
Railway
Shops
Park area
B.BQs
River
Carrum
Country club golf course
RSL
Peggys house
Boat launch place

Peggy prepared us a rack of lamb for tea, one of those pieces with all the bones curling out. Pretty good. Played a bit of darts in the back room, and couldn't believe how bad I was. They showed some American program about "The Elvis Conspiracy," investigating whether he could be pumping around as someone else. Watch out for that, if only to see how stupid America is.

Woken on Friday by an unusual sound. I didn't rush outside to see what it was as it was chucking it down. Ah, that was the noise. Because of that, we couldn't do much Friday, although Peggy and George had gone shopping when we got up. We had some dim sum for lunch, which are crispy balls of meat and veg, hadn't had it before. At tea time Ian and Bonnie had invited themselves over for food. Our bus went to Adelaide at 9:30 p.m., overnight, so we didn't have to leave Carrum until 7:45 p.m. While we were there we'd been really well looked after, and I know Peggy had enjoyed us being there. Say thanks from me if you do write to her. I could have stayed longer I suppose, but needed to keep moving as we didn't want to fall behind. Nice to have a relaxing time in one place, I know Peggy was sorry they didn't take us anywhere, but we really didn't want to go anywhere, so that was no problem.

Yes, it's a big family, fifteen grandchildren now. They all said 'come back next year,' so who knows! Said my goodbyes and got the train to the city. I know you'll kill me if I tell you I never got any pictures of the family. I was going to, but things sort of happened and I never did (sound like a good excuse?). Also, I happen to know that Peggy is going to send some photos to you that she has. I should have really.

We got the bus in Melbourne for another marathon trip to Adelaide, about 700 km and ten hours overnight. With nothing to see outside (dark) and a video to entertain us for the first two hours, the trip wasn't too bad as I slept virtually all the way, waking up just as we came over the hills to Adelaide, dropping down into the city. Adelaide, or South Australia, is half an hour behind NSW and Victoria, so watches went back. With you going forward that means it's now eight and a half hours ahead here, although when we get to Cairns I think it's different again.

Arriving early at the bus station we chatted to an old Cockney bloke over coffee, who'd been in Australia for quite a while and would never go back (that's a few we've met have said that). Told us of all the things to see in the country. The sky was cloudy, but should be OK, so we decided to camp. A campsite was out on the edge of the city centre, although it was actually a 'caravan park'. First impression was that it was another pleasant city; nice buildings, skyscrapers in the centre, parks and greenery all around. The Adelaide Caravan Park was by the side of the city's river, the Torrens, about 2 km from the centre. Being the closest camp to the city it was most expensive, and we paid for a site, i.e. same price as people in caravans, $16.

This was cheaper than going to a hotel though. Camps further afield for $10 or less. The site was gravely, but we got the tent up OK. The site was OK, nothing special. Again there's not a great deal to see in Adelaide, other than the place itself. It's 'festival state', and we'd just missed the main festival here. Going back into the city for early on Saturday it was surprisingly quiet. At the northeast side of the city where we camped are the botanic gardens and parks which are around the river. In the centre, on the river bank is the Festival Centre, a big, white, odd-shaped building, which is near other places like the museum, gallery, library, and university all in the old stone building style. The centre is a grid setup of streets with really only one shopping 'mall' street. Some nice spots, wide streets, etc.

Picked up the mail – thanks for the photocopies, really good. All I can remember of these camel photos is the old bloke who took them. I thought he was going to run off with the camera, as he demanded money after he'd taken them. Funny at the time. They came after us on the camels when we refused. Nice photos of Hayley, 13 months now.

Walking round the city we came across the casino, said to be nice, inside the old railway station. It was a nice building but we couldn't get in, "too casual and shoes too dirty." Lucky I didn't tell him it was the best I had! We had read all about Kangaroo Island, an island just off the coast 150 km south of Adelaide, and seen ads for tours for $99, ferry there and back, night accommodation, tour of the islands, etc. We thought we could do it cheaper, but the tourist office said it couldn't be done, so we booked on this trip for the Monday (details as they happen). We also fixed up the buses for Ayers Rock, Alice Springs, etc.

We'd been saying for a while about seeing Aussie rules football, and found out where all the games were in the city. One was only a couple of kilometres away, so we walked out to the Richmond Oval, arriving just after the start of the game. It's not a bad game really, fairly fast moving, made up of four 25-minute quarters. The pitch is large and so they need big kickers. The quite large crowd, which was there for a small local game, West Adelaide vs Port Adelaide, was very vocal. It was a mix of young and old, men and women, and is probably the biggest sport in the area. It think the final score was 101-89 to Wests, with goals being scored every few minutes. There weren't any punch ups, which surprised me, and by the end I could follow the rules. $7 entry. It was a good hour walk back to the campsite from there, passing a festival on the way.

The next day (Sunday) we went into the city to do some sights. Went in the museum (free) and saw the dinosaur display. Dinosaurs here were different from the ones we had. Interesting and depressing display of animals of the different continents and how man has changed the climate and vegetation of each region. Then we went to the art gallery for a free tour. They've got a really good collection of paintings there, and it was explained how styles had developed and ideas were borrowed. The old stuff was really well done.

Walking around the city it was fairly deserted. Across on the north side of the river we found Light's Vision lookout, the spot where Col. William Light chose the location of Adelaide. From there there was a reasonable view of the city centre and hills in the background. It was next to the Adelaide Oval, where a local cricket match was on. Headed back to the campsite at 10 a.m. and we'd booked on a bus out of Adelaide to the ferry for 4 p.m. Spent the afternoon looking round the city and in parks by the river. The big posh bus had us and a couple of others for the two-hour trip to Cape Jervis and the sealink ferry. Quite a good comfortable trip, the coastal scenery was very spectacular and changing regularly. The ferry was a car ferry, taking about fifteen or twenty cars on an open deck in the centre. The sun set as we went over, another brilliant one. Ferry rocked around a little.

The deal was the bus and ferry to the island, two nights in Penneshaw Youth Hostel, and a day tour around the island. Penneshaw was a small village at the east end of the island, the third largest island of Australia. We were met on arrival by a minibus to take us the 80 m to the youth hostel, being the only two arriving on that ferry. The lady who met us was very excited about our tour and the chance to see penguins that live along the coast near the hostel. There was a little takeaway at the hostel so I tried a kangaroo burger; not bad, but I prefer beef. The hostel was quite good, with all ages there taking advantage of the offer, big kitchen and rooms.

Armed with a torch we went out in search of the fairy penguins, small blueish coloured ones, of which there are loads around this area of the island. Down on the beach near the ferry jetty we spotted some coming ashore and sat on rocks watching them. Great. They actually live behind the beach in bushes and burrows, and you could hear and occasionally see the penguins in the bushes, making a loud screeching noise, and poking their heads out to see who was watching them.

The next day we had a full day tour. The island is 150 km long and had only 4,000 people on it (!) and 1.2 million sheep. The land seemed either grass fields or red dusty shrubland. The tour started at 8 a.m., and luckily we had a really beautiful day. Our first stop, not far from Penneshaw, was Pennington Bay, a large beach and cliff bay showing the power of waves of the Southern Ocean. We moved on along the only sealed road, stopping at Kelly Hill Caves, a series of limestone underground caves full of stalactites, etc. Some amazing formations. Next was Flinders Chase National Park, covering all of the western tip of the island. We visited the remarkable rocks, 500 million year old granite rocks completely out of place amongst the surrounding rock and shrubs, and then Admirals Arch, a natural arch in the costal cliffs. The waves there were massive, tossing around the NZ fur seals living there.

In the national park we walked to an area full of koalas and must have seen a dozen in some trees. We had a lunch there with an emu and kangaroos nearby. After lunch we visited a 'little Sahara', an area of dunes and fine sand quite a way from the coast. Had a ride on a camel, although mine was a bit temperamental. The last step was 'Seal Bay', one of only two places in the world you can walk on beaches with seals (other being Galapagos). Hundreds of sea lions lying on the long beach in amongst seaweed, recovering after two solid days at sea. They hardly bothered as we walked along quite close to them. Only nine of us were on the tour, so that made it a little more pleasant. Good to get so close to nature on this visit to the island. After the long drive back to Penneshaw Youth Hostel we went out in the village to watch the sunset, then to search for more penguins.

Wednesday, we were due to catch the 8:30 a.m. ferry back to the mainland. It was very cloudy, and the ferry trip was really rough, rocking and rolling very badly. Wasn't bad myself, but a German girl was sobbing away near me. Only a few people make the trip over to the island, with a small population and an expensive ferry (normally $56 one way). With that gladly over, the bus was there to take us back to Adelaide, this being a smooth ride. We arrived in Adelaide at 11:30 and had booked ourselves on the bus out to Ayers Rock at 6:00 p.m. So, as Adelaide was hot and sunny, I spent the afternoon writing this letter. I've now moved on, so have more to write to catch up. Now then, listen to this bit.

We got the 6 p.m. bus to Ayers Rock, 1,600 km (1,000 miles away), due to arrive at 2:15 p.m. the next day, not too bad being overnight. The journey wasn't too bad, showing some videos on the way. We'd booked a tour for our arrival at Ayers Rock at 3 p.m., then another the next day, finishing in time to get the bus out to the springs. That was more or less three solid days on a bus. The drivers on the overnight buses change over occasionally. As we left Adelaide it got dark and we watched a video. It took a few hours before we got off the west coast and started heading north into the outback. By this time I was going in and out of sleeping, as it wasn't all that comfortable, and every time I looked ahead all I could see was a straight road. This was the scene for hours. After an evening stop, the next was at 5 a.m. at a small mining town.

You can't believe the distances here, seven hours constant driving in a straight line from one town to the next. I say town, but our first evening stop was at a 'roadhouse' in the middle of nowhere, as was our breakfast stop at 9 a.m. As it got light, the scenery appeared; just flat land, mainly a red dusty colour, with varying numbers of thin trees and white coloured grassy clumps. This hardly changed throughout the whole journey, although the amount of grass, trees, and dust changed in quantity and type occasionally. There is a lot more life (plant life) than I expected in this harsh environment.

The day was of course really hot, and stepping outside meant being attacked by swarms of flies, usually around the head. Time seemed to pass fairly quickly on the coach and we arrived at Erldunda, another roadhouse, to change coaches to go to Ayers Rock at 11:30 a.m. While transferring bags from our old coach to our new one, the driver broke one of the compressed air lines. He couldn't replace it, so a mechanic had to be called from Alice Springs. This was two hours by road from where we were, what a call-out fee! So, by 3:30 p.m. the mechanic had arrived and done the job and we were off to Ayers Rock. Luckily the roadhouse where we were delayed wasn't too bad and was well visited. Due to the delay we would miss out on the afternoon tour. As it worked out, the tour was with Bus Australia and it was the same driver, so he worked out an alternative plan to get all our tours in.

We should have visited the Olgas, a series of massive rocks near the Ayers Rock, and see the sunset at Ayers. That was cancelled, so we were dropped off at Ayers resort area, Yulara, a town set up especially for visitors about 20 km from the rocks. We stayed at the campsite there, as everything is extortionately expensive. The hotels, of which there are four, start at $21.50 a night, while camping is only $9. Putting the tent up was a bit tricky with the ground being solid. We were in the camp about 6 p.m., and sunset was around 7 p.m. We walked to a viewing point in the campsite, but it was cloudy where the sun was so nothing really happened, although we did get to see the rock eventually that day. The camp was quite large, but not all that busy.

The new plan was to get up at 4:15 a.m. to be collected by the bus driver at 5:15 a.m. We packed up the tent in the half-light. The night sky here is so clear, and different to the Northern Hemisphere. There is a band of haze behind the stars running straight down the centre of the sky. Milky Way, perhaps? Always does my head in looking at all the stars, thinking what it's all about.

So, at 5:15 we were on the bus and travelling to Ayers Rock. He had decided we would start to climb the rock as it began to get light and get to the top in time for the sunrise. As it turned out this was excellent, as normally people climb a little later. Ayers Rock is just massive, no other word. A vast red blob, coated with iron oxide (neat!), and the rock is mainly quartz. At one point you can climb up, a mile walk to the 300 m summit. About half of the climb is assisted with a chain as it's quite steep. Warnings are issued about the risks of going up if you're not fit, and a few people have died doing the climb. It was dark when we started, light enough to see though, and was quite bright by halfway. The surface is very rough and there's no really easy part on the climb. It took us 45 minutes to climb (Jon

Walker once ran up in twelve minutes) and we got there just in time to watch the sunrise.

As it got brighter the land around and sky changed colour. Views were excellent, could see nothing for miles. The land around did look quite green, looking down onto the top of the shrubs and trees. We even signed the book at the top! I can see why it's special, as it's so flat, apart from the Olgas. The rock isn't flat on top or symmetrical. The picture postcard side is flat and symmetrical, but behind that it's all ridges and dips and holes, formed by the wind and water. When it does rain here, which it only does (and does seriously) once or twice a year, the rock becomes a place for a series of massive waterfalls. No chance of seeing that today. Clear skies, getting very hot. Glad we did the climb so early, as when we came down around 7:30 a.m. it was getting hot and the flies had appeared. The rock has 300,000 visitors in a year these days.

After the successful climb (!) we had a tour around the base, by coach, 9 km round. We stopped at one spot to look at some aboriginal art on a cave in the rock. The driver explained symbolism used by drawing in the dirt. Over the day he told us endless interesting info. To finish off our tour we got our trip to the Olgas in, these are a massive set of rocks similar to Ayers in nature. These were once apparently one big rock, much bigger than Ayers. They and Ayers were formed when the area was an ocean 600 million years ago. We stopped and walked into a gorge between two of these massive rocks. Quite amazing to look up at the walls. Close up you can't really appreciate the size of the thing though. Ayers Rock, while being 5 km wide is only 10% of the whole rock, going 5 km into the ground too. The Olgas are 34 big rocks, taking 22 km to get round them.

With these tours done, we were in time to get back to Yulara for the same driver to take us on the five and a half hour journey to Alice, another 400 km travelling. This journey wasn't too tough and we arrived as planned at 5:30 p.m. The past week had been some serious touring, with a lot of mileage done. We had got up into Northern Territories with its population of 140,000 and area of, oh, probably five times England, but mostly red dusty land. The land is used for cattle mainly, with some gigantic cattle stations. Each cattle needs a lot more land than in the UK, as there are obviously less per square foot to eat.

The area around Alice Springs seemed a little greener. Dropped into the city centre and came straight out to a hotel, so as yet haven't looked around. Staying in Gap View Hotel for $10 a night. The rooms are like proper hotel rooms; T.V., video, bathroom, only have six bunks in. Big place, pool, etc. Population of Alice is only 25,000, so it should be relaxing. Very warm here. In the summer it can be 50°C in the sun. Probably in the 30s now. When it rains here it's pretty rough too, being heavy and rapid flooding.

OK, that's up to date, now some general chat. When did you say Andrew's (Sue's lad – Canada) wedding was? Will you be there when it's on?

Money situation going as planned. Have taken out another £300 on the Visa, and paid for K.I. trip on the Visa (+ Mark's), so look out for the bill. That will see me until the end of Australia now in mid-May. We'll leave Alice on Monday the 6th, go to Townsville and Cairns then down the east coast. Hope to get out of Australia probably by the end of the first full week in May and get through NZ and California by July. We'll have to hope we can sort out transport in the USA quite quickly. Should be OK.

When I travel from Alice to Townsville, that's another 2,000 km trip taking over 24 hours! All this travelling to see the big lumps of rock in the middle of nowhere!

Had a break and didn't send this, so now it's the 7th and I'm on the bus to Townsville on the east coast. As it's a 25-hour trip I should have some time to kill. Later I may do all the detail of the past couple of days. Firstly, we'll be in Cairns at Easter, I hope you got the American Express address from Mark's mum if you needed it. Anything else you want to send, send it to Sydney before the end of April, as we'll check again there for any other mail before we leave Australia. After April it'll have to go to Auckland, NZ. I'll tell you the address in a bit. You should have it, but use the one I give if it's different.

OK, what else. I remembered yesterday that while we were in Canberra Lisa (who gets wed on the 11th) told us all the things that happened in Neighbours (if you still watch it) and they're at least twelve months ahead. I could easily spoil it for you! So...

Sometime soon I'll be sending a parcel back to you, which will have some photos we developed dating back from Thailand, the negatives of the earlier films I've had done and other bits of info. Oh, and a 6 ft didgeridoo... No, no didgeridoo really (if that's how it's spelled). Hard to write on the bus.

We're now nine hours ahead of the UK. The set of photos wasn't bad, mainly of the Sydney area, some are a bit purple, maybe because of the film. Now we both have cameras, Mark never had one before and I was taking all the shots, so all the films you have are all we've taken.

Started a new sheet so I'll tell you about Alice Springs. When we arrived in Alice Transit Centre there were minibuses waiting from various hotels. Gap View Hotel is a really good place. As it says in the name, it's near the 'Gap', a ... yes ... gap in the mountainous ridge that runs for miles. It's at the south of the city and the only way through in the area. The road and railway run through this narrow gap. When it rains the large, dry Todd River isn't dry for long and this goes through the gap too, cutting the city off. Very flood-prone place, the dry river runs right through the town. The airport is on the opposite side of the gap too, and so this can get cut off as well.

It hasn't rained here for eighteen months, so it's not as bad as it sounds. Being about 35° every day, and a dry heat, it makes no sense to rush anything, so the place has a relaxing, laid-back sort of feeling. The hotel ran a regular courtesy bus to the small town centre, although it's not that far to walk. We had a quick walk around the town, not much there; one shopping mall, nicely done out with shaded benches. There are heritage buildings in the centre, and these are not overshadowed as no buildings are taller than the trees (law), so they're not business skyscrapers. Tourism must be the main line here, with people just stopping on their way to or from somewhere to take a break. Back at the hotel they've got a nice pool outside the bar and we spent the rest of the day just lazing around by it or in it. We knocked up some steaks, etc., on the BBQ on the poolside in the evening. What a life out in the wild!

This hotel seemed one of the places to be in the night, with a live band on each night Wednesday – Sunday til 1:30 a.m. Us and two other English had a good night there, the two-man band was very good, playing songs we knew. Plenty of locals there, as well as the young backpackers.

Sunday was our sightseeing day. Not that much of a list that was worth doing. The first do – I give up.

OK, off the bus now. Twenty-five hours at 100 km/hr (no other traffic) on a straight road, making about five stops (three in the middle of nowhere).

Right, the first place we went to see was the reason the town, and in fact many towns in Northern Territory, exists; the telegraph station. This was the first settlement by white men in the area, as they built the Adelaide-Darwin telegraph here in the 1800's. It's actually about 3 km out of the present town, and meant a walk along the banks of the river Todd, which had more aboriginals in it than water (actually no water at all). The aboriginals, even though modernized by us European-types into jeans and shirts, still like to live outdoors, but seem to spend most of it drinking and aren't too tidy – locally having a bad reputation.

Anyway, being hot and dry, this wasn't a bad walk. The telegraph station was just a few old buildings done up (cynic), but the surroundings made us realize how tough it must have been for the early pioneers, though they had aboriginal slaves at the station. Here also was the waterhole, 'Alice Spring'. We climbed up a hill nearby for a view of the area. Alice is in the river valley and is quite green, but all around is rocky, rough land, no longer flat but quite mountainous (I didn't expect that either). Another small rocky hill, ANZAC Hill, nearer the town gave us a view of the city. It's only a tiny hill, but the town is not built upwards.

Last on the list was a museum, we visited the Flying Doctor Centre briefly before this. The Spencer and Gillen Museum was named after the early station masters whose job was also to study aborigines. The museum had a few displays of their lifestyles as well as the usual museum stuff. Quite interesting.

Not a bad day, the scenery and town are unlike anything else we've seen (what, again?), different to the other cities we've looked down on.

Back at the hotel there was a band on in the garden by the pool playing rock music. Very busy. There are plenty of bikers here; big beards, big bellies, big tattoos, and tiny sunglasses, all in black of course (That's just the women!). All harmless, and with nice bikes too. Hard to believe this place; it's like a holiday resort in the middle of all this nothing, miles from anywhere.

Chatted to a Canadian lad the rest of the evening. So many other young travellers here, all have very similar views and attitudes, even the same as me!

On Monday we had our massive trip.

I think I'll stop here as this could go on forever (like the journey) as I continually catch up.

We've sent a box of goodies back, a set of photos (Mark's), four rolls of film, postcards, etc. If you can get the roll developed A.S.A.P. and send a set of each, with the half of the set in the box that had Mark's writing on it (blue pen) to his mother. Perhaps if they get developed in time you could fetch some out to Canada (?). Should be good photos, although quite a few were night shots, sunrise, etc., so don't know how they'll come out.

OK, hope that's everything. I'm now in Townsville and Magnetic Island, and we will be in Cairns next week.

Hope everyone there is OK, including Sharon and the baby – or is it babies yet?

Will be in touch again before I leave Australia.

Love

David ..

Oh, you should get the box about three weeks from today (today being 9th) so around the end of April.

Address in Auckland NZ;

American Express Travel Service
95 Queen St,
Auckland.

(I think this is it – I'll double check and tell you again in the next letter)

Just got your letter in Cairns, arriving on the 12th (yesterday). Glad everything's OK, and it answers some questions from this letter. Great. Had a letter from Martin, too. Will write again soon with answers to this latest letter.

Doing a dive here I hope. What else, yes, I know the Tories won, so maybe I won't come back! Also enclosed a photo Joanne (met in Nepal/India etc.) sent us, as she had returned to the UK. This was in Pokhara on one of those hot sunny days, about Christmas. I'll write to Cyril and Joan soon too, now I know you've spoken. Say hello to Sharon, hope everything's fine and waiting for the good news, although I guess I won't hear about any events for some time after, unless I can afford a phone call.

Ok, take care.

Love

Dave

13th April

Cairns

up to 20th

Hello,

OK, time to write again, even though I only posted the last letter today. I picked up your letter in Cairns. Hope you got the previous letter and may even have had the parcel. As I said, had a good stay with Peggy, and all's well there. Have written a brief letter to Canada, just saying what I've done and I'm on my way still! I don't know what happened to the tax renewal on the mini, can't remember if I changed addresses, I think so. Glad it's still OK. With the insurance, if you want to use the car renew it but change addresses, otherwise leave it until I return. I hope there's still plenty of money in my account if you need it (let me know the balance next time). Don't worry about the diving certificate if you receive it. I don't need it here as my temporary one is still valid, but I'll need it later if I want to dive in the USA, so we'll sort that out when it arrives.

Right, as I say, at the moment I'm in Cairns up on the east coast in Queensland. The centre was a great trip, some amazing scenery and conditions. This time I'll start with what I'm going to do before I update you on what I've done. Tomorrow we go on a three-day trip up into the rainforest near Cape Tribulation. After that, back in Cairns, I'll do a dive (two actually) out on the reef. Weather here at the moment is a bit poor; when it's hot it's hot, otherwise it showers. Should be clearing up. It's OK as we go south anyway.

Last time I was about to do a twenty-five-hour trip on the bus. Well stocked up, the time seemed to go by reasonably well. As the sun set on the first evening on the bus, the deep red sky in front was reflected on the heat haze of the dead-straight road, just a blur in the distance. Leaving at 6 p.m., by 11:30 we had reached Threeways, which as it implies is just a road junction. We changed buses to a more cramped one with bars on the front because "we may have to avoid cattle or roos" on this road, Threeways to Townsville heading east.

This road was rough, one lane wide and the driver was flat out. This was nothing, at 3 a.m. the driver got off and a new one drove us even faster to Mt. Isa. Didn't sleep much as it bounced around. Land was still dusty and flatish as it got light. Don't need to say much about the rest of the day's travel other than only maybe four stops; breakfast in Mt. Isa, a mining town, and two other food stops, passing through very few towns. At Queensland, well, as we reached the coast anyway, it became large green plains with tall grass in parts stretching out into the distance. As we got nearer the coast around sunset we passed through a few "mountainous" areas, the Great Dividing Range again.

Passing through Charters Towers, an old gold rush town about 150 km from Townsville, we saw plenty of the old-style buildings. Other new sights were the stockmen herding cattle on horses, a bush fire by the roadside in the outback, and another deep red sunset behind the tree-fringed hills.

Arriving at Townsville about 7:30 p.m., we stopped at the transit centre. Here they had a large backpacker accommodation place above the centre, which contained the bus company desks, info checks, etc. Quite an easy setup. It saved hassle to check in here, and the place wasn't too bad and very popular with all the new lazy arrivals. Collected some info on the area to study for the next day. Across the street from the tourist centre, which was only a ten-minute walk from the small town centre, on the opposite side of the small river that runs through the town, was another backpacker place which would let us put our tent up.

The next morning we left the reasonable but impersonal tourist centre accommodation for the "Southbank Village". There was a small lawn there in front of the shacks with the rooms in. We pitched our tent here for $8, and Dwain, the bloke who obviously had something to do with running it, said we could use the kitchen, showers, pool, T.V., free pool table, BBQ, etc. as well. Pretty laid-back really, just let us get on with it, great. The place wasn't exactly smart, but the kitchen and facilities were clean enough and the atmosphere was so much nicer than the busy transit centre (although it was full here too). By early morning we were settled, nearly recovered from the journey, and headed off into the 'city'. A really small place, though very pleasant; river, boats, old-style bars and buildings, as well as a paved shopping mall with all the usual shops. Not that busy in the centre. Nicely done there; trees, water, fountains in the mall, not that touristy. Following the river out to the marina area was a nice walk, although very hot. It was a very humid heat, as opposed to the dry heat of Alice, so a lot more sweaty. Right on the end of the marina is the dead-posh Sheraton Hotel and Casino. We actually got in the casino, as it wasn't busy, in shorts. Not worth going in really.

One attraction here is the Great Barrier Reef Wonderland, an aquarium and OMNIMAX; remember the one in Singapore, the surround cinema, this was the same. Watched the Grand Canyon movie, and as we rushed down the river at full pelt my legs went all tingly, even though I was sat back in a comfy chair. Really weird. An excellent film about the history of the canyon as we went down the massive rapids and flew along and above the canyon. Extra effects added by the group of screaming school children.

I think there are a couple of these cinemas in the USA, too. Leaving here early in the afternoon, we strolled leisurely round the town, as the only other thing to do was climb up 'Castle Hill', a very large rock protrusion in this fairly flat part of the city. We walked up this far enough to get a view over the city. From above the city looks fairly rough and ready, not as well planned as the others. It is quite an industrial place, with BP oil tanks on the docks. There is a long beach here, but as you may not know, swimming in the waters along this coast is not safe, due to box jellyfish or 'stingers'. They are sometimes deadly, and are in the waters until about May. The town is green apart from the very centre, and tiny. Behind it are the mountain ranges, all tree-lined, and some flat plains running down to the coastline.

Eight kilometres out to sea lies Magnetic Island, an island 10 x 15 km, which from the city appears to be full forest with no sign of life. In fact, there are a few villages on there with 2,000 inhabitants. This was our next destination. It is supposedly the sunniest place in Australia, and has some great forest walks and nice bays and beaches. After 'doing' the city we cooked up a BBQ, more steak and chops and a nice fruit salad we made up ourselves. In the evening at the bar in the tourist centre they were having some 'cane toad races', so we had to investigate. There were twenty toads, each of which were exhibited in turn and bid for by the customers, the highest bidder getting and naming the toad. With four heats, the toads were numbered with chalk on their backs, put in a bucket and placed in the centre of a circle. The first two toads to hop out of the 10 ft diameter circle went to the final. Quite funny to see the bucket removed and the toads just sitting there confused, until someone stamped the floor and they all, well one or two anyway, leapt a few inches. All over very quickly. This event is quite common in the touristy places in the northeast, where this immigrant toad is now quite a pest.

The next day, Thursday the 9th, we packed up and went over to Magnetic Island. Trivia – it is so called because as Cook sailed past his compass turned as though the island was magnetic – good, huh! Only 20 minutes on a speedy ferry. The island looks like this:

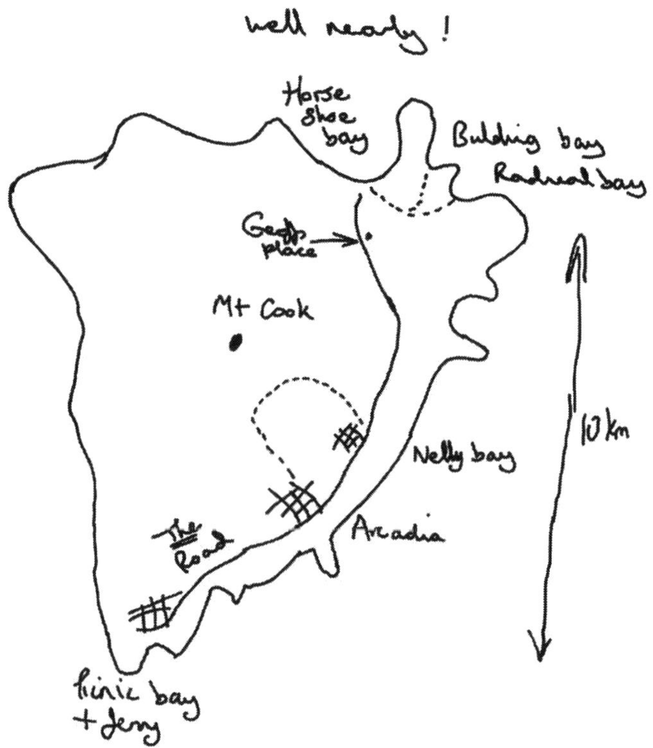

75% of the island is national park, very rugged and forested. When we arrived a few comfy buses were waiting at the ferry place, belonging to a few resorts on the island. We'd already targeted 'Geoffs Place', as it was a resort that had camping too.

Cairns Friday 17th

The courtesy bus picked us up, only us two, and the driver gave us a chat about things to do, etc., which we found upon later use of the bus was exactly the same every time! Being the furthest place from the ferry had the advantage that if we wanted to go to the walk or stops on the way between Geoffs and the ferry we could use the bus and be dropped off or picked up anywhere. Only one road. We got up there and set up our tent, only $6 each. People staying in the little huts (like the ones in Thailand) were paying $10 and this time four were squashed in (compared to two in Thailand). Nice place though; camp area was very green, kitchen facilities for us also. A few coconut trees around, as I found out the next day when a coconut fell on the tent with a bang, and I was in it at the time. We split that coconut after getting the milk out.

Tropical climate here. The forested island is really only eucalyptus, but there are a few imported palms. One of the sunniest places in Australia, or have I said that already. Yes, OK. We got a lift on the regular courtesy bus to a supermarket, probably the only one on the island, and we were picked up as it came back full of new arrivals. Spent the rest of the day lazing by the nice pool there. Decided to have a couple of days to do the walks and then go to Cairns, as there was not much on offer for dining here and it was expensive. Nice sunny day. In the evening we sat around in the open air area with wooden benches, chatting to some of the other travellers. Being a 'resort' place, the Aussie lad working there tried to encourage people to do some silly games, of which the young British lads, just on holiday and able to waste their money on beer, obliged. Could have been Spain! The place had travellers doing all the jobs there, with no sign of anyone in control (no Geoff).

The next day was a little overcast at first, a good chance to do the two and a half hour walk through the hills (Nelly Bay → Arcadia). Free bus there. The path through the forest was quite narrow, but well made. Dropping down into a dip the plants became quite thick and dark green, although no water was in the creeks. Masses of big butterflies were here. Climbed up the hill, spotting a rock-wallaby in the trees. The trees and grass became drier, and a different eucalyptus type. Views from ledges as we followed the hillside around were good, being of Nelly and Arthur Bay. Horseshoe Bay was large and flat behind it. Towards the end of the path we could see Townsville, but it was quite hazy. The final viewpoint gave us views of some small rocky-edged bays. Plant life in this forest is interesting.

Finished the walk in time for a bus back. Treated ourselves to a spit roast of beef and pork, but at $6.50. It was nice, but not worth the money when you can get meat from the shop so cheaply. Chatted to a couple from Ipswich who have travelled for seventeen months so far, doing a diving course here. Very cheap course here too, some taking you to the reef. Conditions not too good at the moment. After a few drinks of punch they sold us very cheaply, they (Geoffs Place) laid on a free bus to a club with a reggae band. As it's a small island, it's one of only a few places to go. Not too good. Had to wait around until the bus took us back.

On the Saturday (11th) we did the other walk on the island, from Horseshoe Bay to Balding and Radical Bays. Nice bays, wide sandy beaches, though you can't swim in the water (stingers!). Very quiet, no one else about on the beach, although there is a resort on Radical Bay. Didn't take long to do, only about 3 km there and back. Horseshoe Bay was quite long, hard sand, no one in the water.

Back at the resort, sun was shining. Played a game of football in the heat with other English lads and volleyball in the pool. Needed the afternoon to relax and recover. Possums and some green, red, and blue birds around us.

On Sunday we packed up, squeezed in the bus, and caught the ferry back to Townsville. We had booked the coach to Cairns and got it at noon for the five-hour bus trip. The Bus Australia pass we have means we have to book our seats in advance, so we need to know when we will leave each place, often nearly as soon as we arrive! They have merged with the two other bus companies (Greyhound and Pioneer) and so things are a little chaotic for them, but we will be able to use all of the buses soon. As we headed up to Cairns it started to rain. We passed vast areas of sugar cane in the flat land beside the roads, with the high Dividing Range in the background. This got nearer the coast as we neared Cairns. Very green countryside.

Was drizzling as we arrived, and we were surrounded by people offering backpacker accommodation. We went to 'Caravella 149', as we had heard of it. Right on the waterfront, esplanade. Bit of a dump. A lot of people, getting in a dorm for $10, with 16 people in, mixed. Clothes everywhere, very messy. About 200 people in the hostel apparently. Lots of info on tours around. The esplanade is full of tour shops and hotels and takeaways. It's a touristy place. A lot of signs and leaflets in Japanese, as it's a very big area for Japanese holidays, with flights direct to Cairns from Tokyo. (A big fact coming later.)

We were given a voucher on booking in for the 'End of the World' nightclub, $3.50 (£1.50) for any meal, so we went to try it. There was a help-yourself salad bar, so we had a mountain of salad to ensure they didn't make a profit, and it was 40 cents (18p) for a glass of beer. They got so many backpackers in over the night that they must have made a fortune. There are loads of places in Cairns doing similar deals, each place tied in with the hostels, who in turn are tied in with the tour operators who run day trips, away tours, etc.

There isn't much to do in Cairns itself, which is why there are so many tours, as there is plenty to see in the area. The main visits are to the reef (snorkelling and diving), or to the rainforest north of Cairns and Kuranda on an amazing mountain railway. On the Monday it was cloudy at first, but got sunny and hot later, with the odd brief shower. We booked a hotel, as we wanted to move from the one we were in. Cairns itself, away from the touristy esplanade, is quite a pleasant town; a small paved mall at the crossroads of two streets, no tall skyscrapers. Plenty of old-style pubs and shops. Streets are wide, with tropical trees in verges down the centre. Whichever street you look down you see tree-lined mountains in the background, apart from the ones out to sea of course. There's no beach, just a water's edge and a few pelicans. As the tide went out it turned to mud flats. Some posh hotels on the palm-lined waterfront, including one over the pier (another exclusive shopping place), with big boats moored on its end. Sat in the mall listening to a bloke playing classical guitar as I read the letters I collected OK. Not very busy. Nice like that.

It rained in the afternoon, and a rainbow appeared out to sea. Ate in the same place as the previous night, only more of a mountainous plateful.

At 7:45 a.m. on Tuesday we were collected in a minibus from the hostel for our rainforest trip. This was a three-day/two-night trip north of Cairns, tours, etc., for $66. Not bad value; accommodation was included, but no food. The choice there was 'Crocodylus Village', in the rainforest, or Jungle Lodge further north at Cape Tribulation near a beach for $69. The Jungle Lodge was more of a party place, so we went to Crocodylus. The weather was OK, so the trip was clear. It must be about 60 km to Port Douglas from Cairns, and then you have to cross the Daintree River. From there is only a dirt road into the rainforest, about another 20 km to Crocodylus and 50 km to Cape Tribulation. As we headed out of Cairns we passed plenty of big, posh resorts built for and owned (as is most of Queensland) by the Japanese, with the compulsory golf course.

Big fact: It's cheaper for the Japanese to come for a week's holiday three times a year to play golf in Cairns then it is to play one round in Japan, so that's why the place is like a suburb of Tokyo. The Aussies have mixed feelings, some obviously like the money aspect they bring, but they are taking over and Aussies are relying too much on the Japanese. (Then complain the British didn't do enough in WWII when they tried to keep them out!)

Back to the trip: Paul, our driver, was excellent value, didn't stop talking all the trip. As well as driving he was really into nature and had a lot of interesting info, as well as gory theories about dangerous animals and plants (crocs, jellyfish, trees). We passed massive sugar cane areas again, which were once rainforest. All Australia was once rainforest. When Cook arrived only about 1% was, now 0.3% (i.e. 70% lost) due to farming etc. Along with cane came cane weed. To remove that they introduced the cane toad (as in races), but that didn't eat cane weed, but ate everything else and is now a massive pest.

Our first stop on the trip north was at Mossman Gorge, an area of rainforest south of Daintree. Beautiful. So much variation of trees and plants. Paul described things as we went through, thousands of different types of life supported on each tree; ferns, insects, mosses, etc. Sixty-five percent of medical products originated from the rainforest. A river running there had drinkable, crystal clear water. Only a brief stop.

Next we had a one hour cruise up the Daintree River, surrounded by rainforest. Weather still good. A flat boat, which the informative guide parked occasionally along the way to show us various things. The river was lined with mangrove trees, with their breathing pipes poking out above the water. Some interesting plant life as well as the fruit bats or flying foxes, pythons rolled up on a tree branch, a small crocodile (river has plenty of crocs) [no swimming], tiny crabs, and so on. Really good. Trying hard to take all this new info in.

After the cruise we had crossed the river and travelled on in the bus along the dirt tracks, travelling through some amazing forest, massive palms and trees growing in solid rock, some nice creeks. Stopped for a couple of viewpoints and a bonus stop at a fan palm area. Walking into the palms, all tall and fan-like at the top, was very nice. Only two square kilometres of fan palms left in Australia, as it felled is good flat farmland.

On the bus there were also people going to Jungle Lodge, so we could stay on, ride up there, and go back to Crocodylus, seeing Cape Tribulation, etc. without paying for it. One stop on the way was Bouncing Stones, a beach full of stones that bounce! (amazed!). These are very dense rocks that don't absorb shock, so if you throw them down they bounce.

Cape Tribulation is where "rainforest meets reef," the forest comes down to the beach and reef comes in to the beach. Very nice.

Arrived at Crocodylus village around 3:30 p.m. It was set in amongst the rainforest, really well done. The main area with wooden tables and floors has trees growing through it, or should I say, it's been built around the trees and is covered in a big canopy like a tent, with open sides so you can see the trees. It has a pool, and the dorm-style accommodation was a few large huts with canvas roofs, all green and hidden in the trees. Amazing place. We were given an "orientation" by the owner to tell us what to do, like walks, etc. Nothing else around in this area, no towns, etc., though there are some good walks in the national park. After making our own tea we chatted to the owner, who'd travelled a lot himself. Later a couple of local blokes came and entertained us with their guitars (not a planned event). Small place, very relaxing.

We had the next two days to do what we wanted. Oh, I should say that at midnight they turned off the generator for electric, so it was dead quiet and we could hear all the noises of the forest while lying in bed.

Planned to do a few walks. Weather still good.

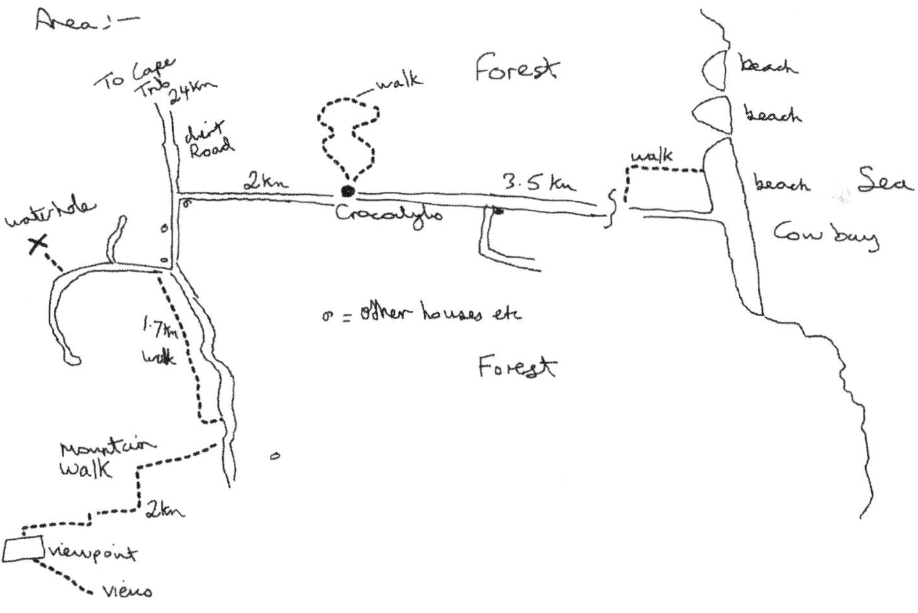

Started off on the morning of Wednesday, the owner took us to a mountain walk by bus. Three and a half hours to do that walk, 1.7 km walk to the waterhole and back. The mountain walk followed a dirt road up through the forest. The last bit was real jungle stuff though, scrabbling between trees and plants on no real path. Loads of life and plenty of mossies, who took a shine to my repellent and took loads of my blood. No real views from the top after all that, due to all the trees, although we did see Daintree River Valley and the coastline. The 1.7 km walk was better, finding an amazing massive strangling fig tree (won't describe – wait for photos). Fought through 6 ft high grass that had grown in an area obviously cleared for a house. The forest was great, no spot the same, so indescribable. Loads of different palms, (palms aren't all the coconut type!), creeping plants, ferns, and even the fungi was interesting.

Carried on to the waterhole. A short walk through some forest got us to the small waterhole in a small creek, about twenty feet across, with a waterfall at one end. The hole was surrounded by the forest, the canopy of trees completely covering it from the sun. Had to have a dip, even though the mossies had scared off previous walkers. The water was so cool and clear.

Walked the two kilometres back to the hotel for 1:30, exactly three and a half hours walking. A little later we started the orange rope walk at the back of Crocodylus. This is a long walk through the rainforest, taking me a very slow two and a quarter hours, as I was keen to take my time. This walk was excellent, following the rope which in places was lost in all the debris of the forest, fallen branches, etc. Some trees, plants, etc., were numbered and I carried a sheet with related info on it. Again, great palms, nice creeks. Saw plenty of fish and turtles, and an orange-footed bird that kicks up a massive mound of a nest, even though it's only chicken-sized. So much life on the floor in amongst the leaf litter. Ninety percent of the light is absorbed by the canopy, so very cool in the forest.

As if we hadn't done enough walking, after tea at 8 p.m. we went on a guided 'night walk'. With a battery pack strapped on to us, thirteen of us and Jamie the guide went out for three hours in the forest. Unfortunately it was a full moon, so it was quite light, but we still found masses of life; birds asleep (only fluffy balls on small branches), insects, lizards, frogs, toads, eels, catfish, and heard so many sounds. Excellent. Me and Mark were left alone for a half hour (part of the walk), turning off the torches and listening to the forest in the darkness. Spooky. Heard a lot but didn't see much. I wasn't really sure where to look, although I had picked out some things earlier while in the group.

In the night it really rained hard, beating down on our canvas roof. Still raining a little in the morning, although it cleared by 10, so got the free ride down to the beach at

Cow Bay. Walking through the forest just before the beach there was a spot for cassowaries, but we didn't see any. [Big emu-like birds]. The beach was nice, about a quarter-mile long with rainforest behind it. Hard sand, rocky ends. Walked along it and to the next two beaches. The sea was quite choppy. The mist hanging over the forested hills behind the beach was quite a sight. We walked back to Crocodylus and halfway back it rained, we got soaked. We had expected it, though, so not too bad really. Still warm enough for shorts and a T-shirt – very humid. Back in time to dry off before the minibus collected us at 3 p.m. for the trip back to Cairns. Rained all the way nearly, but it had been raining in Cairns since we left so we had been lucky. Got back about 6 p.m.

Phoned up this other backpacker's hotel, "Gone Walkabout," and they picked us up in their van. The smallest hostel in Cairns, only around 40 people. Smaller and friendlier, rather than the 200 or so in Caravella with the Tannoy calls for anyone they want to speak to! Nice little place, we got a little room 'out back' with two bunks in, so only us. There's no TV, so it's quiet. Walked up to the supermarket after we'd had a good chat with the owner. It was near closing, so we got plenty of bargains, the main one being the hot barbequed chicken going at $2.99 (£1.30). It actually went down to $2 as the store closed. Whole chicken. Told you it was cheap. Cooked up two packs of 18-cent noodles (9 pence) and had a meal really cheaply.

Spent another evening just talking to other travellers, this time a Danish couple. Have made so many friends, who after a couple of days we leave and then meet more new ones. Chatted a lot to an Australian couple when in Crocodylus. With staying in all these popular backpacker's places we have met all the travellers but not many Aussies or locals. Never mind. The ones we have, though, have been really friendly and outgoing, 'no worries'.

Thought the rainforest trip was brilliant, really worth it. So sad to hear of the destruction and damage and what we have left. Even though most of this forest is National Park and World Heritage it is still privately owned in parts, so the landowner can do what he likes and no one can touch him. This area of forest is special, even more than in Brazil, as it was there when Australia was Gondwana, the great landmass of Australia, Antarctica, and South America, etc., and some of the species of plants have remained unevolved there for 175 million years. Hard to believe.

Mon 20/4

Had the Friday off, just walking round Cairns. It was hot and sunny in the morning, but rained a bit in the evening. It is quite a nice place. Just stayed around the hostel the rest of the day, again talking to others, playing cards with another English lad.

Saturday we had booked on the diving trip out to the reef. We had hoped the weather would be good and it was. There were a few cheap trips going out to the reef by sailboat, etc., but we decided that we should go with a better boat especially for divers. Cost is $99 for the day trip, two dives. The boat was pretty fast, and though the water was choppy we had a fairly smooth ride. The reef is only a few miles from Cairns, but we went out to the outer reef, taking one and a half hours, better diving there. There were about thirty people on the boat, some snorkellers, some doing diving courses, and just a few of us 'certificates'. It's unfortunate in a way, in that the cheapest way to dive the reef is by doing a course. On a course though, I suppose there's no time for pleasure diving.

Also on board were a few introductory divers, people who are taken out to the reef having never dived before, and taken down for a 'hand hold' dive. A bit dodgy, but the instructors are always there. One girl had paid $100 to do this and was too terrified to go down. Shame. We had got out to the reef in good weather, but with black skies ahead. We pulled up about 100 m from the reef. From sea level you could only see a colour change in the water. When the sea is lower the reef does show out. We were in 15 m of water, the reef is in about 5 m. All the gear was set up for us already on the boat; BCD, tank, and regulators, so it only took five minutes to get on a wetsuit, jacket, mask, and fins, and in we went. After swimming around for five minutes I worked out that I hadn't enough weight to sink, so had to go back to the boat for another weight. OK after that. There was a little current.

We dropped down slowly, getting to 14 m and swam around the bottom. At this depth there wasn't much coral, mainly a sandy bed, but came across the occasionally big patches of different-shaped stuff. After swimming around for a while it didn't seem to be getting shallower as it should have if we were heading for the reef. Visibility was probably about 5 m at that depth. Had no problems. After looking around for a while at some interesting stuff we went to the surface to see that we were by the side of the boat, not having made it to the main reef area. Still, we were pleased that we had managed a long dive with no problems apart from me not sinking at the start.

After a lunch break of an hour and a half we started our second dive. We should have gone to another reef, but the weather ahead was bad so we stayed in the same place in the good weather. The boat faced the reef and we got off the back, meaning we had a long swim to get to the reef. On our second dive, refiled with air, we dropped just under the surface and swam in the direction of the reef. Swimming on the surface is very hard with the waves against you. As we neared it we dropped down, must have been to 11 m, and swam up to the reef. Keeping down was a tricky job as it became shallower heading between the coral, sometimes as shallow as 3 m, but managed it no problems. Forgot all about the diving things as we swam through some brilliant coral, all shapes and sizes. Where it was 3 or 4 m we could see the colours too. Lots of fish around, some small shining blue ones were good, all hiding in amongst the hard coral. Hard to describe it all, but so much of it was a brilliant experience. Also found a giant clam, about two feet long and had some blueish life inside, as it was open.

I went down and kicked a little sand over it and it snapped shut. It's best not to touch anything, firstly in case it's sharp or dangerous, and second not to damage the reef. It's quite special, very different to the coral forms in Thailand. Didn't see any big things, although the divers doing the course in the open water out of the coral saw sharks and sting rays. Oh well. Swam for about a half hour and my air ran down quickly – must have had a leak somewhere. This was a brill dive; no hassles, seemed so easy, and we stuck together OK. Have to do this another time before we leave. It's very tiring diving, and we have been quite drained since doing it.

Returning to Cairns on the boat we went through some rain storms, quite entertaining as the boat was tossed around. We went past the cheap trips in their slow boats and were glad we'd gone on this one as we got through the storm quickly. Next time I go down I'll get some pictures. We had a camera this time, but didn't use it as after our first dive we didn't think the visibility was good enough. In the reef though, away from the sandy bottom, it was fairly good, although there was no sunshine to brighten up the coral. A good day, felt very pleased.

Sunday we had arranged to go with the hostel to Kuranda, a town up in the mountains and rainforest, about half an hour by road from Cairns. They have a big market on Sunday. The main reason for going, though, was to ride back on the scenic railway ($17 one way, $29 return). We saved $12 by going up by hostel bus. The markets were nothing special, mainly arty junk; earrings, paintings, nothing I would buy, so arriving at 10 we had a lot of spare time to wait for the next train to Cairns at 12:30.

One attraction in Kuranda is the 'bungee jump', where stupid people pay large amounts of money ($70) to leap from a cage dangled by a crane, about a hundred feet up, being stopped from certain death only by a big elastic rope. It's a craze here and in NZ. Not for me. It's all over in a few seconds.

Anyway, the train journey is special as the line was built in the 1890s using only picks and shovels and hundreds of Irish, as they built it along steep cliffs, made fifteen tunnels through the mountains and built bridges across the ravines. An achievement of engineering for those days. Built when Kuranda was a tin-mining town. Nothing there now, bar busloads of tourists. Some amazing views of gorges, Barron Falls, and Cairns plains as we rode along the side of a mountain. A nice clear day. The train carriages were old-style too, and we stood out on the platform at the end of the carriage for a better view. Good trip, but not worth $17. Took an hour and a half to get to Cairns.

Spent the afternoon back at the hostel with the two Danes. There is a tiny pool in the hostel, which has a button to turn it to a jacuzzi. Pretty good. Nice afternoon, sunny for a change. In the evening we went to one of those places that does a mega-meal and salad bar for $3.50, where I had masses of roast pork.

Everyone here seems to be doing diving courses as they are good value, and we've been giving the new starters the benefit of our experience! Nice and relaxing at this hostel.

We've moved the flight forward by one week from Australia to NZ, as we've got plenty of time to do what's left and haven't missed anything. One month should be plenty in NZ, as it's only the size of the UK really, although there is so much to do – good reports from all who have been there. May be snowing in some places!

OK, will tell you more later on. Hope all's well and as normal. May call soon to see if there are any new arrivals. What else – I'll probably remember after I've sent this.

That's it I think.

Lots of love

David .

Also. Tax rebate. I should have a tax rebate of £1,300 or £1,400 for last year. Did I sign a form? If not, could you get a form to me and I'll have to sign it and try and fill it in. Can't miss out on that.

Thanks.

Byron Bay

8/5/92

Hello,

It's been a while since I wrote and loads has happened so be prepared for a real long letter (longer than usual!) Hope all's well still. I guess I'll be in NZ by the time you get this. I don't think I've much general stuff to say, just that we're still having a great time here, with only a few days left in Australia. Since Cairns we've travelled down the coast and really only have a stop in Sydney left. We had a few days at Airlie Beach/Whitsunday Islands, Hervey Bay/Fraser Island, Noosa, Brisbane, Surfers Paradise, and now Byron Bay.

I think it was Cairns, Sunday the 19th I wrote after going to Kuranda. It was a bank holiday on Monday, so we spent the day lazing around. Cairns was deserted, all the shops were closed, although wandering around I met a lad I knew from our stop in Sydney, and spent an hour catching up on our tales. A very hot day, the wet season looks like it's over, so we sat in the sun and at the pool chatting to new arrivals. Kim and Dorte, the Danish couple (Kim the lad) were to start a diving course, but came back as Kim had failed the medical. He would have to have tests the next day to see if he could go on. The stay in this hostel in

Cairns had been great, I felt like I knew or had spoken to everyone there. No T.V. to occupy everyone's time, you see.

Tuesday the 21st we were off from Cairns to Airlie Beach, nine hours away. It was a great sunny day and we didn't have to get the bus til 2 p.m., so we had more spare time. Heading back south now from Cairns to Townsville the scenery was the same as the trip up (obviously), but seemed so much nicer with the sunshine; past the mountains and beaches and forests and plains. We arrived in Airlie Beach at around midnight. No terminal here, just a bus shelter right on the waterfront. We could have gone to the backpacker's places, but we wanted to camp as it was nice weather and half the price. Decided to stay out until it got light, to save a night's accommodation.

Airlie Beach is a small place, the place to go to get to the Whitsunday Islands, a group of seventy-four different sized islands. A few lively pubs about, so we found a quiet spot and settled under a sheltered park bench and table at the end of the bay. When it was light we could see what a nice spot it was. After a morning cuppa we went in search of the campsite. A map on the main street showed it was one and a half kilometres away. It was a clear day, very hot, and we walked out of the town to the 'Island Getaway' campsite. It was pretty good, the usual standard; pool, BBQ, T.V. area, camper's kitchen, and grassy area for camping. Put up the tent and headed straight back into the town to see what was on offer. We wanted to do a dive and see some of the islands. The small town area was basically one street lined with tour shops, souvenir shops, and takeaways, etc. The street ran along the area behind the two little beaches and that was the 'town'.

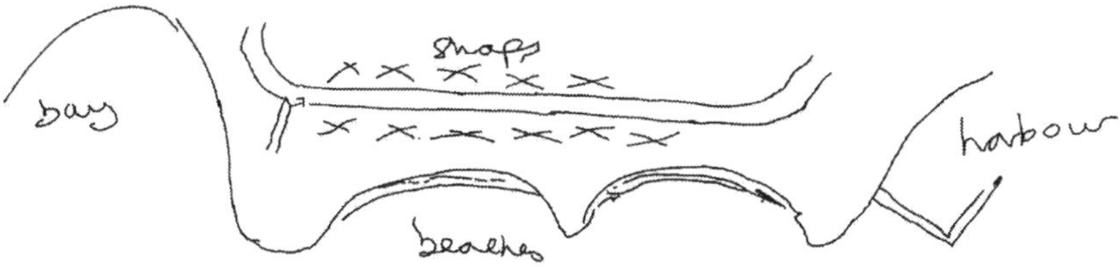

There were plenty of island trips, road trips, and dives on offer. There were cheap dives around the island but we decided to pay extra to go the extra 50 km out to the reef. Airlie Beach was mainly a place full of backpackers, with the real holidaymakers going directly to the resorts on a couple of the larger islands, being able to fly direct from Sydney or Brisbane. One other thing to do in Airlie Beach was to go up a nearby hill, Mount Roger, for a view over the bay and islands. We did start to walk there, as it's in yet another national park, Conway N.P. The national park info office told us it was 5 km, and as we turned to go back and give up a bus came along, of which there are very few here.

The walk to the mountain was in itself 6 km, through more eucalyptus woodland, forest, grass, and trees. The climb to the top was worth it, a great view over one end of the islands, some completely tree-lined and others fairly barren, disappearing into the distance. We walked back down and through more woods, and back to the campsite. In the day we'd done over 15 km. Finished off the tiring day with yet another barbeque; pork chops and veal steak, very cheap too.

The next morning we booked our dive trip out to the reef, $100 all in. We also hired a camera, $25, to get some photos. It was one with manual focus and expensive, so I hope I got some decent ones! We had the rest of the day to look around, although it didn't take long. Really the water here still has a risk of stingers, but people were in the warm water. It's also a popular spot for sailing, the waters being full of private boats. Had another leisurely afternoon just around the beach, with some great houses on the end of the town on the waterfront.

On the Friday we had our dive, going with the Whitsunday Diver. From Airlie Beach the islands are only a few kilometres, with a bit of coral around between the islands. The real reef is another 50 km, two hours by boat. It was a great clear day, the sea was dead calm, unlike in Cairns. We were collected from the campsite at 8 a.m. and set off on the smallish boat around 9. There were only about twenty people on it, most doing certified dives, though there were a few students. The boat took us past and through the larger islands, so we saw this as an island cruise as well, saving us another trip! After two hours we arrived at the reef, Bait Reef in fact. The Great Barrier Reef here makes the ocean look light blue and you can see waves breaking over it where it is shallow. We stopped for our two dives inside the Bait Reef, which is in effect a reef lagoon, an area of 10 m deep water surrounded by a circle of coral, with a little opening to get the boat in.

The 'lagoon' was probably 200 m diameter. This meant the dive was very safe, never getting into the current, deep water, or far from the boat unless we went out of the entry. The sun was shining and so conditions were perfect. Our two dives went really well, getting thirty and forty minutes. Even though we went 10 m or so, the best coral was only two metres, easy for snorkelling. We saw so many small fish and some really big fish near the boat, maybe 3 or 4 ft. We were asked to dive with an older woman who was on her own. One group of divers went 75 ft, or 25 m, which they shouldn't do (max of 18 m) so they couldn't dive a second time.

Took a whole roll of 36 photos of us, coral, and fish. At just below the surface, say at one metre, was the shelf of coral, covered in so many different colours and shapes of coral, and teaming with

fish. This shelf stretched on for a long way it seemed. When the tides are low this is sometimes exposed. At lower than 6 m colours fade and so the effect isn't as good, but obviously the variety of shapes and forms is still easy to see. I hope these pictures come out so as you can appreciate the things I've seen. Just amazing, a different world. Really enjoyed both dives, a real thrill, and such a beautiful spot, worth every penny and conditions so much better than Cairns. That's really why we had to go again. That's diving for a while, until I get my proper certificate. I haven't had it yet, I'll have to let them know. It's great to do, getting in the wetsuit, etc., but it's tiring and hard to get out of the water with all the gear on.

We had all of Saturday to recover, as we planned to get the bus out in the evening for an overnight twelve-hour trip to Hervey Bay. Saturday was ANZAC Day, with parades and special events all across Australia (and NZ). As I've said before, remembrance of war dead and war veterans is a very important thing to them here. In Airlie there was an outrigger boat racing competition. The outrigger is the long thin boat with a 'stabiliser' and six paddlers.

There were boats and teams from the area around, such as Mackay, with a whole series of races both for men and women. The people in the boats all looked very fit and it looked really tough, as the 'sprints' were over 2,000 m and took over ten minutes. An even hotter day, and so exhausting watching it from the banks.

The crowd there were mainly involved in the competitions. Spent more time on the beach and back at the campsite pool. We knocked up some barbequed burgers and eggs before getting the bus at 11 p.m. The bus was nearly full when we got on, having to take the seats at the back where normally the driver sleeps. It's always a bumpy ride there. We stopped at 1 a.m. for a 'meal break'! Kept waking up hourly through the night, but slept enough I think. Even down this 'populated' east coast it's still hours between places and roads are long and straight.

We arrived, after a brief stop in the strange town of Bundaberg and travelling past banana and pineapple areas, in Hervey Bay at 11 a.m. There are two reasons this place is on the popular tour list: one, it's the gateway for backpackers visiting Fraser Island, and two, during the months of August – October whales visit the bay and can be seen there. I would have really liked to have seen that, but we were too early. We'd go to Fraser Island, though. Around Hervey Bay, which is a bay probably ten or fifteen miles long, are plenty of little towns that all merge into one, with such original names as Torquay, which is where we are.

On arrival we were mobbed by backpacker representatives all around with their courtesy buses. 'Koalas' said we could camp there, and we'd been recommended the place by others on our travels. We collect so much advice on things from other travellers, and give plenty too! We had met Nicki, a girl we'd met on Magnetic Island, and she we went to Koalas too. The hostel was excellent, we were camped at the back, but could use all the facilities. They had a large pool, nice kitchen, and a main room. It was just across the street from the beach. It was beach, a few trees, the road, and then us. The beach was long and straight, calm water, very quiet. Walking around, it was very quiet overall, not much around. Plenty of holiday units, a family could get a unit for $30 a night. Cheap. It showered a bit although was still warm. We wanted to find out about the trips to Fraser Island, of which we'd heard so much.

Fraser Island is a beautiful island and different to every other in that it is probably the largest sand island in the world. More details later! Various trips being offered, day trips for $46, but the hostel ran a three-day/two-night trip for $59. We went to a meeting about the trip to find out more, with a video of the island. Looked excellent. We had been dubious about spending say $100 to go there, but as it turned out we were so glad we did. These trips for $59 include a rental of a four-wheel drive for a group of eight, all the camping gear, the ferry, and permits. The island is mainly national park. On top of the fee we'd have to pay petrol, food, and drink. We didn't put our names down this day, but decided to go on the Tuesday and try and find some people to go in a group. On Monday the hostel had four groups of eight going, so it's a popular trip.

We spent the evening talking to Phil, an Irish lad. He was coming up the coast and told us of the dolphin show at Coffs Harbour. He said if we contacted someone we could swim with the dolphins. When we were in Brisbane I called the guy and that's OK, so looking forward to that, it will be Sunday the 10th. See, you get some great info. A lot of the stuff we've done we've just learnt from others as we've gone.

Monday we were woken early as the groups loaded the trucks for their trips. The weather wasn't too bad, although again in the afternoon there were showers. We had a walk along the beach and esplanade. Didn't seem much going on, but we did find Pialba, a small town with all the shops, etc., in it. By the afternoon we had our meeting about our trip. There were twenty-six people. The lad in charge (?!) went through everything and suggested groups. He listed Mark and I with six Germans – imagine that. Luckily there were two Germans who wanted that group, so we were out of that. Phew! Nicki said she was with us, so we had a group of three. After a bit of reorganization we managed to sort ourselves out with some Irish and English we'd been speaking to. There were actually nine in the group.

By the time we'd worked this out the girls in the group had already made a shopping list for our three day's food.

It cost us $14 each, for masses of fruit, big steaks (massive), all good stuff. So, in the group we had me, Mark and Nicki (Kent), Paul, Annamarie and Lorraine (Ireland), Andrea (Eng.), and Nico and Silka (Germany). Paul, Mark, and I went down the bottle shop to get the booze while the girls went to the supermarket, getting some 'slabs' of cans and boxes of wine. Four litres of Mozelle costs $6 and it's not too bad either. When that bit was all sorted we tucked into a $2 pizza. The others had a great apartment-style room with its own kitchen, bathroom, and T.V., so come 11 p.m. all the lads were there watching the weekend English football highlights. A bumper show, as no one knew Sunday's results, which as it turned out got Leeds the league.

Tuesday, we got up before 7 a.m. and packed up the tent and what we needed for our three-day 'safari'. We then had to spend the next two hours sorting out camping gear, packing the truck, checking it over, and sorting out details with the rental company. The mechanic then told us where to go and what to see on the island and things about the trip. The island is, as I say, mainly sand. It's about ninety miles long and ten miles wide, with many freshwater lakes to visit. There are no roads or towns on the island, just a few houses and sandy tracks. On the ocean side is a 75-mile long wide, hard sand beach, which is used as a road, and is brilliant to see and drive along. We packed up and surprisingly had plenty of room inside, with three in front and six sideways in the back. The ferry ride over was only a half hour on a small vehicle ferry. The weather had picked up and was looking good. I've enclosed info on Fraser Island to save; maps, etc.

Once we got on the island we hit the sandy tracks. These were excellent, just windy single-width tracks through the forest. We travelled for 10 km to Central Station, stopping to decide a plan. We headed south, as the ferry had brought us to the middle of the western side. The track was rough and windy and so we were going only 30 km/hr. There was some strange noise from the back, so we stopped and checked the wheels for flats – OK. Then, ten minutes later, we were going slowly down a gradual slope when someone in the front asked if "that was our wheel" that had overtaken us and was heading off down the hill! At the same time we stopped moving! Leaping out we did discover that yes, it was our rear nearside wheel.

Someone went off in search of it while we stood in disbelief. After we realized the situation we all cracked up laughing, but thought how lucky we were. It was also lucky in that although we'd lost all six wheel nuts the studs were fine, and the axle and wheel drum were fine, falling in the soft sand. Jacking up the truck was impossible in the sand. It even started raining!! As it turned out it was only five minutes and the only time in the three days. Luckily we'd blocked the road. I'd got the spare out and taken a nut off some of the other wheels. The trucks arriving behind us were also full of backpackers, a few of which gave us a hand lifting up the truck. We wedged a wheel under the axle and dug a hole to drop the spare wheel on the drum. Once the nuts were on we were OK. Paul checked the other wheels and all the nuts were loose.

Mark just reminded me that after the wheel had passed us (!) Nicki asked if it was our spare and should we drive after it! It could have been very dangerous if it had come off on the tarmac roads on the mainland or at 80 km/hr on the beach. We returned to Central Station and called the island's mechanic. While we were there we had a brief walk to a creek there. Walking down to it I thought it was covered in scum and froth, but when we were closer it was actually perfectly clear water with a white sandy bed, surrounded by rainforest. The mechanic's house was about 10 km away, which on those sandy roads takes half an hour. When we arrived he couldn't help us until he'd finished his game of darts! He then attempted to replace the lost wheel nuts while still holding a can of VB in his right hand. Him and people with him all looked a little out of touch (polite version). We said, "should you check the suspension is OK?" "Didn't think of that."

Within half an hour we were back on the road, heading back inland from Eurong on the beach. We drove up past Lake McKenzie to Lake Wabby. We had arranged to meet one of the other truck groups there. They never turned up. Found out later they'd broken down, clutch trouble, getting to the mechanic just after we'd left. Anyway, this lake was stunning. It's actually being taken over by a moving sand dune, so on three sides are forest and on the other is a sand dune sloping down straight into the green water. Great to roll down the sand dune straight into the water. That was us cleaned up a little, as I was very oily from my mechanical efforts after our wheel trouble.

Leaving the lake, as it had been very hot, I drove. We had been taking it in turns to drive and everyone seemed pretty sensible. It began to get dark very quickly as we went steeply downhill from the lake to the beach. The 7 km took three-quarters of an hour, the steering making quite a nasty noise. We arrived on the beach in darkness. The permit we had allowed us to camp virtually anywhere on the island, so we found a reasonable spot on the beach. While driving around there we came across a couple who'd set up camp nearby.

In the light from the truck we set up our three four-man tents, which were easy to put up, while the girls, in their own words, 'did the girly things' like getting tea going. We went off in search of decent firewood, getting enough to keep us going for the night. We did really well, everyone was well-organized, as we produced a brilliant spaghetti Bolognese over the wood fire. We did have a gas stove, but that's no fun.

Settling down around the fire with our drinks, the sky was really clear and we could see the silhouettes of dingoes on nearby dunes and hear them as they howled. Dingoes are harmless, but will pinch things if you leave them out, like babies (Australian joke – ref. the women at Ayers). They're a bit like purebred wolves. We had a great night, with Paul mainly keeping us entertained. Everyone got on really well, we hadn't stopped laughing all day.

Our plan for the next day was to drive up the beach to the top end of the island. To drive on the beach you have two hours before and two hours after low tide (around 12 p.m.), so we couldn't rush off in the morning. No one felt like rushing after all that cheap wine anyway (apart from to behind the bushes). We cleaned the dishes in the sea, packed up the tents and ate our three-for-$1 pineapples (cheapest ever). As we were about to leave, the couple we saw the previous night came walking over. They couldn't start their Jeep. 'Have you tried drying the plugs' I said. We went over to find the engine was soaking. I dried the plugs, etc., and within a few minutes they were started. [All favours repaid – wait til I get to Noosa and you'll see what I mean].

Another brill day, we cruised up the beach. You have to watch the creeks that run out on the beach making soft patches. Brill though. The sea on this beach is pretty wild and full of sharks, so not safe. After a short drive we reached a creek, Eli Creek. Clear waters running out of sand hills into the sea. Beautiful. We said we'd camp here later, after going up and back along the beach.

Our next stop was at an old shipwreck, rusting away in the sand at the water's edge. Interesting. Boiling as we had a drink looking at it. Drove on up the coast. We stopped at one of the few populated spots, 'Happy Valley'. There we found probably the most miserable groups of Australians we'd ever met! We had rubbish to dump, but the bloke said we could only put things we'd bought in his shop in the bins. We wanted water but the taps were padlocked and wouldn't be unlocked unless we bought enough, even though nearly everyone had bought ice-creams. We moved on up as far north as we could go, having a dip in the 'Champagne Pools', rocky pools frothed up by sea waves. We had to be quick as the tide was cutting off the beach at Indian Head.

Turning round we stopped off for lunch at a small place with a petrol station and a picnic area, laying out a big spread. Trying again to fill our water bottles we were told 'if you want water you'll have to pay for it'. Ten litres cost $1! On our return to Eli Creek we saw wood on the beach, throwing it in the back of the truck for firewood. This time we could set up in the daylight. The spot was perfect, on the wide sandy beach, in the soft sand, right by the side of the creek with the sand banks and trees behind the creek. There was even a toilet block on the hill. We set everything up really well, and had time to play. We did silly things like have races with empty cans down the creek. Following the creek upstream it narrowed down to four feet deep and four feet wide, so it was quite fast, with trees and plants right on the bank. You could float and be carried by the water right the way to the beach. Amazing to float down this water past all the greenery.

This night we had a good fire and barbequed some big steaks and had them with salad. To keep our fire going someone acquired a large piece of wood that looked very much like a piece of something other than a tree. More steak, beer, and wine later and we had another excellent night.

On our third and last day (Thursday) we got up early and took our time to clean and pack up. We had until 4 p.m. to get to the ferry. A short drive down the beach and back inland. We stopped at Lake Boomanjin, supposedly with turtles. A massive red coloured lake (dyed by leaves), and we patted the water to attract turtles – no good. I did find a couple of shin pads and with twigs set them up in the parking area.

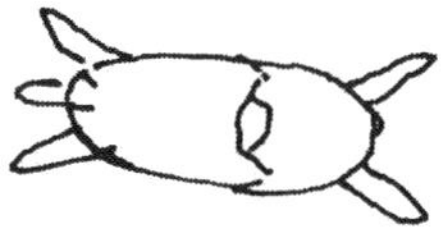

Mark was driving and stopped in front of it. Some of the girls did think it was a turtle – they saw it move (?). Funny at the time. We headed on another 20 km to Lake McKenzie. This lake was different again. An amazingly white sandy beach there. Water was cold but clear. Very large lake. Had lunch there and saw a four-foot iguana too. We got to the ferry early, on the fumes from our petrol; on the island it was 97 cents/litre instead of the usual 65 cents. Made a cuppa while we waited and talked to a German who'd been with the German group. He'd had a really boring time and wished he were with us! Our Jeep was by far the dirtiest, having been through some oily black puddles on the inland roads.

Back to Koalas by 5 p.m., we had everything to sort out quickly as three of us were off at 7 on the bus. Paul gave the rental company hell about the wheel and loss of a day (not bad really) so they gave us $100 compensation. It was $85 in all for three days (including beer).

Great trip, beautiful island, good group. We have lots of addresses now. That evening the two girls left cooked us tea. More of those boxes of cheap wine. We booked in a bed this night as a treat. It had taken a while to get the sand out of everything and get it cleaned, as we can't use soaps, etc., on the island. I'm sure sometime we'll see some of these people again.

Friday morning we were off to Noosa, only three hours down the coast. Said our goodbyes and caught the bus at 11 a.m. Slept most of the way, fairly drained from the previous few days. We thought Noosa was only a small beach resort, our first stop on the 'Sunshine Coast.' In fact it was a big resort made up of again lots of small towns very close together. The main town was mostly the Sheraton Hotel, very upmarket. We were dropped near the main beach area, and being sunny we headed the 1.5 km to the council campground.

At Noosa there is a series of rivers flowing out to sea that wind and form a very broken up land, joined by bridges. The campground was in an excellent spot. Only $10 for two, we pitched up right on the side of the river, which was actually a beach. It was starting into a bank holiday weekend and getting busy. The area is a haven for fishermen, our little beach had a few on it and the river had plenty of little boats going up and down it with fishermen in. We had been accompanied to the camp by two young English girls with a minute tent and a minute spending urge. They are probably the tightest people I've ever met, living off bread for weeks and talking of money all the time, even more than me! The money they'd saved on food they'd spent on medical bills, both having been very sick! We did a little shopping in the nearby streets. Tea was, guess what, a barbeque of steak cooked on a real wood BBQ. While cooking we chatted to an old Aussie couple who'd started a three-year trip round Australia with a caravan, a jeep with a boat on. Good luck to them!

The smoky steak was excellent. Camping next to us was a young bloke from Cardiff who told us how easy he'd found it to emigrate – or get emigration papers (too old for a working visa). Great campsite, watching a new couple put up a new tent, "Pole 1 into pole 2! Not like that!"

The next day we had a whole day to see the area. We hadn't realized Monday was a bank holiday, so we had very little money to last us til Tuesday. Woken up early by boats, fishermen, and babies at 6 a.m. The area behind us had been filled up by mansion-sized tents with all mod cons. After brekky we walked into Noosa, along the main beach, which was quite nice, and into the national park. First place down the coast where it was safe to swim in the sea. Very hot. One of the N.P. walks was along the coast and headland. The coastline here is, in the N.P., very rugged and rocky with small beaches.

The walk took us past the calm blue sea, Hell's Gate, an area of deep cliffs and rough water, and through more eucalyptus woodland and forest, but different again. After some rough shoreline we came to Alexandria Bay, a half mile straight beach, then Sunshine Beach, a thirty mile straight beach, fairly empty, good surfing waves. Not much of a town there, but walking back to the campsite we came across the big shopping area. We did our usual, 'get somewhere high for a view', climbing a hill up to Laguna Lookout, looking over the river and beach.

Heading back to the campsite we met Jon and Julie, the couple we'd rescued in Fraser Island. After a chat they invited us to their apartment for a drink. It was a great place, perched on the hillside at the end of the beach, they had a balcony view over the area. $160 a night, although you could have six there, which with three bedrooms is really cheap if there are six (expensive for two). Posh. On their massive balcony was a spa bath, so you could sit and look over the area while in it.

A few drinks later and we were offered tea, a barbeque of chicken, salad with salmon, mousse, and biscuits. It was fortunate, as we'd been to Coles and already bought our tin of soup, meaning we had nearly no money! They were both 30, single (tut tut), living with their own parents, and quite well off. Australians and just on holiday. Nice couple. Walking back to the campsite at 12:30 there were still people fishing on the river.

Sunday we were moving again, off to Brisbane, but not til the afternoon. Another hot day. Sat by our little beach. The fishermen had some big catches today. The guy who was looking after the campsite showed us photos of western Australia, as we'd missed it; gorges and canyons, etc., different again.

Had an easy two-hour trip to Brisbane, getting a courtesy bus to a backpacker's place, 'Sly Fox'. The place was only a few minutes from the city centre, across the river. It was an old hotel which had obviously dropped its standards to attract the backpackers and still had the carpets, brass beds, brass fittings, tiled bathrooms. Doesn't sound special, but it was the Victorian style, 'a touch of class' as they called it. It works for them because instead of charging $50 a night for a room and getting no takers, they charge $10 and put five in a room and fill the place. The hotel had an open flat roof with our kitchen and tables and chairs on, so we had a view over to the built-upward city centre.

Brisbane is a very built up city, around a wide river. The north side had the usual tall shiny bank and insurance tower blocks, built between the city's 'heritage' buildings, the nice old ones dating as far back as, oh, 1900. On the Monday it was 'Labour Day', and there was a union march through the city. Other than that it was deserted, virtually everything was closed. Brisbane isn't known for having much to see, and apart from the heritage buildings and the usual shopping malls it was true. It has a nice botanical garden...

Walking around in the evening a drunken beggar asked me for $3 for the bus home. All we had between us was $2!, not that we considered giving him any. Comes to something when a beggar wants more than you've got. We hadn't enough to pay for accommodation, so had to leave Mark's passport as security until Tuesday morning when the banks opened and we could get money. On Tuesday, apart from a little more city wandering, we went on a free brewery tour, the 'XXXX' brewery. All the say twenty people there were backpackers. Really interesting to see the virtually completely automated plant bottle 1.7 million litres of beer a day! Mostly bottles and cans here. A lot of beer. Three weeks to make the brew, 20 million litres in the plant. After the tour we had a chance to sample the beers for free, too.

So, after our brief stop in dull Brisbane we were off again, moving the one and a half hour trip down to Surfers

Paradise on the 'Gold Coast.' This area is on a massive beach, very commercialized, the vast number of skyscrapers casting shadows along the beach. We went to a small 'guest house' for backpackers called 'Trekkers'. It was one of the most expensive at $14, but probably one of the nicest, with some very friendly owners and guests. We had four in our big room, our own bathroom, quilts on the bed, and a nice pool.

As with all the places we've stayed, it was full of young backpackers from all over. Being quite a way from the town area they ran regular minibuses down. The hostel was near to Australia Fair Shopping Centre, biggest in the country, with the usual indoor malls, air conditioning, shining floors and plastic plants. Surfers Paradise itself was a load of cheap shirt shops and Japanese jewellery shops. Loads of Japanese here. Off-season. It's a real Australian equivalent of Spain I guess.

In the evening the hostel had a trip down to 'Cocktail and Dreams' nightclub, where we had free entry and free drinks for one hour, then two for the price of one for two hours. Very busy and lively, good music, and full of backpackers. Everyone who went spent the next day taking it easy around the pool.

Down on the beach it was very busy and hot, with only a few surfers, the waves weren't massive, but the surf stretched up and down the coast for miles. Tuesday evening we had a pool contest in the hostel, with the twenty-five or so people taking part. I was third or fourth and Mark won, the prize money $27. The people who ran the place were really friendly, and we were waved off when we got the bus out the next day to Byron Bay.

The weather at Byron was pretty good and so we went to a backpacker's where we could camp. No courtesy bus this time, but they laid on a taxi for us. The place was about half a kilometre from the very small town and beach. The camping area behind the wooden two-floor structure of dorms, kitchen, and lounge, a big pool, etc., was on a little island. The hotel had free bicycles, and so after we had upped the tent we cycled to the town and out to a walking track. Byron Bay has quite a good long surfy beach with a rocky headland at one end. The walk went around the headland up to the lighthouse and 'most easterly point in Australia'. Nothing but sea. Once again we found ourselves coming down the hills through eucalyptus and various other kinds of forest and rainforest. Checking out the town took all of two minutes. It started to rain really heavily, which it did on and off for the rest of the day.

Saturday was better, so we spent some time down at the beach. There was an old wreck just out from the shore, so we snorkelled out. Not much of it was left, but loads of fish were around it. Plenty of dolphins were swimming around in the bay, popping up out of the water, but I didn't meet any when I was in the warmish water.

In the evening we barbequed more lamb and steak, and waited in anticipation of the FA cup, being shown live at 12 a.m. Coverage before the game was awful, but we had the ITV commentary. Pretty good game, I expected them to win 2-0. It was raining again in the evening and we hoped our tent would be dry by morning when we packed it up. It was nice and dry inside, so it proved itself.

I'm continuing now I'm in Sydney. I got your letter from the 23rd of April. Thanks for that. Glad you got the parcel and maybe the photos back by now too! The India photos were packed up at the P.O. in Delhi on their own. I did fill in the form, but couldn't see what good it would do. I'll send it in my next parcel soon.

We left Byron Bay early on Sunday the 11th, for a four-hour trip to Coffs Harbour, where the 'pet porpoises pool' was. We planned to stop here to do this, get the evening bus out, and travel overnight to Sydney.

We arrived at 2 p.m. in Coffs, and got a free lift up to the porpoise place. Smallish town. The show started at 2:15 and took one and a half hours, with three dolphins performing various amazing things, along with a few seals, sealions, and sea leopards. They also had penguins and fish. Not bad, the place was family run and probably short on cash. The children there loved it. After the show we saw the trainer, Greg, and he let us in with the dolphins. Brilliant. After a while swimming around and throwing balls to them, he got fish and got them to play. They towed us round the pool, leapt over us, tail-walked between us, and lay there while we patted them, tickled their tongues, and fed them fish. Amazing animals, tough skin but soft. They don't let many people do this so as not to stress the dolphins. We were in for probably half an hour, and a lady there took some photos, so I hope they come out. What a way to finish an amazing three months in Australia, doing so many things I've always wanted to do.

Now, we're in Sydney after the overnight journey, another nine-hour trip. It's colder than when we were here last, but we can remember our way around, seems like we've never been away.

OK, that's Australia 'done', I'll have to try and sum it up sometime, when I look back at the massive list of things we've done, all of which have been excellent.

What else. I'll be sending some more photos soon, for you to get developed. We'll be in the USA, LA I guess, if it's still there, in early/mid-June, so will get up there to see you. NZ will be pretty cold now, so I hope I can put up with it. I may even have to buy a jumper! When I get to NZ I'll be changing say £400 on plastic, if you can pay off my debts with them. I'll need it clear when I get to the US, in case I want to buy a car or van.

Say hello to everyone, and hope all's well. Good to hear Sharon seems fine. I thought the baby was due mid-April, that was why I phoned, but I'll call soon as I guess it'll be on its way about now.

I've also put in a couple of postcards, if you could post them for me, as it's cheaper than posting them from here. Thanks. Add the cost onto my ever-growing bill!

See you soon.

Love

David.

P.S. Mail you want to send before end of May goes to Auckland. After that may as well hang on until Canada, and you can bring any over with you (along with all the photos!). Mark's told his mother to send anything for him to you before you leave and after the end of May, if that's OK.

New Zealand

May 1992

Hillo,

Hope all's will! (Kiwi accent!) So, firstly, congratulations, a new addition. Glad to hear the baby and Sharon are well, apart from the name choice. Just kidding, Naomi's not bad! Still, looks like it's left to me to keep the family name going, two girls, unless of course they're thinking of more expensive children! No doubt I'll get up to date on all this when I see you, as there's not much else I can say.

OK, I'll bore you with more tales now. In this letter I've attached more of a diary list of my events, I'll explain later.

Oh, one thing I should mention is another package winging its way to you (hopefully), with another five reels of film, two books, postcards, and a Cartier watch I found in Bondi Beach. I could have sold it for $20, but decided to keep it. It does work but the battery's run out. Have it if you want, Dad. Posh, hey (P.S. it's a Japanese fake). The films are marked. One's the diving film. If you can get them developed A.S.A.P. then hopefully they'll be back in time to carry even more over to Canada! Hope the other sets of photos are good. I wonder about a lot of the ones I've taken. Still, even if they are just a blur I'll know what it means – been there, done that. You may be able to work out what's what from my letters.

Right. Since I last wrote we've come over to NZ. We had a couple of days in Sydney before our flight. We were keen to survive the last bit on the money we had left. We stayed in a cheap hotel again in Kings Cross. There were 'cooking facilities' (a ring thing) in the room. Mark was cooking bacon in the room. It was hot so I opened the door, letting all the smoke out. The fire alarm went off, and we had to leave the building (apart from the ones watching TV who didn't hear!). Even the firemen came.

The time we had there we used mainly to work out what we could do in NZ. The alternatives were to go to some contacts in north NZ and try and borrow a car for one month, to get a travel pass for the trains/buses, or to go on the 'Kiwi Experience', a special bus trip that tours NZ over eighteen days. With this we could get off in one place and catch the next bus a few days later. Prices were about the same for each method.

I was quite sad to leave Australia after such a good trip, but looking forward to NZ, ignoring everyone who said it was freezing.

We had a good flight to Auckland, only three hours. I laughed at the American crew, who were all so nice and pleasant to everyone to extremes – "You're welcome." You'll see when you get to Canada! Only sea to see as we flew. Arriving in Auckland around 6 p.m. we could see the big bay the city is on. It was the first time we'd landed and hadn't heard "It's 6 p.m. and 30°." This time, "It's 6 p.m. and 4°." On with the extra T-shirt.

Waiting at the airport we were both collected by customs along with all the other backpackers and our bags checked. They were quite good about it, asking jokingly if we'd tried the drugs on our travels through Thailand and Nepal. No problem. The tent had to go and be checked for imported dirt. Needed a clean anyway!

After getting through we checked the info for accommodation. Lucky again. We've hit NZ off-peak, so prices are a lot lower than expected. The 'Hilton' in Auckland was only $10 with breakfast and Kirin the minibus driver would take us there for free, even buying us a coffee as we waited to go. The trip into the city wasn't bad, it's a big city. The hostel was OK, but was cold in the dorm room. It was located on Queen Street, the main street in the city. The streets were all hilly, the town centre being down the hill ten minutes.

After walking for five minutes we were stopped by a bloke with a pen and paper. "Could we do a survey?" OK. He asked 'if we could be anyone who would we be,' (I said "me"), 'if we could do anything... blah blah.' (I said "travel the world!")

After this he said he'd tell us how to achieve this (but I already had?!). He took us up into a room with 'dianetics' books everywhere. We did a questionnaire, which turned out to have 200 questions to determine our personality, loads of stupid questions. From the answers my personality profile was produced (enclosed) which he said told me in myself I was fine, but I was as bad as I could get otherwise. It would mean I should buy the book and maybe go on a course to save myself from disaster! I told him I thought it was all rubbish, or was that my -80 critical personality coming out!

The city was nothing unusual, tall buildings in the centre. Some good news we had was that the Kiwi Experience was only $300 (not $400). Now $3 to £1, so it would be best to do this. We spent the first two days in Auckland working out our plans and wandering round the city. The weather was good, although cool. It did rain a little, but the sky was clearer than expected.

We decided to go on the 'Kiwi Experience' tour of NZ starting on the 16th. This way we could go to virtually all the things we wanted to without any hassle, as it was mainly used by backpackers and stops off at the main things, not just a bus service. As it turned out it was excellent, just what we wanted; people of our age, lots of activities organized, going to sights and accommodation with no hassle, even supermarket stops to get that cheap food in!

NZ seemed a little cheaper than Australia, too, what with our free breakfast as well. Auckland was a very spread out, hilly city. There's not a great deal to see here, but it is quite a relaxed place.

We set off on the Saturday, quite early, on the Kiwi Experience. Now we are in Queenstown after two weeks on this trip. NZ is a beautiful country and we've had a great time with the others on the trip, with the bus of forty.

I'm writing a separate diary thing for this trip, and I've put in what I've written so far. Basically though, all's well. On schedule still for Canada. The weather's been excellent, not too cold at all. The place I'm in now has a great view over a lake and mountains. Queenstown has a real ski resort feel, the ski fields just opening. Just in case I don't get up to date with my diary bit (I won't), I'll mention the main things I've done in the south island.

One night we had a 'hangi', a meal cooked in the ground the Maori way, then a lively night in the pub where we stayed. One guy played guitar and I had a go at piano as we performed a few songs. What a star. Put in a photo of the occasion someone took. Also a photo of the hot stream at Huka Falls. Went on a helicopter flight over the glaciers in the mountains on the west coast. Just amazing. The glaciers are massive. The flight was brilliant, flying over the mountain peaks and spiralling down, landing on the top of the glacier, high above the clouds.

Since we arrived in Queenstown, myself and Mark organized a four-day tour of the south for thirteen of us and hired a minibus. The scenery down there is just spectacular, Fiordland in particular. More in the next instalment.

OK. Must get this letter off as there's a card in it for Chris. Pass it on. I'll be in touch again with more details.

See you

Dave.

16/5/92 KIWI EXPERIENCE DAY 1.

We were collected after our free breakfast at 9:30. It took us another half-hour to go around Auckland and collect all the others, being a mix of international backpackers, mainly European and North American, with our Kiwi driver/guide, Grant, a graduate himself. The weather was quite dull, and although it wasn't raining it was too dull for a view over Auckland. We stopped off at Domain Park, where Grant told us briefly what was in store for us. After this we headed off down the centre of the north island towards our first destination of Waitomo, following the Waikato River, the longest in NZ. As we followed this through the rugged pasture land of limestone hills and cliffs, cows, and sheep, we all introduced ourselves over the microphone. Grant would also keep us informed on all the little places we went through, Maori history, natural stuff, and info on stops and activities, in between playing a suitcase full of tapes. NZ has around three million people, with one million in Auckland, so it's very unpopulated overall. It was once very forested, but it has been turned into farmland reminiscent of the UK, only a lot more rugged.

We stopped at a small town called Huntly, on the banks of wide Waikato, opposite a power station. The sun was shining but it was very cold, or 'fresh'. Getting to know the other travellers rapidly, all obviously friendly as usual.

We only had relatively short journeys, having another short trip to Waitomo, where the limestone caves are an attraction; black water rafting was also one on the list of activities, and glow-worms. Our accommodation was for all the bus in the cheap end of a very posh-looking hotel in the small town (almost village). They wanted to keep us out of sight of the 'guests', as the normal rooms are over $50. We had a good room for two, a bathroom, but no cooking facilities.

It was clear, so we went for a walk down by the caves, being taken there by bus. The first walk was through the rainforest, along a very steep-sided valley following the stream to a natural bridge (where?), the rocks and cliffs worn by the river. Surrounded by moss-lined trees. Different yet again, nothing this rugged and mossy in Australia. Back out of the forest we, a group of six of us, walked through the countryside, following a river, then up and down the hills back to the hotel, a half-hour walk. We went through loud cows, ginger pigs (free-range), sheep of course, and hills with pink spots. Nice walk, great hill scenery, rainbows too as the sun shone with rain in the distance. The ups and downs are much more frequent and sharper than ours. We were walking through open field, hills, then went through a couple of large rocks, and suddenly were in thick forest without even expecting it. Amazing.

Back at the hotel we had a barbeque lined up in the bar just in front of the hotel, and Grant had got us a happy hour. A band was there. We got some cheap drinks, a schooner (half litre) being only $1.75 (80p). Lamb chops BBQ. After eating up Grant took us back to the forest for a walk in the dark to see the glow-worms that live there, little specks of green light. A full moon lit the night, making it very clear. Interesting walking through the forest at night in this light.

Returning to the bar and getting in eventually, had a lively night, even though the band wasn't too good. The 'locals' were very large and mean looking, but the Kiwi Exp. crowd is pretty good. Lucky to have a heater in our room.

17/5/92 Day 2 TO ROTORUA

Off at 9 we had a short drive on this clear day (still cold) stopping briefly at the Arapuni hydroelectric power station. The gorge it is in is quite deep, palm-lined, and a long way down from the suspension bridge. The station was built into the base of the gorge cliff.

A shopping stop on the way to Rotorua at the supermarket to get a few items and we had another entertaining trip, arriving around midday at the Kiwi Paka Lodge at the edge of steaming Rotorua. We are now in the volcanic active area, with thermal activity all around, steam rising out of the ground in the parks, gardens, and street drains. Very strange and smelly, being hydrogen sulphide from the sulphurous activity. The hostel was really nice; our (the group's) own kitchen, a nice lounge, a cheap pool table, and good rooms with L-shaped bunks.

Before heading off for another walk, that is those who weren't doing the dodgy white water rafting with the seven metre waterfall drop (!), had a few games of pool and Bernie kept us entertained with his pool talent. Just behind the hostel in the park were big areas of activity; steam and boiling mud pools. The town centre was very quiet being Sunday. The town area was surprisingly large, being an unusually flat area.

Later Grant collected us and drove us out of Rotorua to a few of the lakes. Rotorua is on a large lake, but there are many other smaller lakes around. The last lake we reached, Lake Tarawera, had as a backdrop Mount Tarawera which violently emptied in 1886, blowing the top off it and covering a wide area, and the pink and white terraces that had formed as a natural wonder there. Two smaller lakes were green and the blue lakes reminded me of Canada, with the Canadian pine plantations on the hills around the lakes. We had another 'great walk' around the blue lake, Lake Tikitapu, following the shores through massive straight trees and gigantic fern palms. Still fresh! Great scenery.

Back at the hostel we'd worked up an appetite and six of us sorted a simple spaghetti Bolognese. Played cards in the evening, some very silly games. We even went to a Maori building to see a show of Maori singing, dancing, pom-pom stuff, etc. Brilliant, the singing was very Polynesian (like you imagine Hawaii). The war dances and haka were good, with the performers sticking their tongues out and stamping. The blokes were massive.

18/5/92 DAY 3 TO TAUPO

Again another early start. A clear day, not too cold in the night. We set off on another short drive, stopping for ten minutes at NZ's largest mud pool, bubbling and steaming and smelling strong. Weird, as it spurted molten mud from spots all across the 10 m pool. Our next 'appointment' was at the Lady Knox Geyser nearby, which erupts at 10:15 daily! It wasn't completely natural in that to make it blow soap is dropped down the geyser hole. The area was covered in extinct geysers. After a few minutes the geyser bubbled then suddenly blew a fountain of water 30 ft in the air from its white cone base. It was hot water and a cloud of steam and spray formed a rainbow. The water builds up underground under pressure and when it blows it spurts for an hour or more, thousands of litres of water.

Another half hour drive and we reached the 'Wai-O-Tapu Thermal Wonderland,' NZ's most colourful thermal area. Walking around this area was just unreal, surrounded by activity and a vast range of colours of rock and water from all the various minerals. The one and a half hour walk took us past big craters with boiling water or mud in the base, churning out more hydrogen sulphide. Is it safe to breathe? The most impressive bit in this large area was the terrace area and champagne pool which boiled and steamed with different colour patches. Have a leaflet with all the sights there on to save listing them here.

After this we moved just a little down the road to a hot stream Grant knew of, hot water steaming down to a small waterfall and pool. Had time for a dip – great, but watch out for meningitis. Not too cold getting out either.

This busy day meant we moved off again, having a lunch by the Huka Falls virtually down to Taupo now. Here a wide river is forced down into a 30 ft wide channel and rips down it with more force than I've seen before, although this was still low level, falling over the 7 m Huka Falls at the end. From here was an hour walk along the river to Taupo. The path followed the river, but up and down the hills on the bank, through a different form of woodland. At the end of the walk our reward was a hot stream that flowed into the icy cold river. Those brave enough to dip could sit in the hot water or move out into the cold. It was weird to stand where they met, the top half of my body was hot while my feet were freezing. The main river really was cold, the hot stream sometimes too hot. Spent quite a while soaking in the hot water.

Still sunny as we left for Taupo. The hostel there was pretty comfortable, a small room with a few bunks in, but only $9. A local club, 'Club 66', had a special deal for backpackers, a meal and beer from $5 (less than £2), not bad food. We had a good night there, most of the crowd staying til midnight, taking advantage of the cheap drinks. It was only a small place, with mostly our mob in there.

19/5/92. Day 4 TO OHAKUNE

Leaving Taupo early we passed the very large (almost sea) Lake Taupo. The nice clear day meant we could see right across the wavy lake to our destination, Tongariro National Park, with its three snow-capped volcanoes. What a view. We drove around the lake, taking an hour or so. We called in at the national park info centre, where Grant showed us what we were to do on a model landscape. A walk went up the mountain of Tongariro to some hot springs, and you could go right to the top and look down into the crater. The volcano is in theory still active, the lake being formed (Taupo) by the biggest eruption ever known. It's still steaming. I'd like to have gone up there but we didn't have time, as it's a whole day's walk and we only had time to go to the springs.

After a brief walk around the small town of Turangi we moved off to drive out to the start of the walk, in the middle of nowhere. It was around 11:30 and we had until 3 to get up and back on the two-hour walk uphill. The first half was a climb through forest alongside a stream. Suddenly we rose out of the trees to a long area of smallish brown shrubs, which went on up the mountain until the active area, which was lined in spiky clumps of greeny yellow grass. When we reached this shrub area we became exposed to the icy wind, although it was still sunny. Clouds were moving in fast around us, but luckily it remained nice for the whole walk. We stopped for a lunch break at the steaming area in the side of the volcano, most of the group making it all the way there. Scrambling up the unstable soft rock and earth of greys, orange, and greens there was a great view of Lake Rotorua at the base, behind a band of planted pine. The lake is used in hydroelectric generation. Very windy up there. The top of the mountain seemed a long way off. It didn't take long to get down, running part of the way.

A good walk. Of the bus load (around 40) most had got up and back easily. A couple of lads had decided to go to the mountaintop, which we'd been told not to do. As we had to leave around 3 and they had not returned and were nowhere on the track, we left without them. Their own fault, we had to move on as we wanted to play the 'Ultimate Game' near Ohakune this afternoon. It would take an hour to drive there. We had twenty waiting to play this game, which is actually paintball, so some jumped off at the hostel and we went to the game place and got kitted up with overalls, goggles, and guns.

The game was two teams of ten, playing in a small area of pine wood, each team at opposite ends of the wood. We had a flag for each team and had to get both flags to win the game, shooting the opposition. Great fun. Had four games and won all four, in the last game I ran right through the opposition, got their flag, and ran back without firing a shot, getting the opposition to 'surrender or die' by rushing them! Got hit a few times, splatted by paint. Quite painful. When you're hit you have to leave the game for a minute. I got hit in the face mask, and when I said I wasn't dead (doesn't count) I got shot in the ear, which really hurt (but didn't count either). It got quite dark at the end, making it hard to tell the greens from blues. I must have done well, as I shot or surrendered at least ten enemy and only got hit three or four times.

A hard day, we went to Ohakune to stay at a hostel there. This was full, so we were taken to a nearby motel to stay there at same price, $15. Bernie and I had a room with a TV and bathroom. Not bad. We had to walk through the deserted small town to the hostel where the others were, as we were cooking between us again. The rooms there weren't bad, with a kitchen and lounge area in each.

Bernie, the trombonist from Dublin (or is it Tim?), knocked up a stir fry, pretty good. The T.V. here is a mix of American, Australian and English mainly. News is poor, some of the headlines being about a bloke who tried to get an emu (dead) through Heathrow Airport. Wow! They show our comedies, 'Only Fools and Horses', 'One Foot in the Game,' etc. We had a small heater and real bedsheets, so not too cold.

20/5/92 DAY 5. TO WELLINGTON

An even earlier start, hard to get out of bed. We would have a good while on the bus today, having to get right down to Wellington. Leaving around 8 we travelled through more agricultural land and pine plantations. After an hour or two we stopped off at a place for the bungee jumpers. It wasn't a town, but a spot over a deep river gorge. A road bridge provided a good spot to let people jump off the 150 ft drop with only a bungee rope around their ankles. The setting was nice and the day clear, a nice time to die. I wasn't really interested in doing it, but a few of our crowd did jump. Being $60 it was cheaper than usual. Looking straight down from the bridge you could see the pebbles at the bottom of the shallow river, which wouldn't help if the rope broke. Everyone survived, so it was good to watch. The jumper free-falls for a couple of seconds, the rope comes into play, slows them down, then they bounce up and down, upside down, until they are lowered into a raft on the river, untied, and it's over.

After all this excitement we had another hour's travelling before a stop for lunch at 'Flat Hills', which wasn't really a flat hill, but an area of steep grey cliffs along a river valley. We stopped at a cafe, tourist spot come farm. A few did horse-riding and jet boating there, but only for an hour and it began to rain.

A couple of hours more and we'd reached Wellington. About 4:30, so no time for sightseeing. Not much to see anyway. We were dropped at our hostel, 'Rowena's'. Nice place, big lounge area. Right on the hillside so we had a good view of the city surrounded by hills, lying around on a semi-circular harbour area.

The hostel had $2 meals, so easier and cheaper than cooking. After a while we went into the city to meet others at Molly Molones, an 'Irish bar'. Quite lively, but pricey (though cheaper than the UK). Our two missing persons made it here, after hitching down from the national park to catch us up.

21/5/92 DAY 6 TO NELSON

Up too early again, though time for breakfast today. Left the hostel by 8, a nice clear day again, in time to sort ourselves out for the ferry, leaving from the dock in Wellington at 10 a.m.

Big ferry, with a train in the centre, a cinema, and loads of lounges. Quite cold outside as we headed south. The trip was three hours and forty minutes. It was a good journey over. Getting near the south island you could see the snowy peaks. We headed into the Picton area through the Marlborough Sounds, a channel between the mainland and large peninsula, with small islands in the channel. Very scenic, tree-lined hills sloping steeply down to the water. Arriving at Picton, the hills behind the small port seemed massive and impressive. Beautiful day. We had a drive along the northern coast to Nelson, following a very spectacular hillside road, winding along the rugged coastline. We had a brief stop at Pelorus Bridge, a 40 m bridge over a picturesque gorge and river. There's too many great scenic views.

Nelson looked like another nice small town, arriving in the evening time. This time we'd been booked into YHA. The YHA was a large wooden place, reminded me of the Adam's family home from the outside. Inside it was really nice; lounge (no TV), duvet. There was even a guitar and a piano, so I had a mess around while I was cooked tea. The advantage of this group travel is the international mix, so were cooked a 'Swedish' meal. The group of eight of us (four men and four women) had a game of Trivial Pursuit, but I forget who won!

DAY 7 TO WESTPORT

Headed inland to Westport on the west coast. Most of the way we followed the Buller River and Buller Gorge, with some roads having very steep drops. The river is wide and pebbly, but quite low on the water. At times though the river level can rise 20 m in places when the snow melts. At one point we had to get off the bus as Grant took it through a stretch of road which was very narrow and cut under a cliff. Interesting drive down getting to Westport early in the afternoon. Westport is an old coal mining town, though not much is going on now. There's a cool smell in the air from a mine that's been burning for 60 years. We were dropped off at Bazil's Hostel, thirteen of us.

There was no one around so we went in and claimed beds, the doors were open and the fire was on in the lounge. We wondered for a while if it was the right place, as it was just like someone's house we'd invaded. It was right. Most hostels are good, but like hotels. This was someone's house, they lived in one room and shared the kitchen, lounge, etc., with us. A hot coal fire, the ornaments, photos and all the little things you'd have in your house. A nice change.

Spent the afternoon walking around deserted Westport. Another small town. Where does everyone go?

Eamonn, from London, cooked a shepherd's pie. Lucky we had the use of all the kitchen utensils and oven. Some hostels only have rings and saucepans. Good stuff, eight people in this effort.

The rest of the bus crowd were staying in the Black and White Hostel, which was also a pub, so we went down there for a while. The locals don't really make as much of a Friday night as we do at home, most leaving quite early.

Day 8 – TO ROSS

Set off to Ross, again leaving early. First stop was out on a peninsula not far from Westport, now being on the west coast, at a spot famous for its seal colony. On the rocks there, in the rough and cold sea, were quite a lot of NZ fur seals. The coastline around this area is rough and rugged, battered by the big waves. It was interesting to watch the seals, as the large ones slept and young ones played in rock pools frothed up by the waves. It was a great day again.

As we headed down the coast we made a few stops for ten minutes to view the landscape and coastline, one stop being at a small beach of pebbles with worn ledges spraying up water as waves broke. Further along the coast we stopped at the Pancake Rocks near Punakaiki. The rock formations here, which were through a forest from the main road to the coast, were really unusual, being like stacks of pancakes I guess. They had been worn down into pillars and ridges. There was also a blowhole there that spurted as waves broke. Mark almost slid to his watery grave after being stupid enough to leap out to the blowhole. He'd have been washed away if it had blown, too. The power of the sea is frightening, even just watching the waves break is enough. The road that followed the coast along the rocky front was pretty good.

Another stop in the afternoon was at yet another ghost town, Hokitika. It was a Saturday, yet no one was about and the shops were shut, apart from the greenstone shop! Greenstone is a sacred stone for Maori's here, but is carved and sold as jewellery, etc.

Before arriving in Ross we stopped at a famous pub apparently, selling some strong local beer. The pub in the middle of nowhere, an old wooden place lined with hats, had become famous from a TV ad.

Getting into Ross in the dark we were all staying at the Empire Hotel in some rooms separate to the main hotel. The building was mainly the pub, an old-style place nicely done out with a big log fire. This night we had a 'hangi' meal lined up by the hotel. When we went for it, it had already been going for three hours. It is an old Maori method of cooking. The technique is to dig a hole in the ground, light a fire in it, cover the fire with sacred hangi stones (although they actually used angle iron) til they're hot, remove the ashes, put food on the stones (bars), pour on water, and cover it with dirt. The food is then steamed in the ground. Here the food was in stainless, foiled trays covered in sackcloth then earth. We had lamb, chicken and fish, and veggies cooked in the ground. The taste was really unusual, particularly the veggies. We're still alive, so it can't be too bad! Hard to describe; smoky, steamy.

After this we spent the evening in the pub. Quite a night. One guy on the bus, Mike, was a guitarist, travelling around with his guitar. He was going to play a few songs, and as there was a piano I had a go playing along. Not bad, though hard to keep up with him. Another lad, Karsten from Denmark, had a harmonica so we all tried to play along. Great fun. Everyone was quite impressed. So were we, I think.

DAY 9- TO FRANZ JOSEF

We didn't have to leave until around 9, so why did everyone look so awful? We only had a short trip to Franz Josef and the glacier there. Arriving in the area early, we went down to the area of the glacier. The glacier was coming down the mountainside quite low into the valley. The valley was full of grey rock and pebble going back for miles. The glacier is retreating, as at one time it came right down. From the car park out of town the front of the glacier would have been a one-hour walk away. With the blue sky behind the snowy mountains it looked impressive. We had a group photo on the bus there too. We were all staying at the Franz Josef Hotel in the virtually non-existent town of only a few shops and houses. One of the things to do there was go on a helicopter ride over the glacier. We got some groups together to try and get a deal. I'd never been in a copter before, what better place. For $90 (£30) we could get a half hour flight and land on the glaciers. We arranged all this for this afternoon, as it was nice and clear, although we had a free day in Franz the next day. After checking into the hotel, which we took over, we had a little time before walking the ten minutes back to town for the flight. The hotel was quite good.

By the time we flew it had become a little cloudy around the mountains but was still clear overall. The helicopter took six. We climbed in, put on our belts and headphones and lifted off without even feeling it. We flew out of the stony valley, up over the tree-lined mountainsides out to Fox Glacier. Just amazing. As we got higher above the cloud the snow and rock was so clear. We seemed to just go over the peaks and then the ground below would drop away. It was good when we dived down and leant into a turn. We climbed up over the blue ice glacier with its massive chasms, landing right up on top of the glacier field. Views from here were spectacular, solid ice but not that cold. Flying back down the Franz Josef Glacier doing sharp turns we seemed to be right down at the glacier surface. In the front seat it was a real buzz. Seemed over so quickly as we landed back down in the valley by the town. It was good how we came down below the clouds perched halfway up the glacier.

After this excitement Grant had planned a beach trip for us, having spent the afternoon making up his infamous pumpkin soup. We went the 10 km to the beach with intentions of having a beach fire. He told us we'd have to collect wood, so we thought it would take time. In fact, the grey sand beach, flat and half a mile long, was covered in wood. We virtually had to clear a space in the wood to build the fire! It was so dry it lit quickly and it was good to sit around it as it got dark and the icy wind blew. Grant warmed the soup and some garlic bread in the fire and it was good stuff. Mike even brought his guitar!

DAY 10 – FRANZ JOSEF

No bus travel today. Up by 10. Kit, a young English lad, was keen to do a walk, as there are some good walks in the area. There was only us interested, but everyone else missed out. We walked for seven hours, but it was brilliant walking. Heading upward along the hillsides we got great views of the river valley, the river from the melting glacier.

The walk would take us along the mountainsides to a viewpoint over the glacier. The wood and forest we walked through was so green, lined in mosses, with small streams and falls trickling down. As we got higher we had to cross gullies of rock debris that had been formed in the mountainsides. High up the views were great. Some of our gang had gone on glacial walks, and from our high point we could see the small specks of people on the massive ice flow. On the way back we thought it may be easier to go down one of those gullies or screes to the river bed. We did get down easily, but we couldn't get across the river, being fast and icy cold. We followed the river, but we were forced back up onto the real path. The last hour back followed a road, so we hitched a lift only to find we were only five minutes from the town... Just crashed out, trying to solve a slide puzzle.

They said it was impossible.

DAY 11 TO MAKARORA

We would have set off really early (7) if the bus hadn't had a flat battery! Eventually we got off and reached Lake Matheson, which should have reflected Mount Cook. It was nice, but a bit too wavy to reflect (postcard!). Nice day though. We headed off along Haast Pass, stopping off at a salmon farm. Even with a rod here the salmon weren't to be caught. Travelling on the bus is good fun, as everyone has a joke or something and the crowd are pretty good.

Makarora, where we stopped, was just the hotel. The place had a few big wooden huts as accommodation, triangular shaped. It was quite cold. A nice setting. There was also a main building which was a little like a village hall! The lad there was doing a barbeque, an excellent one. It was going to be a party night, as there was nowhere else to go and only our crowd there. Brilliant night, everyone really in the mood for a good time. Bernie was our DJ as everyone danced around.

DAY 12 TO QUEENSTOWN

Left Makarora early, but not too bright, to Queenstown. A couple of stops on the way at Lake Wanaka and the puzzle centre, with a massive maze (didn't do it). The puzzles were too hard, but we spent ages trying all the various types. Some impressive holograms there too. Getting to the Queenstown area we had a stop at one of the bungee jump sites, from an old bridge over the gorge we'd followed. It was about 50 m high, and a few of the group dived. The water here was deep enough for the victims to get dunked in. Grant did a backward jump, getting dunked to his ankles.

Arrived in Queenstown as it got dark. Seemed only a small town on the lake's edge. The hotel, another Hilton, was on the lake shore. A nice place, four in a room with its own bathroom etc. Out the window you could see a hotel or something on top of the mountain; with its lights it seemed to be hovering in the sky.

DAY 13 QUEENSTOWN

A free day. We had this day to sort out a trip around the south. Queenstown seemed how I imagine a ski town;

surrounded by peaks and very scenic. Like a Pokhara of NZ, very quiet with small streets. A lot smaller than expected.

We had a group of thirteen off the bus and a plan to travel the south for four days, so we had to collect info, sort out a bus hire, etc. It worked out well, hire of the bus was $350. Only problem was that Monday 1/6 was the queen's birthday, so a bank holiday and a lot of things in Dunedin would be closed. The lake and park there were nice to stroll round. Mark and I made the plans for this trip.

On the Friday we collected the minibus from the track centre at 9. It was a thirteen-seater, three years old with a gear change on the steering column. Being the 'tour guide' I started the driving, with four of us in the rental agreement. It was yet another great day. We drove out first to Coronet Peak, a mountain about 20 km from Queenstown. There was a windy road up. The peak is a ski resort which was due to open the next day. No snow, but the snowmakers were on full blast. Great view of the valley and other mountains in the area.

Our next visit was to a small town, Arrowtown. It was obviously once a gold town, with plenty of nice old-style buildings in its small main street. Found a great pie shop, taking Andy five minutes to list the types of pies on sale. An old gaol and Chinese settlement there. We then headed off towards Te Anau. Planned to stop at a winery on the way, but we didn't see it so we never did! Driving along the mountainside following the lake shore was excellent. After windy roads we went into the flatter area and suddenly hit fog or mist. As we dropped down to a lower level we came back into the sun.

Arriving at Te Anau, about 250 km from Queenstown, around 2 p.m. we were back in the mist that was hanging over the lake and town. Temperature only 3°. Nice spot; our hotel was on the lakeshore, the town only very small, just a few shops. A bit cold to walk around, but we did a little anyway. Staying here the night. Our hostel was pretty good again. The rooms were in a separate block, but electric heaters meant it was very warm. In the main block was the lounge and kitchen. Nice wood fire to lay in front of.

Jan and Tracey had volunteered to do a group meal for each day, although a vegetarian one to cope with our veggie members. Three days tea was only $6. They cooked a good tea.

Our plan for the Saturday was to drive up to Milford Sound in Fiordland National Park, which was a very scenic 120 km drive. The roads were quite icy and very windy ← as in ~~~ Not

The mountains were impressive. As we neared Milford we passed through a 1.5 km tunnel cut through a mountain. We had already booked on a cruise of Milford Sound, a waterway between mountains.

The 1 hour 40 minute cruise was great, the Mitre Peak and some waterfalls there were outstanding. The sides of the narrow channel were steep, tree-lined rock. The sun was shining and the water was calm, but it was cold in the shade of the hills. Impressive looking straight up from our little ferry boat.

After the cruise we headed back to Te Anau, where we were staying again. We planned to do a walk at a spot on the way back. Key Summit was a climb, but rewarded us with a superb view of the valleys and seemed so close to the snow line. We went up through woods to a mossy bog, with brown and yellow moss. At the peak were frozen pools that gave reflections of the other snowy peaks. The lakes we passed on the road also mirrored the sky and mountains. We got back easily before dark for another laid on meal.

Sunday (31/5) we had a bit of driving to do, with a visit to Invercargill and getting to Dunedin on the east coast. A two and a half hour drive along a 'scenic route' through very misty land. We reached the south coast and saw the sun, after getting through a 'sheep jam', with rolling waves and mountains. The scenery was constantly changing! Some nice little towns on the way. Riverton was a small, boat-filled harbour town. Invercargill was a brief stop, having a long shop-lined street. Quite industrial. Nothing special.

We went out to the bluff, and south of Invercargill there was a lookout hill over the coast showing Stewart Island

and the aluminium smelting plant! We headed straight off then, back inland with me driving, through small towns and landscape similar to our own, more similar than anywhere else I'd seen. A three-hour drive to Dunedin, arriving as it got dark, we dropped down into the large, lit up city. It was too dark to see much of the city, though we did a brief 'tour' as we looked for our hotel in the centre, even after a guy's 'push'. The hostel was just off the main street, Princes Street. The city is supposedly modelled on Edinburgh and very Scottish. The hostel was a bit like a nursery, with drawings of Walt Disney characters on the doors. Tired.

We had until the afternoon to see the city, so we started with a drive to a couple of sights in the morning. One was the steepest street in the world, which people actually live on. Mark and Jon tried to run up and down it. It was hard enough just to walk up, and they both gasped for air after. We didn't dare drive up. I did drive up to Signal Hill, which was high enough to give a view over the big city, coast, and peninsula. The city is in a harbour in a flat bit on the coast.

Parked up in the city and had a couple hours to look around. It was a nice place, a few good buildings. One long main street, Princes, George Street, and Octagon. The area was filled with the usual shops, etc. The Cadbury factory and brewery were closed for the queen's birthday so no tours were being offered. We had missed the rugby by two days (NZ vs Ireland).

The drive back to Queenstown followed a gorge for ages. 300 km trip. Around Cromwell was a new lake being filled for hydroelectric. It cost millions to build the dam, as they had built it on a fault line.

Just crashed out that night, back at the Hilton hotel. Tuesday was a free day, just catching up with myself, as things have been non-stop for ages. Walked around the lake a little.

We were off again on Wednesday on the Kiwi Experience bus. It was a different driver and crowd to the one we had previously. We had a long trip to Christchurch, leaving at 8 a.m. and arriving at 6 p.m. The bus stopped a few times on the way, at Mount Cook and the lakes in that area. Lake Pukaki is a massive, milky-white, manmade lake used in hydrogeneration. Looked very spectacular. Another lake in the area, Lake Tekapo, was also picturesque. Here we saw a small church and a dog statue to honour the sheep dogs that worked in the area in the past. Later we hit the Canterbury Plains; vast, dead, flat, glacially-formed land between the coast and mountain, with Christchurch at its heart.

The city looked good, even in the dark. Said to be very English, with the style of stone buildings. It even had a cathedral at its centre. Our hostel, the Stonehouse, was about five minutes from the centre. Good rooms for three.

Free beer too. On TV was the 'State of Origin' rugby league from Australia. It must have been the hardest play I've ever seen, probably some grudge between Queensland and NSW. NSW came out winners.

The next day, a whole one in Christchurch, I'd decided to take advantage of the opportunity to ski. In the area was the recently-opened Mount Hutt Resort. It was cheap, too. I got a bus out there taking two hours, over the plains and then the steep windy road high up the mountain. The resort didn't have much snow, but enough for the different-sized runs. For $59 I got a package; ski hire, lift pass, and a two hour ski lesson. Conditions were good, a sunny day, and I got very hot in my hired jacket. It felt odd to have the solid boots on my feet, and even stranger with skis.

The lesson was good, only three of us, learning to move, stop, and turn (in theory). After the lesson and a break I had three hours to play around. I spent one hour on a small slope with a cable tow lift getting the hang of moving and stopping, before moving on to a bigger slope for an hour or so. Had my 'last go' about ten times. I bet it can get quite addictive. Good fun; good to try it. A great view over the plains from high on the mountainside. Some people commented on snow quality (looked like snow to me) "a bit icy". What's that mean, easy to fall over? Plenty of people took tumbles, while I had to control myself so as not to fall from laughing. Saw two victims brought down from high on the mountain by sled-stretcher, to make me concentrate harder. Enjoyed the day, may go in Europe one year, but not in the near future. It's still a bit snobby and too expensive.

Christchurch was a nice place, I got to see it in daylight as we left on the bus to Kaikoura, further up the east coast, early the next day. The trip up there was a reasonably brief one, reaching the dramatic coastal road, skirting the sea and steep-sided hills, after an hour or so. The road went through tunnels in these hills where they jutted out into the water. Mixed weather, but bright when we reached Kaikoura. Our first thing was to do a 'whale watch' here. In the waters off Kaikoura can be found various species of whale. There is a shelf of shallow water for a couple of km, which then drops off sharply, allowing whales to get close to the shoreline, and so easy to spot. The whole watch would involve getting on a smallish boat (thirty people) and chasing them around for three hours. The new-looking boat had a raft-like tube all around it, which made it look a little safer. We raced out over the big waves, thumping them hard occasionally. Just along the coast were a couple of humpback whales which were ducking in and out of the water surface. They seemed small, but apparently humpbacks are. Everyone was pleased we'd seen a couple of whales, but this was nothing.

After half an hour watching these swim around in unpredictable directions we went out to sea a couple of kilometres, where sperm whales were to be found. These float on the surface for around five minutes and then dive for around forty, so they just lay on the surface relaxing. When we saw them they were just massive, thinking at first that it was a floating log. They blow occasionally and then made a few moves before diving. Got a few of the classic tail shots (I hope) as they dived. Must have seen four or five of these. Got reasonably close. Impressive. The food supply here is excellent too, for the whales. The whales have battles with giant squid (largest found was 27 m!!).

Heading back to Goose Bay to have another look at the humpbacks, we saw a few feeding on the surface, swimming on their sides in and out of the water. Came really close a few times, as our boat rocked with us fighting for photo positions. Even the boat driver (?) hadn't seen whales feeding here before.

From the boat the coastline looked very odd, a line of mountain peaks appearing only above a low band of cloud. Out at sea it was bright and sunny. It was an expensive experience, at $85, but where else can I do this?

Had a stay over in Kaikoura at Moby Dick Hostel, a strange blue/pink coloured place. Nice fireplace. Just played a few silly games in the night. (Not Trivial Pursuit again!).

The next morning we were off to Wellington, via Picton and the ferry (Saturday). It wasn't too bad until we reached Blenheim (sunniest place in NZ, and the shakiest after the earthquake here) where it was raining! No stops, apart from a wait for the ferry. On the boat trip, which wasn't bad, we watched the NZ vs Ireland rugby match, in 'Windy Wellington'. Arrived just too late in the city to go and see the greens get stuffed, although they did remove three of the New Zealand captain's front teeth! Lucky the training staff bloke was a dentist. (59-6). Very wet and windy on crossing, so we didn't brave the views (seen it already anyway).

In Wellington as it got dark we stayed in the trekker's hotel come backpacker's, in the red light area. A proper big hotel, but not too nice. A few of us had a night out in the city, checking out the local pubs. Pretty good, very similar to ours on Saturdays.

On the Sunday we had a full day on the coach to get us up to Auckland, having 'done' the north island already. You can get off if you want, but there's no need to really. We went a very similar route to on the way down, but did go through an unusual black lava area covered in light yellow bushy stuff, an area the army uses for tank exercises (No good for much else). Other than that we had to keep ourselves occupied, as there were no real stops. Arrived in Auckland in the evening, being held up by a traffic jam on probably the only stretch of 'motorway' in the whole country. Went back into the weird 'Hilton' backpackers. Searched for another couple of people we said we'd see there (off Kiwi Experience earlier) but never saw them until an hour before we left the city on the 11th.

We were back on the 7th and would fly out on the 11th, so we had three days to look round the north. The best way was to hire a car. We'd got two others, Jane and Ian from Balsall Common of all places, interested in coming along, as there is a lot to see in one of the few areas we hadn't covered. This bit is the area north of Auckland.

Up here, too, was the Maori family we had an address off. On the Monday morning we rented a car, which for three days cost us only $135 (£40) between the four of us. It was a Toyota Corolla diesel, so cheap on petrol too, and seemed newish. By 10 a.m. we were off, so easy. From Auckland we headed north over the harbour bridge, getting a good view of the central city in the sunshine. Up to our first destination and this family at Kaitaia would be a six hour drive, but we planned to make a few stops along the way.

There was an east coast and west coast route, so we took the west on the way up. We stopped by the dirty-coloured river in Dargaville for a picnic lunch before moving on up what they jokingly call Highway 12, a rough, windy, loose, chipped road. This would take us through a kauri forest, that is forests with these thousand-year-old kauri trees in it, massive diameter and height trees. A nice half hour walk through the green forest with plenty of these gigantic trees between the smaller standard types. Just north of this walk we went to a fire lookout over the large natural forested area, and then a stop at the Tane Mahuta, or 'big tree' to us non-Maoris. It was humongous, 13.7 m diameter, 17 m to the first branch! And it was around 1,500 years old. The bark on these falls off as it grows, so has a rippled surface.

As we got up north we took a car ferry for a twenty-minute trip across an inlet rather than cutting back inland. The country around here was still very bumpy and agricultural (sheep and cows). We got into Kaitaia around 6 p.m. and dropped off the others at a nice backpackers before calling in on our contacts. They had a small wooden bungalow on the hillside overlooking the area, which was basic but OK. Nice people. There was the older couple, Mary the daughter, and her son Uru, who was only four and very energetic and noisy. He wanted to play all the time we were there. Nice kid.

Even though they were Maoris it was so different to our lifestyle, looked after us OK. Chatted to May and her cousin Alice, who turned up. May works on the local radio and had a request played as we listened.

9/6

After a cuppa in bed and a cooked breakfast (!) we collected the other two and headed off for our day to Cape Reinga and Ninety Mile Beach. Of this thin strip of land at the top NW, the west coast is one long beach of flat sand

and rolling waves. Right at the top, 120 km from Kaitaia is the cape, complete with a lighthouse and signpost (London 19,000 + something km!). Here you could see where the two seas split, the Pacific and the Tasman; the Tasman being a lighter blue. Odd.

The road went up to the cape close to neither coast so only saw the planted pines. At the top at Te Paki, we drove down to a vast sandy dune area, stretching right over to Ninety Mile Beach. Some of the dunes were massive and very steep, hard to climb up. No real views from the tops, but we could see where the dune area met the green tree area. Heading back to Kaitaia we stopped at the lower end of Ninety Mile Beach, which was deserted. It is actually only fifty miles long, but still impressive as the sun set over the sea. Arriving back in Kaitaia, May and her mother had gone to a Maori funeral. Their custom is that a close relative would have to spend three days with the body until the burial, staying in the marae, or meeting house. We spent the evening talking to George, the son, who had a few stories of his days as a gang member in Auckland.

Next morning we had another breakfast and Mary sang us a Maori song just before we left. We collected the others and started our return journey along the east coast. This road took us past a lot of bays of all sizes and through some small towns, one nice one being Kerikeri. Here was a 'stone store', the oldest stone house in NZ (1835). Across a small inlet was the 'Rewa's Village', a small Maori village of small straw huts with tiny doorways. Oh, it was historical, not a residential place.

Carrying on along the coast we had a lunch stop at Paihia, a picturesque spot by the Bay of Islands. Very hot, getting up to 18° in this winterless north. Waitangi was nearby, the spot where in 1840 the Maoris signed over to European rule and to accept the queen (or was it king?). Caught another car ferry trip across another the inlet, getting over to Russell, yet another nice quiet town. The views of the Bay of Islands from the small peninsula weren't as good as I'd hoped, but still very nice. Seen too many nice things now, you see.

The road down to our overnight stop at Whangarei, pronounced with an F, was a windy, gravelly, up and down road, quite dramatic in places. Took quite a time to cover the ground. Found the YHA perched on a hillside overlooking the big industrial city. Here a city is anywhere that has 20,000 people, yet there are only a few cities. The YHAs are always comfortable. Had to be careful with hot water, etc., as there was an electricity shortage due to the lack of rain in the south at Pukaki, etc., for the hydro scheme. Big problem, could be bad in a few more weeks.

Leaving the YHA in the morning we stopped at an 80 ft waterfall in a suburb of the city, supposedly one of NZ's most photogenic. The drive to Auckland was only a couple of hours and the weather was OK. Stopped off at Mount Eden in Auckland which overlooked the city, sprawling out in all directions, the bays, and One Tree Hill. There is a mass of multicoloured roofs of mainly single-story houses.

Had a couple of hours in the city before having to return the car and go to the airport. Just before leaving we met Eamonn and Terri, Jon and Tracy, and Gerald and Sarah, all in the space of five minutes. NZ is small!

Returned the car OK and were taken to the airport. The flight to LA was delayed two hours, so we had a long wait.

So, NZ. Had a "choice time, eh". Most of the sights were "full on", not that much time to "gel out". Then of course is the classic... "eh, how ya doin', haven't seen you fa... Eh, how ya doing" etc.

Beaut country.

LA 17/6/92

Hi y'all, ← I pick up accents easily.

Made it to the USA, now settled in LA for a few days. Got in on the 11th after an eleven-hour, two-hour delayed flight, only to discover that I had arrived six hours before I had set off!?? Do I have to go through another whole day? Anyway, made it eventually. Had a bit of a hiccup to get the plane. They won't let you on the plane unless you have a flight out within three months. I thought it was just a flight out, so we had to change it rather rapidly. No problem now I'm here.

There's no problem with LA now. We're staying at a friend of Mark's cousin's, and she has a nice apartment with a pool, etc., just 100 yards from the beach (Baywatch use it sometimes), so we've no problems. It's a few miles from downtown, although people still talk of the riots, etc. We'll be here for a while trying to sort out our transport, maybe buy a van. Whatever I do I should get up there when you're there.

Not long now. Hope everything is under control. This letter isn't a long one, I'll save that til I see you. This, I'm afraid, is a request letter, a sort of shopping list of things I'd like you to bring, if that's OK.

Firstly, the easy ones; obviously any photos you have. Hope you had the package in time. Next, the tapes I sent from Bangkok, well at least U2 and Genesis. Also, if you have room, my new trainers, white ones. Should be somewhere in my room there if you can find them.

Right, now the tricky one. I need say £1,500 or at least £1,000 in cash if you're allowed to bring it. There's not a problem with money at the moment, but I figure that if I do buy a car or van (which is cheapest and easiest in the long run) and get money using my Visa card, I'll be stuck until it's paid off (and you're in Canada so it may be some time). Also, it will save Visa fees, and should see me to the end of the USA trip. I have no traveller's cheques now. I'll use the cash to buy traveller's cheques here to be safe. My limit is £1,300 or, say, $2,000 US. I don't know yet how much I'll have to spend on a vehicle, but it'll probably be most of that with insurance and registration. So, don't worry, I'm not stuck (yet), but I can see that I may be if my Visa is full. Mark's is full, nearly, and his is being cleared soon, but it is quite expensive here.

OK. I'll phone soon, before you leave, to let you know my plans. At the moment I'll say that I'll be up there your second week, give you a week to do what you want, etc., but I can be more precise later (hopefully quite soon). Anyway, we're quite settled here for "however long" it takes to sort out something.

The weather is excellent and it should be in Canada, too. As for NZ, we had a great time; beautiful country, and we made some good friends. They had an electricity shortage when I left as it hadn't rained enough to power the hydro system. Millions of brilliant photos.

Flight over here was long, plane was on a massive 747. The Americans are OK, mostly friendly, very mixed races. I worried when the first bloke we spoke to was telling us about how to properly shoot an intruder so he doesn't sue (try dead!). OK. Been fine though, the city is massive, with big roads and loads of concrete. Standard of living for most is pretty high. Some nice beaches. Travelled up the coast a little. Some more unusual scenery, very dry looking.

OK, sorry the letter is really brief, but I want to get it to you before you leave. The 'fine detail' of all my tales is here with me, so you can see that in Canada!

Bring over anything else and leave Chris and Sharon with all your info, as you may not want to go back after seeing how people live in Canada!

Hope Chris, Sharon, and the children are still fine. Right, must finish. Unfortunately over the past month or so I've had very little spare time to write, or when I have I've been too tired. It's all go, this travelling job!! The reason I must dash is that the sun is just dropping behind a building, so my afternoon by the pool is almost over!

Can't wait to see you in Canada. As I say I'll phone soon to see what's happening, and make sure everything is OK with my financial requests. If there's a problem we'll have to work something else out.

Hopefully you get this soon.

See you on this side of the pond!

Love

Dave

PS. A little card here to send for NZ info if you could (address on small card). Hopefully will get some nice brochures and pictures from them. Thanks.

Summerland, BC,

8/8

Hi,

First of all, Happy Birthday Dad. I know it's probably late but my excuse is I lost track of the date, though I remembered it was the 11th. Hope you had a good day if you did celebrate (?!).

Since you left the days have flown past, and we've travelled all of 250 miles in three weeks. We stayed at Sue's until the next Wednesday, went over to Salt Spring for a day, staying at the motel that the relatives of Mark's run. Nice place, so we have been taking it easy here for a while.

So, you missed all the fun of the wedding and the do on Friday before. Still, sounds as though you had a good trip back. After you got the ferry it was a hot day. I started checking over the van, even the hubcaps were hard to get off – it needed a special pronged tool which we didn't have – though a corkscrew worked. In the evening Alexi turned up and we went down to Victoria to the wedding rehearsal where I found out that I had to stand at the front with Andy and Debbie, as well as Dave and the bridesmaids. Didn't take long to sort it out. Nice cathedral inside. Back at Sue's, she had laid out plenty of food for the people who came back. Us two and Alexi left everyone else to it as we ate our way through most of the food.

Saturday morning Dave collected Andy early and went into Victoria. We had plenty of time to get ready, having to get to the church around 12:30. John looked quite presentable in his brown suit, though we had to cut open his jacket pockets, and Mark was kitted out in Alexi's trousers and shirt and Cyril's shoes. When we arrived Andy and Dave were just going in the back door of the church. They had the jackets with tails and pink ties. After a half hour people started wandering in so I had work to do, waving them in the right direction. There were only maybe fifty people so didn't take long, having to sit the mothers last. When Debbie arrived at the doorway, I had to head up to the front and stand next to Dave. She looked pretty good in a beaded dress.

It was interesting to see the service close up, both were shaking a lot. It only took half an hour, and there was no singing. From the church we had to go up to the governor general's garden for photos. This took ages, the photographer getting everyone exactly where he wanted them; "move this foot, move that finger, John take those things out of your pocket (after we'd gone to the trouble of unsealing his pockets)." Then he took one photo before going on to the next. Plenty of photos of the wedding party (all us dressed up mob), but no big group one.

Even though this took ages we still had an hour or two before the reception meal, so us 'wedding party' went to a pub nearby, all wandering in dressed up. Shame no one else was in there. They got a parking ticket outside the pub, but the officer ripped it up when Debbie walked out in her dress. Getting to the reception at around 4, it was in the basement of the Harbour House, very hot in there, a small room too. I sat at the top table with the wedding party, Sue and John sat opposite Jean and Alec, so John was quite relaxed. Once done everyone headed to get outside as it was so hot, having to avoid all the broken cups the waitress had dropped – not once, but twice. The cake was excellent, and looked good after Cyril had brought in 'Plan B', a tinfoil-coated piece of plywood placed on top of the bottom level to stop the rest of the cake from sinking into it!

Sunday morning, Andy and Debbie came for the truck and left for Whistler. We took Sue, John, and Alexi out in the van, down to a park and beach on the Saanich Inlet. A nice hot day, nice walk in the woodland there. A few small boats were around, but overall it was very quiet. There were storms in the night, a lot of lightning flashes but no thunder, some heavy rain. Sue said John got up and asked if he should 'get them inside'. She said, "they'll be alright in the van." He meant the dogs!

I spent Monday working on the van, changing the oil, plugs, air filter. We got a new (used) tyre fitted on the back. Sue and John were off to the US on Tuesday to see John's brother so we decided to move on on Wednesday, and the weather was pretty poor too, raining most of the day.

Wednesday morning we got the ferry over to Salt Spring to spend the day at Cyril and Joan's. I guess we spent the afternoon out on the deck, as it was another great day.

We got the ferry over to Tsawwassen on Thursday, the one that leaves Long Harbour, and stopped a couple of times on the way over. A nice scenic route I guess, so the two and a half hours didn't seem too long. Getting over to Vancouver around 2 p.m., we drove around the outside of the city past the university (which is a big place with a big park of its own) and along to the Kitsilano (where Alexi stays). There's a nice beach area there and waterfront looking across to the city centre area. Vancouver is cut up by waterways and has bridges across from the south to the centre, then more bridges across to North Vancouver. It seems a nice place, though the residential area of tower blocks next to the centre was quite rough and ugly. Across on the north side where the land rises up quite high it was cloudy. As the evening came on we headed over to that side and westward to get out of the city. There was a park there which was up the mountainside, so we drove up there to camp. There'd have been such a great view over the city if it had been clearer, though it did clear up as it got dark and the lights came on.

I think I'll leave the letter for now, as I want to get this away to you. We'll be headed for the Rockies soon, and we want to try to get over to the east before the weather changes.

OK. Hope all's well and I'll be in touch again soon, as I've still a lot to write. I would imagine you've had some of the NZ photos back by now. Should be good.

Love

David.

24/8/92

Somewhere near Moose Jaw, Saskatchewan

Hi,

Time to drop you a line before you wonder where I've got to. OK, so now we're starting our long haul across Canada toward Montreal. We've been taking it fairly easy travelling from Vancouver to Summerland where I last wrote from, and through the Rockies to Calgary. Now it's pretty flat and the weather is mixed, so it's get-across time. Travelling 300 miles a day (not too easy, but not too hard on flat straightish roads) it's going to take eight days!

Now, firstly I've enclosed a little diagram of my journey up through the states so you can work out what the photos are (perhaps). Just under three weeks of travelling, 3,000 miles and plenty of sights. I think the last letter ended in Vancouver, so there's plenty to tell since then.

On the Friday (24/7) we went in search of our contact, who was the daughter of people we stayed with in Summerland later; this was Caren. We found the house OK, one of those numbered street systems, 24th. Nice area. Vancouver freeways are very busy. Spent the day sightseeing, checking out the museum at the university (interesting Indian artefacts, but too much to hold any real interest), the big park just next to the downtown area, and Stanley Park, with nice tree-filled areas. In the evening we went to a laser show at the planetarium, which was a light show accompanying music of U2. The blokes running it used the planetarium effects (stars, sun, moon, etc.), slides that shone all around the domed roof, and a group of powerful lasers that drew shapes and patterns all over, such as spinning worlds, or any object that fitted the songs. Very impressive stuff. Now when I hear the songs I see the images. We went back to Caren's house in the night. We camped in our van out on the street, which was fine until the morning when it got boiling hot.

Saturday, Caren was working, so we took a trip up to Whistler. I mean, I couldn't let you see something I hadn't either! It was a great drive, up and down the side of the inlet. I hope you visited the places I mention as they were all quite impressive (if you'd not already seen loads of waterfalls, glaciers, etc. – sorry, not boasting). Our first stop was Shannon Falls, the second highest in BC. Squamish was a nice little town, obviously a big logging area with the booms in the lake.

In the town of one street was a steam engine, the Royal Hudson. It was in good condition despite the hundreds of people hanging off every bolt for a photo. The Brandywine Falls just appeared as a massive drop out of nowhere. Driving up that way you could see some impressive glaciers on the mountaintops. Whistler was obviously a nice ski resort, though not much was happening in the summer. A lot of developing of Swiss-style alpine resorts (do the Swiss own the rights to mountains or what?). Didn't stay in Whistler long. Drove back to Vancouver via a few provincial park stops, a few lakes, etc.

On the way down the hill into Vancouver the engine started making a terrible whining, clunking noise. Oh no – I thought that was it. Overdone it on those hills. The noise was intermittent, which puzzled me. Looking at the running engine I could see the alternator pulley moving a bit as it rotated. I hoped that was the problem, not a broken piston or ring or anything like that. Luckily it was freewheel time down into the city. We had arranged to go out, so I put off any repairs until the next day and crossed my fingers. We had a good, but expensive, night out in the 'Gastown' area of the city, a paved (cobbled) street with some bars down it. The 'Town Pump' had some band on, and so we spent the night in there.

So, crawling out of our boiling van (another hot day) sometime in the afternoon the following day, I figured the best tactic was to remove the fan belt and see if the noise went. Sure enough it did. No problem. I figured I'd pull out the alternator and check it out, and if necessary replace it. Then I remembered, since when has working on a car ever been no problem. The van was air conditioned – so it must have a fan – where's the fan – on the end of the alternator – behind that plate – yes – OK – but it's behind all the engine. So, I could slacken off the alternator, but I couldn't get it out because the fan inside the big metal air ducting was bigger than the gap between the engine and engine compartment! I couldn't remove the plate because the four bolts holding it on were hard to get at because of all the engine piping, etc. Thinking I must be missing something obvious (but not convinced), I went and bought a manual, hoping that under chapter 6, section 37, part 2 it wouldn't say 'remove engine'. In fact, it only said 'remove carburettor', so not too bad.

Even so, to get the whole thing out was very awkward, having to lift up the whole air duct cover to be able to force the fan and plate through.

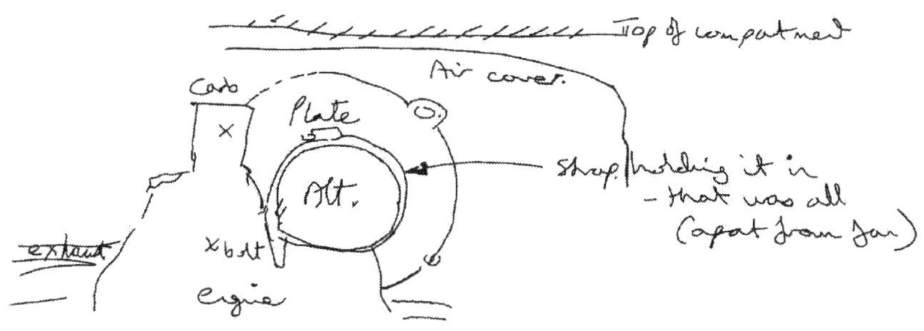

So, I got it out, and the spindle sounded loose. Took it to a repair place the next morning and the guy said the front plate was worn – 'a common problem' – so why is it so hard to get out. He'd see if he could fix it. I gave him that day to get a new plate, otherwise we'd have to buy a reconditioned one for $130. That afternoon we toured the city centre, going over from north Vancouver on the 'SeaBus' ferry. Not much special; more shops and shops and tower blocks. In the evening we went down to Lonsdale Quay, one of those harbourside shopping arcade places, for a meal with Caren and Rob (her boyfriend) to a 'British' bar/restaurant. Steak and kidney pud!

Tuesday (28/7) we went and saw our repairman. No good. The replacement plate is hard to come by, and VW doesn't sell them as separate parts (obviously), so may as well get a good one. So I did. Fitted it in very rapidly, it slotted in nicely and with no trouble. The engine started the first time – no generator light on the dash, so seemed OK (?). We have had no trouble anyway since then.

Wednesday we were back on the road again, if only to do a 250 mile drive to Summerland. It was a fairly easy drive following the freeway out to the small town of Hope. From there we headed towards the USA and Cascade Mountains then back up to Princeton. This road followed a river valley; more icy cold streams and endless trees, until we reached the warm Okanagan Valley area where the hills became treeless and a dusty, browny-green colour. Heading north now past Penticton we reached the lakes in the valley, surrounded by the fruit-growing businesses of peach, apple, strawberries, etc.

Summerland was just a few miles north of Penticton, this medium-sized town being on the south end of Okanagan Lake. The motel run by Marjorie and Malcom was between the two towns. They were glad to see us. It was a nice motel, with seventeen rooms quite nicely done out.

There was a pool and hot tub out the back by the side of a lawn. They've been running the motel for fifteen years, so they have it well worked out now. A few years ago they had a major rebuild. Malcom being an electrician by trade meant that he did most of the work himself. While we were there they were nearly always full. They're a bit more upmarket, charging $70 a room (for four people), so they earn well. Then, come winter, they close up and go off touring in their VW Westfalia as Malcom does electrical work. Not a bad way of life at all.

Basically, without going into detail, we were spoilt to death while there, having use of the pool and tub too. The first week of the two we stayed it was boiling hot, 35°. We were staying in their van during the night. It was good to put up our feet and laze a little, as we had a big trip ahead.

I think I'll just mention some of the things we did while there. Penticton was a nice little town, very spread out. Summerland was quite small. Along the lakeside were plenty of beaches. The first weekend we were there it was a long weekend (like a bank holiday), so it was very busy with people up from Vancouver, etc. Saturday night was busy in Penticton. The previous year there had been a riot in the town. Because of this, masses of police had come to the area. There was no trouble this year.

One thing to do is to hire a rubber tube and float down the river channel between Okanagan Lake and Skaha Lake south of Penticton. It's 8 km, but only going halfway takes one and a half hours. Very relaxing and popular. Had a go at windsurfing. Obviously the lakes mean lots of water sports. It's not easy, well, balancing is, but the wind was blowing into the beach so I couldn't handle getting out.

Had some trips out with Marjorie and Malcom, mainly when they had to go and shop, etc. Spent plenty of time on the van, checking over a few things and cleaning it up. Marj was keen to help us clean it and supply us with everything we lacked. Now we've got quilts, pots, new curtains, etc. Most stuff was motel stuff they had spare, or scrap.

Overall the weather was good, though there were a few thunderstorm days. We were in the daily routine when it was time to go, and it was hard to leave the comfortable life.

Time came to move on, leaving there Friday the 14th of August. We had a 150 mile trip to Christina Lake, an easy trip to break us in. First we went south towards the USA before following the border. To stay in Canada meant we had to climb up and over some serious hills, as the easy way round was over the border. It was a hot day and arriving at Christina Lake in the early evening it was a good chance to cool off in the 'warmest lake in BC'. Chatted to a bloke from the Canadian army who was travelling across the country. Had spent a few years in Germany. He liked it, but was glad to be back. It's quite a scenic area here, with more lakes and trees. We spent the night in the van at a car park out of town used by boaters who park up and boat across the lake to campsites on the uninhabited side of the lake.

On Saturday it was a 'sport day' in the town. There were softball matches between local town teams and a tennis competition. Watched a bit, the 'local' teams with their average players, and it was quite entertaining. Drove on toward Nelson. As we approached this area along the Kootenay Canal we passed a series of hydro dams. Hydroelectric is the main source in this area. Nelson is the 'heritage capitol of BC' with buildings dating back to, oh, the early 1900's!! Nice location on the river, we could see it well from a viewpoint on a hillside above town. We also visited the small local museum. Quite a Russian-inhabited area.

Still a hot day, so we went to the 'beach' on the riverside for a dip. Drove on through Balfour following the Arrow Lakes, past Ainsworth Hot Springs up to Kaslo. Here, the small town (800 people) was deserted. Nice location on a lakeside with a mountain backdrop. There was an old steamboat parked on the end of the 'beach'. We pulled up for the night just outside the town in a perfect spot by the side of what looked an icy, rocky river, surrounded by trees.

Woke up by going in the river the next morning. Heading into the Rockies. This was where the real touristy bit begins. Actually it was partly covering bits I'd done on my last visit to Canada. Driving north along a quiet, windy road we reached Nakusp, where high in the mountains are hot spring pools. Went up there for a dip in the two pools, one was 42° and the other 38°. It was 28° up in the air! Very relaxing, and draining too. Chance to clean up, though. Some spectacular scenery on the road up there, waterfalls and rivers. Drove up to the Galena ferry, a free BC ferry across the lake, to allow us to drive on to Revelstoke. Wondered about the ferry after the recent accident when they pulled off from the dock as someone drove on in Nanaimo (Vancouver Island, two dead). Still, we made it safely over to Revelstoke, a logging area. Visited the impressive hydroelectric dam there, part of a big network of dams. It was built in '83, so it's more efficient than Hoover, yet smaller. Quite a structure. Camped in the pull-in off the main highway, now on to the Trans-Canada Highway, up on the hillside above a grey river and opposite the CPR railway line.

The next day we headed into the national parks, a collection of five covering the Rockies and another couple before there.

I'll finish this instalment here, before it gets really interesting. A couple of things to mention in this letter. Firstly, it's slow going trying to get time to write these letters, and now I've moved 1,300 miles since the time I started this letter. On the edge of Lake Superior now. Everything's still fine, chugging along nicely. We'll go to Montreal for a while, Quebec and Toronto next week sometime, so September 7th or around then. Secondly, we hit snow around Edmonton and Calgary after the Rockies. Freak weather, like snow and back to 20°. First time it had ever snowed in August. I said the weather patterns are messed up. Florida's being blown away, too. Hope it's still there when we reach it!

Also, just up from Calgary is the town of Olds, so I had to call in there (that's where the stickers came from). Population of 5,000, not much there. It was named after George Olds, who was a Canadian Pacific Railroad controller in the 1890s. I even saw his signature on early railway tickets in a museum in Calgary. So, great-great-uncle George! Have to investigate that. Got a pack of info on the town too, and left my name in the visitors book!

What else. I haven't a clue where you can next write to. After Toronto, it'll be New York, Washington, somewhere between there and New Orleans (maybe visit Elvis, if he's in), then Florida. So, maybe New Orleans is a good target, but I'll let you know once I'm back in the US, if they let us in.

Photos. A few more rolls on the way soon. Hope the NZ ones are good and you can get an idea of where they were.

Warning: Open one of the packs with care when you get them developed, as I was informed there's one of Mark's 'moonie'. I was on the piano at the time and know nothing of this. With my camera, too! Check!

Doing alright so far, we only paid for one night's accommodation since our arrival in the USA. After all my fiddling, the van is cruising at over 33 mpg, which I reckon is pretty good. (Malcom's Westfalia only does 28 and his is an '81 I think).

That's it for now. Hope you don't worry that you don't hear much these days, but after a day's travelling we crash as soon as it gets dark.

A few facts: We have done 7,000+ miles, which has cost us $168 US (£100) and $300 Canadian (£130). Another 1,500 miles in Canada and 3,000 miles in the USA to go.

I'll write again after I get your Toronto letters. Say hi to all there, hope the kids are fine, and looking forward to Christmas. I'm sure it's all that now (well it is September). Say hello to Princess Diana when you speak to her on the phone next, as I hear she's available on a chat line these days, though not as available as Fergie. Still haven't seen the photos.

Think that's it.

Love

Dave.

P.S. Now forward a few time zones, so now only six hours behind.

Toronto

21/9/92

Hi,

So I'm writing to you from Kim and Heather's in Toronto. I'm fine, they're OK. Got the letters alright. Glad you managed to keep track of me up to here. It's been quite a while since I wrote. Hope you managed to get anything you needed to off to Washington DC. Having a nice time here. Yesterday Jo and her husband Phil came over and Cyril, Joan, Sue, John, and Andy phoned, so we all had a chat. Jo said hello, and that though she hasn't seen you, Mum, since 16, she'd have recognized me anywhere. Had a laugh at Sue about what you'd said in the last letter.

Before Toronto we had a week in Montreal and Quebec with a couple of friends we made in NZ, and had a great time there. Most people speak French, which was interesting, and the cities are very different from the English/American style of the other Canadian cities, with old stone buildings, small streets, and some sort of history.

After we leave the girls here, we'll be going back into the USA via Niagara Falls, NY, Washington, then Tennessee and New Orleans. John had given me his mother's address in NY, so we should be OK to stop there. The van seems to be fine. We'll be trading in our flight from NY, and will pick one up later on when we get to Florida perhaps, rather than having to return there. We should get into better weather too, as NY gets cold in November.

Oh well, if all's well there, then I guess I've got to do an update on the journey since I last wrote. There's loads to say, though I guess I can keep some of it short. I think I was heading for the Rockies. August the 17th it was. We'd been parked up overnight just off Highway 1 before the national park area of the Rockies and the Continental Divide mountains. Before the Rockies we'd have to get through these. It wasn't too tricky driving through Mount Revelstoke National Park and then Glacier National Park. In the centre of Glacier was Rogers Pass at 1,300 m. There were plenty of glaciers on the rugged mountaintops. This area is famous for its very high snowfall and avalanches. One of the interesting things to see in this area was the remains of the original battles to get the first railway lines through the hostile surroundings. Some good models and walking trails showed how wooden sheds had been built over the lines to prevent avalanches blocking the lines.

Dropping down from Rogers Pass into Golden, a real nothing town, though in a nice location, a valley between the two mountain ranges, we then had another gradual climb into Yoho National Park. This is an area on the west side of the Rockies. The highlight of this park was the Takakkaw Falls, the second highest in Canada, falling straight down over sheer granite cliff faces. The railway would be near the road, then disappear through the mountains, spiral through, and reappear later. After Yoho was Banff National Park, beginning on the west side at Lake Louise. Because we got to Lake Louise in the late afternoon, the sun's position spoilt the views of the lake, but it was still impressive. Kayaks were around on the white-blue lake, with two peaks and a glacier backdrop. It's actually quite high up, a cold (6°C) glacial lake. It was a warm day, but a nice cool air in the mountains. We drove from here to another lake, Lake Moraine, which had a different colour and another mountain and glacier backdrop. The water had different colours of blue with the effect of the sun. We pulled up overnight in an area off the road to this lake. In the night I heard noises outside the van. It's bear country round there. I didn't dare look out the window.

Early the next morning we went back to Lake Louise before the hordes of tourists arrived. Beautiful, perfect colours. The moon was still in the blue sky just above the mountains. The big, big posh hotel there attracts the tourists, which is a shame as it spoilt a great place. I mean spoilt it with the numbers of people, as the hotel itself is quite impressive.

Next we headed south to Banff, stopping about halfway at Johnston Canyon. Nice drive, quiet tree-lined road. The canyon was a great walk, along a suspended walkway on walls of the canyon. The water was so clear, and the canyon was deep in parts. Limestone I think. Along the roadside to

Banff were spectacular mountain formations. When we arrived at Banff we drove straight to Sulphur Mountain Gondola (which I did before) and went up. It was a clear day so we had awesome views of the sea of mountains. The gondola is pretty scary, up to 7,500 ft in eight minutes, with a rise of 695 m; at an average of 51° on 2,100 kg of steel cable. A real fresh feel up there.

After admiring the view for some time we went into the now Japanese-owned town, with the one street of souvenir shops. Didn't stay long, though I guess it's a nice place to stay, in such a stunning area. Cruised up from Banff, now north, back past Lake Louise onto the 'Icefields Parkway' (Highway 93). It's a good name because all the way along to Jasper you pass glaciers. The first were 50 m thick and icy blue. Plenty of light blue glacial lakes. It was hard to take it all in as there were plenty of different glaciers and lakes. One glacier came down into a lake (Peyto), which we viewed from Bow Summit, the highest point on the parkway at 2,000 m.

For the night we pulled up in an area at the start of a glacier walk, surrounded by signs warning of a recent black bear sighting. They're the ones that climb trees, so are hard to escape from. To add to this, there were some wicked thunderstorms in the night, which started some forest fires, as everything had been dry before. It was really nice in the morning, though, and good for the first stop we made at the Columbia Icefield. Mark did the snowmobile tour I did before, and I walked up to the front of the Athabasca Glacier, which comes right down into the valley next to the road. 500 m from the glacier it's warm, but as you get closer it gets really cold. This massive flow is only two percent of the whole icefield that covers a vast area.

Between this icefield, on the border of Banff and Jasper National Parks and Jasper town, we had a good list of touristy things to see, so breaking up the hundred-mile journey. Stopped at Sunwapta Falls, a steep fall in the grey coloured river, then Athabasca Falls with the now-wide river gushing through the small channel. Showers were constantly passing, coming in from the west as we headed north. We drove along a steep and windy road to get to Mount Edith Cavell with the Angel Glacier dangling off the side into a grey lake with ice floating on it. Further down the valley the next lake was a bright green, which seemed very odd. The area here was treeless and rocky due to avalanches. Breaks in the showers were long enough to have a walk around there.

Getting into Jasper we were virtually out straight after, as there was nothing there; very few open streets, a few tourist shops, cafes, etc. We drove out to the nearby lakes, past Medicine Lake, which changes level with the seasons and flows out through underground channels, on to the Maligne Lake, a 22 mile long narrowish lake. Very scenic there. Plenty of deer on the roads as the sun set. Stayed over at a lookout area over the Jasper Valley area.

In the sunny morning of Thursday the 20th we did a 5 km Maligne Canyon walk, which took us from the top with its narrow, 50 m deep chasm of 3 m wide to a wide, rocky, shallow river. Limestone had been cut away over thousands of years. The water was clear, and there were great views from the banks of one of the six bridges along the walk.

After this we'd virtually done the Rockies and headed out to Edmonton. Just before leaving Jasper National Park we had a really scenic drive, with lakes of different colours, elk standing in the rivers, and mirror lakes. We stopped at Miette Hot Springs, another natural hot pool (actually two) at 40°. 22° in the air. Again it was a steep windy road off the main highway to get there, but it was great to relax there. Really draining. So, after this interesting week we were heading for the prairies. Before getting out of the Rockies we had to climb to 1,600 m, which was the highest point on Yellowhead Road. It confused me, as when it got "flatter" we still seemed to be going up, yet in my rear-view mirror we seemed to have come from downhill. I guess it was flat enough that the horizon at eye-level was miles away, like being in a bowl. Mind you, it wasn't as flat as I imagined (it did get really flat later). We stopped at Edson, a small town 110 miles from Edmonton. There was a fair on, though it wasn't busy that early, but it was a good place to get some cheap food and coffee. It was clear at that time, but by the time we had found a place to stop, a free campground near Evansburg (with BBQ, toilets, etc.), it was drizzling.

In the morning it was still drizzling, or was it snow? As it was now cold and miserable I had to fix the heater cables, using bag ties (those wire things) to fasten them. Obviously in California they didn't ever need them working. There's not much to see in Edmonton, apart from West Edmonton Mall, the biggest shopping centre in the world; five million square feet, 800 shops, an ice rink, a few cinemas, a water park (with a massive pool and wave machine, water slides, etc.), and an amusement park, all indoors. The amusement park had three loop roller coasters fitted very neatly into a tiny area. Also in the complex was a big 'pool' with a life-size replica of the Santa Rosa at one end and submarine tours of this pool at the other. Very impressive, but the shops were pretty typical. In the city was a fringe festival with street acts, but this was a bit of a washout. Watched a movie for $1 in the mall before leaving the city. Stopped overnight in a rest area on the highway south to Calgary. The rest areas are great, little blocks with toilets and hot water nearby, so we would even have a wash in the morning. By then it was clear but cold, getting down near freezing.

On Saturday we had a dead flat, dead straight drive to Calgary. Stopped at Red Deer to shop. The store had tubs of bulk stuff, from rice to cake mixes, just having to scoop out as much as we needed. We left with a box full of plastic pots of all sorts of cheap stuff.

Our next stop was at Olds. I had to see what it was like, as I mentioned before. 5,000 people, in a town surrounded by flat yellow wheat fields.

When we got to Calgary it was snowing slightly, and the flashing signs told us it was 5°. Out with the woolly hat. Very quiet city. Walkways join buildings in the city centre 15 ft above the ground level (due to the bad snow they get). Very clean, though plenty of tramps. I guess they were the only people outside. One area was an 'old style' paved mall, though still the usual tower blocks and flashy malls. Parking seems like a big business, and there are car parks everywhere.

We spent the night parked in a car park at the bird sanctuary just on the edge of town, though did check out some bars in the city which had tried for an English feel (no!), King's Horse and Fox & Firkin. Some band playing in one.

Early Sunday were woken by bird spotters, loads of them. Strange creatures with bobble hats, glasses, and binoculars. Oh, and plastic macs. Funnier to watch them than the birds on the nice trail there. We then did tourist stuff. Fort Calgary (no longer exists) told of the history of the city and the British fort. The city was even quieter. We went up Calgary Tower (190 m high) and the view was good, the area very flat, seeing nothing for miles. Sat and watched a snow storm moving across the west side of the city, getting close to the tower. Could see the storms miles away. Moved out of the city that afternoon on the Trans-Canada Highway (1) again, the start of our long eastern trip.

About a hundred miles from Calgary was Dinosaur Provincial Park. Though it was mixed weather it wasn't too bad. We got there eventually, after my "don't you trust me" navigator had taken us on a major detour. The 'Badlands' of the park were outstanding. Odd. Lower than the normal plains, this area of softer land had been cut and eroded by rain and wind leaving soft stacks of earth in bands of colours. The 'layers' were from different ages and erosion has exposed dinosaurs from 75 million years ago. A rich area for fossils, as you can imagine. They say it was once the edge of a massive interior sea. Had a walk on the soft, slippery trails and checked out some of the interesting finds. Timescales are beyond imagination. Got back to Highway 1 and a rest area near Brooks for the night.

Long drive from now, so Monday we basically just drove. In Medicine Hat they'd had lots of snow in the previous week, though it was OK this day. First time it had ever snowed there in August. There was still snow on small hills nearby. Flat drive into Saskatchewan, getting further between places. Agricultural land now. Stopped at Moose Jaw, where I last wrote, in a picnic area for the night. It had a shelter, so we lit a fire as it cooled down. We had driven 300 miles, as we would every day for the next week.

Tuesday morning (25th) carried on to a 'pioneer village and museum', which had an amazing collection of old buildings and endless 'junk' from the early 1900s. Everything there was really interesting; old cars, tractors, and even a homemade ship built by a guy intending to sail to Finland. (?!)

Drove to Regina, the provincial capitol. A smallish city, not a great deal there, though it is the headquarters of the RCMP (mounted police). We had made it in time for a drill parade. The museum had history of the RCMP from 1870. There was a nice park area, but nothing else to stop for, so we drove another hundred miles or more and stopped at a rest area on the Manitoba border (Friendly Manitoba).

The next day we carried on, with a few rest stops, across the flat land to Winnipeg, a very spread out city. Down in the 'Forks' area was a riverside market, quite nice. The river here freezes in the winter so is a great spot for sledging and skating. We walked through the built up city centre without going outside, again in interlinked, suspended, enclosed walkways. A bustling centre, quite nice; more Eaton's, Bay, etc. shopping malls.

Tried to find a place to pull up for the night near the city, but had to go 25 miles before finding a spot by Lake Winnipeg. Here was what we'd been expecting – loads of big mosquitos. Took some serious bites while trying to cook tea. Had coils to burn inside the van to kill them and luckily it worked. It was really the only place we had trouble with them, being on the edge of a lake. In Winnipeg it was no problem, as we were well away from the lake.

Spent some time in Winnipeg in the morning of the next day, before heading on towards Ontario. At last the scenery began to change (though once it did it was the same for another three days!) to trees (pine, mainly) and small lakes with bumpy roads. Near Kenora we skirted the 'lake of woods', on a big lake with 15,000 islands and 65,000 miles of coastline. The small towns had gone from growing wheat to logging and pulp mills. One town had a massive smelly pulp mill and not much else. Pulled in to a picnic area for the night by the shore of yet another small lake.

The water was clear and good for a wash in the morning. Drove on. Can you get sick of trees and lakes? Swampy lakes, lakes of different colours. Crossed a time zone into Eastern Standard Time (six hours behind the UK). The highlight of the day was an hour break in a laundrette in Thunder Bay, a city/town on the edge of Lake Superior. Looks like an ocean, can't see any sign of another side. In Thunder Bay was Centennial Park, with some old log pioneer huts and a nice lake park. Chatted to a guy there who runs trips to Nepal. We had our T-shirts on!

Just outside the city is the Terry Fox monument, near where he ended his effort to run across Canada in '81. If you didn't hear about him, he lost one leg from cancer, and died in his effort to run across Canada to raise money for research. A national hero. Another picnic area stop for the night. It was great, this free stop, even though we shouldn't really have done it.

The next day (Saturday) we drove along the shore of Lake Superior. Had a dip in the cold water, though the day wasn't bad, sunny and around 17°. Passed Wawa town with its two-ton statue of a goose. Here was the 'High Scenic Falls', which were I suppose, though the lake at the top was used for hydroelectric generation. Stayed over in a picnic area there over the rainy night.

This all sounds pretty dull, and now I'm just listing the day 'diary'. Hope you've not gotten bored yet, but you should try driving 300 miles a day for a week. We tried hard to find interesting things to do, but as there was not much we were better off getting to the east quickly.

Sunday the 30th we headed south to Sault Ste. Marie on the US border and the junction of Superior and Huron. Lake Superior Park covered fifty miles of shoreline and was pretty scenic, in between the showers. The deciduous trees here were changing to a blazing red, so we had a full range from green to red. Stunning. The normally calm lake was stirred up to a sea with big waves by a storm out in the centre. Some nice beaches and sheer cliffs, too. Heavy rain as we stopped for lunch.

It brightened up in S.S.M, so we saw the locks that keep the 20 ft difference in level of the two lakes. The town was better than most, as it was less spread out. A great riverside picnic spot for an overnight stop.

A better day on Monday, driving through Sudbury and North Bay. Stopped at a flea market/auction in a small town along the way. Weird people, speaking some French. All grubby, with those hats and few teeth. The men were as bad! They were auctioning all sorts; a can of bolts – started at $1 – went for $3. If you have seen 'Southern Comfort,' it reminded us of that!

Got near to Deep River before stopping on the side of Ottawa River. We'd made it. We would take our time now, only another day to Ottawa, then short trips. Had a less-travelled day, only covering a hundred miles on Tuesday. Spent an hour or so walking around Deep River, a nice little town, very green tree-lined streets. Built as a town for employees at Chalk River Nuclear Research Centre, where Cyril worked. A couple of little beaches, too, on the river bank. Nice day, but not beach weather. Visited the nuclear place, with a free tour of the massive plant. 2,500 employees and six nuclear reactors used in research and medical isotope production. Started in 1945. Some good displays and a good tour. Wore a safety badge and checked for contamination on leaving. Clean (well, of radiation!). Nice setting on the riverside.

Followed this by a tour of Rotorua Forestry Research Centre, where they experiment on planting and harvesting of trees. Thing is it takes years to prove a test, with some areas planted over fifty years ago. In the nearby town of Pembroke, fiddlers were converging in a campground for the fiddle and step dance tournament. Funny to see pianos outside caravans, and we heard a few people playing.

Got within 25 miles of Ottawa that night, so it was easy to get into the city, the country's capitol, the next morning. A nice day for once. Parking was a problem, again being expensive. Cost $12 for a day's parking. Still, during the day we toured the Parliament buildings, impressive stone structures. Ottawa is on the south side of the river, and Quebec province is on the north side. Nice inside Parliament; again, they use our system (is that good?). 125 years of confederation this year. One MP for 96,000 people.

A canal runs through the city centre. In the winter it freezes and people skate to work. A very commercial, laid-back city. Quite pleasant sitting on a bit that sticks out into the river and looks back over the city. Some free concerts were on in the park outside the art gallery, playing Irish music. Very hot today. Walking around, we went through a very cheap vegetable market area and quiet pedestrianized mall.

Staying in the city the next day too, so drove out fifteen miles to a picnic area for the night. Cooked up some sweet corn with our steak. Sweet corn is popular and cheap here. Great.

Raining the next day, but it did stop, though misty. Spent the day in the art gallery (laughing at the usual rubbish) and the Canadian War Museum (which was pretty good, though we're also blamed by Canadians for the thousands slaughtered in France). It was a good city, and we felt quite impressed.

It was only a short drive (150 miles) to Montreal. Here we had phoned our new friends, Marjorie and Jannick, who we knew from NZ and would be put up at Jannick's house for our stay. Her house was in Outremont, not that far from the centre. It was a quite a nice area with tree-lined streets, flower beds, and nice brick or stone terraced houses, each with their own balcony and wrought iron staircases out the front.

We arrived spot on time after finding our way through the concrete maze of freeways and overpasses on the industrial outskirts. I won't go into detail, but we spent time catching up with each other's travels and three hours going through their photos of NZ, Australia, Thailand, and Malaysia (four month summer holiday trip, as both are students). We were in Montreal a week (visiting Quebec City for a day in that week) before coming slowly down to Toronto.

I'll fill in this story next time, but I want to get this letter away now. I've put the New Orleans address in, so you can write here up to say the 10th of October, as we'll be there in a few weeks. Nothing else for now. Money's fine.

Hope you all enjoyed your little trip. I'll be in touch again soon.

Love

David.

Address :

American Express Travel Agency

150 Baronne Street

New Orleans, Louisiana, USA

PS. Did you get the letter and card (Birthday) from Summerland, as you didn't mention that (mainly about the wedding I think)?

Put in a few assorted cards for you to get an idea of the places in this letter! The 'multimedia' experience.

16/10/92

New Orleans

Hi,

wrong 26/10

OK, I think this'll be a brief letter. Nice to talk on the phone. I thought I'd better call on my birthday. As I said, my first letter was coming from Toronto, and I put it in with four rolls of film in a jiffy bag mailed from there on the 21st of September. Hopefully you've had that by the time you get this. There'll be some good photos on those, from the Rockies and Quebec mainly. I'm unsure of whether to send the next load, we've six rolls to develop, but if I do they'll be in two lots of three, and you can get them all done in one go and developed as MATTE (tick box on the envelope). Seems better if they're matte. [Not going to send them now. 26/10]

OK, I hope the other letter turns up as it was long and had detail on Vancouver → Montreal. I won't mention any of that in this letter. A brief update then: Called in to Toronto around the 18th of September. Kim and Heather are great, they put us up at their cosy little flat. From there, we crossed into the USA no problem, down to Niagara Falls (check your maps now) and across through Albany to Boston, Cape Cod, Philadelphia, Atlantic City, New York (staying at John's mother's, which was just across the river from NY), Washington. Followed Blue Ridge Parkway all the way down to Knoxville in Tennessee. That was 3,200 miles in nearly four weeks, costing £80 in petrol. I'll go into more detail later on. [Probably 4,500 miles now]

So, everything seems OK at the moment. Had quite a good mix of cities and nature. No problems really, apart from getting moved on a few times by park rangers, etc. Still, we've done well I guess, spending most nights parked up at rest areas (like motorway services, only better), so costing nothing. Money's lasting out very well, as there are no major expenses.

I'm updating this now after Nashville, where on Saturday the 17th we actually checked into a motel so we could have a night on the town. Pretty good to have a real bed, a TV, and a hot, full bath. I'll save this day's details too, and try to keep it in order I suppose.

I can see that I'm a long way back, and so probably won't go into much detail, but I'll give you an idea of some of the things we've been up to.

Had a great time with Kim and Heather in Toronto. Nice girls, seem happy enough where they are and know what they want. Did the touristy thing here and went up the CN tower, tallest in the world, going up over a thousand feet in sixty seconds. Below was the SkyDome, with its sliding roof. It's the stadium the Blue Jays baseball team plays in and we could watch them playing quite well on this clear sunny day. We could also see the sprawling metropolis and adjoining cities going round the lakeshore.

Left there on the 22nd of September and drove the hundred miles to Niagara Falls and the US border. As the falls is on the border, we viewed them and went on the platform at the base (in our free plastic bag coats) on the Canadian side first. On paper the falls aren't as high as a lot we've seen, but looking at the 36 million gallons of water a minute that flows over they look awesome. The Horseshoe Falls kick up mist and spray, making rainbows on the sunny, perfect day. Very busy there. We drove over the border no problems, though had to go and fill in a form for a fresh three-month visa (so we've got til the 22nd of December). There is a different angle to view the falls from on the US side. You can even walk to the 'island' between the two falls. Seems like you can stand right on the edge of the drop. As the sun set it was quite impressive, it almost seemed to turn green. At 8 p.m. they turned on spots to illuminate them, the mist shining white. Very impressed. Now only fifty percent of the total river goes over the falls, as the rest is diverted for hydroelectric generation.

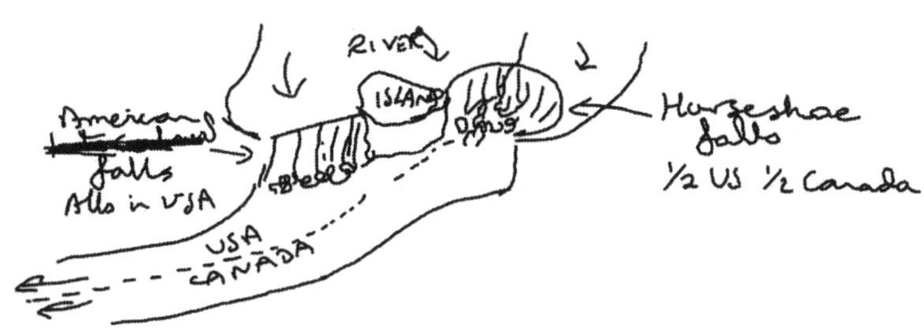

Spent the night in a state park, but it was closed for the season so we could park up for free. In the clear morning we could see Toronto across Lake Ontario. Spent the day driving along the lakeshore, past the small communities and smart lakeshore properties, communities that seem to survive on agriculture and antique sales. Plenty of apple trees in this area. East of the nothing town of Syracuse, heading into New England, the trees were just beginning to change colour as autumn, sorry, fall, approached. The villages here were very nice, the slatted wooden-style houses (though probably now UPVC) surrounded by trees and no fences, no hedges, no visible signs of a house owner's own land. Seems so much better for that. Flying USA flags by front doors. Another overnighter in a state park on a lake. The state parks are something else. Very well set up, usually. Loads of picnic benches, barbeques, and often camping places.

Drove eastward the next day through Albany. Stopped here when we saw a Clinton/Gore rally and thought that the next US president may be there, but wasn't. Had a look and tour around the capitol building, as Albany is actually the capitol of New York State (No, I didn't know that either!). Not much of a city really, mostly commerce. The view from the observation deck in a tower block showed that it wasn't too big. The capitol building was another prime example of vast expense to create a place for the politicians, though very nice inside the stone structure of the 1800s.

Moved on east, passing through the spotless and grand town of Williamstown, with its smart college and old college buildings. Mainly stone and brick houses, making it much different to most other towns in the area. The road rose and fell up and down over the hills and mountains, with gradually more and more colourful trees. When we climbed right up to a hilltop on the Massachusetts border (trying hard to get that Bee Gees song out of my head), we had a view of the tree-lined hills and river valleys. It's funny, but everything we see or go to has either a song or T.V. show or movie going through my mind. Living over here is like being in a film, I'm sure.

Next stop was Boston, where they film Cheers! We parked up on a roadside stop, all legal, only to be woken up at 12:45 a.m. by a policeman. Had to stand in front of his vehicle. He checked licenses, registration, details, and then said 'have a nice night', so we then knew it was OK. First we thought we'd be in trouble. Mark said that when I went into the van to get the documents he pulled his gun on me. Lucky I didn't see that.

Anyway, nice to know that it's OK to stop in these places. Driving into Boston I'd read that "drivers and pedestrians here are somewhere between homicidal and suicidal," which proved to be spot on. To avoid the chaos of the city centre on this now Saturday, we planned to park on the outskirts and get the metro in, but unfortunately it began to rain, so it was not nice for walking about. Instead, we stayed in the outskirts in the Harvard area. "I went to Harvard University." Well, OK, I was there half an hour! Quite nice, some grand old stone buildings. Avoided the rain by watching a movie then driving to the outskirts to a state park for the night.

Sunday was dry and clear, and free parking, so we drove in as far as we dared. There is a 'freedom trail', a big red line that guides you around the city to points of interest; a lot of historical buildings surrounded by shiny mirror glass tower blocks. Unfortunately most of the 'points of interest' were about the American Revolution, as this is where it began. There was the Boston Tea Party, where tea was dumped in the harbour in protest to British tea taxes in 1775. There was a big battle, one of the first, on Bunker Hill. The colonials (Yankees) dug themselves in on the hill. There were 1,200 Yanks and 2,200 British, and it took two hours for the British to take the forfeited position, yet the Americans seem to describe it as a victory. Very odd. As well as history, there were some nice city areas; the posh markets and cafes in Quincy Market and Little Italy.

Left Boston going south along the east coast getting down to a state park just after Plymouth, where the replica of the Mayflower (Pilgrim's boat) is moored. Tiny boat carried a hundred or more over in the 1620s. Really touristy area now.

Just south of here was Cape Cod, a big sandy hook, and actually the area where the pilgrims landed. A national park is at the top, but driving out to Provincetown on the very top narrow end took us past lots of motels on the beaches. The national park was untouched, with dunes and lakes and grass and long, long beaches. Provincetown was a nice, small street town of old houses, similar to any old town on the Devon coast, though the beach there was full of poles and boat moorings and launches. Hot, sunny day, so we strolled along long beaches in the park. The beaches had steep dunes behind them, very narrow with a very sharp drop into the sea causing big waves.

Drove on to Providence, the capitol of Rhode Island, which is tiny; in fact, we drove through the state into Connecticut in a half hour. Very scenic though, this area now full of red and green and yellow trees on the edges of lakes, wow. Pulled in to look at some of this and got chatting to a guy taking out his canoe to do some fishing. It was around 6 p.m. He invited us, so we paddled around the lake, under a road bridge they'd built through the lake. He supplied us with Bass beer while he tried to catch bass (no good). Stayed out on the lake until the sun set and until dark. Relaxing and calm out on the lake. So still, with the mist settling as it got cooler.

On Tuesday the 29th of September, we headed down to New York, a nice 'scenic' drive along country lanes through more colourful trees. Seemed easy to get to John's mother's house, which is actually in New Jersey, so we could avoid NY City. That was in theory, but we ended up being forced through Manhattan at 3 in the afternoon. Not too bad really, though lots of road works in the city. John's mother was in a good spot for us, a safe distance away but easy to get in by bus and tube (not worth driving in).

She'd cooked us a stew and a Slovakian cabbage roll, which was excellent. Nice to get a shower and bed and have a meal cooked. She was a great lady, though as she's old she could only put us up two nights, so we had one whole day to sightsee NY. John and Sue phoned us while we were there and all was well. Planned our sightseeing very carefully to make sure we could do it all in one go.

Bright and early we set off, getting two buses to the subway across to NY and the World Trade Centre. Very diverse and run down in Jersey City. In lower Manhattan, where the W.T.C. is, is all the commercial stuff; Wall St., etc. It's so clean, full of white people with suits and big, big old buildings. The tower blocks are all so close and high, you'd never know that the sun was shining, as you're always in some shadow.

The WTC buildings are the tallest in the world, one having 110 floors. Visited the NY Stock Exchange where a viewing platform let us watch the hectic paper waving on the floor, full of T.V. screens showing latest prices. (Trading places). A short walk from there we got a ferry from Battery Park to the Statue of Liberty. It seemed smaller than I imagined (though it was tough to get up 350 steps to the view from the crown). Good views of the cramped Manhattan skyline from the ferry. Not too busy. Interesting inside the statue, a maze of framework keeps the bronze plates in place.

Caught the ferry back and the subway to the Greenwich Village area. This is an area with cafes, clubs, handicraft stores, etc., but really a pit. Very grubby and run down. The whole city is chaos on the streets and crumbling away, scaffolding all over. Hard to describe the mid-Manhattan area; smaller buildings, wider streets, but still a mess. Horns blaring, yellow taxis everywhere. The Empire State Building was just a little north, so we went up that to the 80th floor (1,000 feet) and 102nd (1,250 feet). There are nets around the base to catch masonry that's falling off. Great building inside. Views from the top on the clear day were amazing. So built up.

One patch of green; Central Park. Manhattan Island is skirted by river. Not so built up off the island, in Brooklyn for example. Strolled north along Broadway (another song) past cinemas and theatres. Nothing special, a lot of neon and billboards. We went up to Central Park and caught the tube and buses back before it got dark. The tubes weren't too rough, no graffiti! Crossed back to Jersey City, like I said, a real slum area. The people living there have wrecked the place, burnt out buildings, graffiti, etc.

Mary's area just south in Bayonne is quite pleasant, and it was odd on the bus how suddenly it changed from no white to all white passengers. Tea was waiting when we arrived! It's tough to think that you can't step out after dark without fear of being massacred. TV news was as bad as any horror or violence movie, only for real. Glad we'd done it and were getting out the next day. Lucky Mary lived where she did. I guess NY is a good place for a tourist, it's certainly good to see so much famous stuff, but hell otherwise.

Mary had been telling us of trips to Atlantic City, a gambling city just south, enough to make us take a trip down there. Drove along the wild Atlantic coast. Endlessly built up, one little town rolling into another, though most of the motels, etc., seemed deserted or derelict. (This trip was 150 miles!) The whole coast seemed spoilt by all this. Lots of deserted holiday homes all crammed together in a few spots.

On the outskirts of Atlantic City it was quite swampy land. City only 30,000 (tiny). The residential area was a real mess, more ruined houses. The only saving grace of the city was the casinos on the boardwalk on the seafront. All the big names were there; Caesars, Sands, and three of

Donald Trump's, including the biggest, flashiest of all: the Taj Mahal. Though none of them were like the outrageous ones in Las Vegas, this one had big coloured domes and massive chandeliers. They were all full of OAPs throwing 25¢ into slot machines. We spent the night in the Taj Mahal, well it was the best! In fact, it had a free car park and was open 24 hours so we crashed in the van in there. Easy! Still, they got a few dollars as we lost in the casino. Too expensive to play anything but the slots. Roulette or card games were a minimum of $5, maximum of $10,000. The boardwalk was quiet. Slept in the van, and at 8 a.m. people were still going strong in the casino. Big area (football pitch) full of these flashing, jangling things. Jackpots were probably hundreds of thousands.

We had no reason to stay here longer, so we headed inland to Philadelphia (Freedom – Elton John). Now in Pennsylvania. This was the big place in the independence era of the 1870s. Declaration of Independence was written here, agreed upon here, etc., even before they'd finished fighting with the Brits. Parked up at the end of Benjamin Franklin Boulevard with its wide street and international flags (Champs Elysees of PA). Ben Franklin was a main man in the independence saga, as well as a great scientist. City Hall, a great big stone effort of 1907, had the tallest tower of the time at 500 ft. Views from here were good, showing the big city which is not built upwards too much. Very hazy, polluted sky. In one area were the heritage buildings, restored well, of independence. The Liberty Bell, Independence Hall, red brick with white cornering, cobbled streets. Quite nice area. The visitors centre had a movie on history. Learned a lot about independence and who did what. One little street showed the real old houses, though it was only a 6 ft wide cobbled street, just around the corner from wide streets with flashy shopping malls.

Another impressive structure (not out, but inside) of 1800s was the Masonic Temple, though we had to roll up our trouser legs to get in! Inside were seven halls used for meetings. Each was in a different style, one was Egyptian with hieroglyphics and sphinx, etc., another Greek-style (pillars and statues), etc. What was impressive as well as the amazing detail and accuracy of all this was that the marble pillars or wooden beams (Norman style) were all just normal plaster tarted up to look like whatever, and done well. It fooled me!

Drove west out of the city to a nice state park. We got moved along as it got dark, before stopping overnight in another state park. In the morning we were at a lakeside, with hardy fishermen out on the misty lake. Spent the morning relaxing as it was a great, hot, sunny day. Took our time driving down more country roads south toward Baltimore. On these back lanes we came across communities of Amish, driving their horse-drawn carriages along the road, in their hats, beards, and costumes (ever see Witness- for real). All corn (sweetcorn) fields here, and harvested by horse and donkey-pulled equipment, by workers still in costume. Men wear braces and straw hats, women wear lace hats and strapped dresses. Bonnets I guess. Funny to see them so neat, yet in the fields. It was like being in the past.

Stopped at a state park on a riverside in a bit of a steep-sided river valley; rocky river, nice trees. Seemed safe, but a ranger booted us out at 12:30. This one was closed but we couldn't stay. Drove on to a service station on the main highway. The next day we headed on through Baltimore without stopping, and on the 30 miles to Washington DC. Being a Sunday the city was quieter on the roads and had no parking fees or problems. We checked out the Washington Redskins stadium on the way in case they were playing, but they weren't.

At the heart of the city is the Capitol Building and the 'mall', a two mile long rectangular area lined with national buildings; museums, galleries, monuments, etc., all free!! Walking in to the centre to the back of the Capitol Building it looked impressive with its clean white dome and big marble steps. Went in and had a free tour of the building. Under the dome is the rotunda, a big circular 'room' with six massive paintings of American history. There was a detailed painting in the dome and a brown and white painting circling the lowest ring of the dome. This told history, too, but it was clever as it looked three-dimensional. Very smart inside. In another hall were statues; every state supplied the government with two statues of its most famous or recognized children. Checked out the House of Representatives and Senate rooms. In the House of Reps there were no desks, only seats. Obviously these were quite immaculate too.

Getting out and to the mall side, the building looks straight down over a 'reflecting pool' to the Washington Monument, a 555 ft needle, down all the way to the Lincoln Memorial.

The sides of the mall are flanked with the grand pillared stone buildings, of which there are many around the city, including the Smithsonian buildings. On the grass area were some medieval costumed people displaying old armour, etc., from Europe. At the river's end was the large marble building housing a massive statue of a seated Lincoln and carved inscription of his inaugural speech. Apparently he saved the Union in 1865, before being shot. Also near there was the Vietnam Memorial, a black marble construction containing 58,000 names.

Checked out the Air and Space Museum, which was excellent. They had the Wright brother's plane, some Apollo spacecraft, rooms full of whole planes, and nuclear missiles. Had a cheap IMAX movie, one of those massive-screen ones. Saw a film made from the space shuttle of the earth. Brilliant, but depressing, as man's destruction can be seen from up there.

While in DC we stayed overnight in the rest areas about 25 miles from the city. It made sense, as the nearest campground was twenty miles and $25 for a tent site!

Our next day was boiling hot. We drove around the city on the ring road to the southwest side, in fact now Arlington, Virginia. DC is very small, being only Washington city. The suburbs are either Maryland or Virginia. In Arlington was the cemetery where JFK and his brother are buried. A nice location on a hill looking across Potomac River to the landmark of Washington. There was an inscription of his inaugural speech, too, "ask not what America can do for you..." etc. Quite a few people there.

Spent a while in the city centre trying to locate our mail, but the address we'd told you was a little out of date (if three years is a little!). Then we visited the zoo! Well, it was free. Saw the giant pandas given to Nixon by the Chinese in the 70s. The male was big and lazy. Nicely kept, but the animals were in smallish enclosures of mainly concrete. Rhinos and hippos were cool. Near to the zoo was Rock Creek Park, a large area of grass, picnic areas, and the pleasant little rocky river. So close to the city centre, for the people to have a break from city life. Mind you, this city was not chaotic or full of high rises, but more official, with those grand buildings.

We still had loads to see the next day, so we drove in part of the way and caught the clean, comfortable tube right into the city centre. We would have done the White

House tour, but billions of people were being shuffled through so we decided it was unnecessary. Queued to go up to the observation inside the Washington Monument. It was a nice sunny day, so when we did get the lift up we had good views up and down the mall. It was built in the 1800s. We then strolled around the fence around the White House. The previous day we'd seen the president leave in an army helicopter from the W.H. lawn! Nice area with Lafayette Park at the back and more state buildings and statues.

Visited the National Geographic Exhibition Hall, which displayed things on world history (physical) with computer interactive displays and a 17 ft diameter globe, which rotated to pinpoint things of interest. Educational. Some great photographs and books available. In search of more photo stuff, we visited the Ansel Adams exhibit. He was a photographer from the 40s and 50s (black and white) who took amazing photos around the California area (Yosemite etc.). Class.

Still had time to do the FBI HQ tour, an hour or so. It was a newer building, and the tour told of what they do and all the data they hold on everything from paint types to weapon types, millions of fingerprints, etc. This building was like a massive data bank that agents use to call on when investigating crimes that are interstate (so becoming federal). (Silence of the Lambs). Finished off with a live firearms display, with a 'special agent' demonstrating the lethal weapons the other agents use. Frightening. They need good stuff, though, to combat the massive amount of mad gun users.

Another interesting place was what used to be Union Station (rail) now converted to a mall. It was a grand place, as you imagine the old stations. Caught a movie, then took the metro out.

The last thing we had to visit the next day was the Pentagon. A five-sided, five-floored, five-ringed building; the biggest 'office' block in the world, with 24,000 people. This is where all the forces are run from. Had a tour. Inside are shops, too, like a city. The corridors are full of flags, models, medals, and memorabilia. There's even a five acre area in the centre! Drove west out of the city into Virginia into rolling hills and fields.

Over the next week we'd drive along the Blue Ridge Mountains, a 580 mile drive heading southwest toward Tennessee. The first hundred miles was Shenandoah National Park, and the 'Skyline Drive'. The road, built by welfare workers in the 30s, climbs up to 4,000 ft, winding along the ridges. Overlooks, picnic areas, hiking trails, and other points of interest are spread all along it. It took us three days to cover the hundred miles, doing plenty of walking to stunning waterfalls and up to mountain peaks. All good exercise. The second night we even 'back country camped' in our tent. Luckily the weather was clear and there was a full moon. We tried to get away with parking up in the van, but a ranger said we had to go down the trail and put up our tent in the woods. No proper sites here; there were only the sounds of rushing water and birds (no bears luckily) to accompany us.

All the mountain ridges, right down to Tennessee, were covered with trees changing colour. It was about peak time for full colour. All the time we'd stop and admire the colours from high viewpoints on the drive. It got even more amazing further south. So many reds and bright yellows. Wow: A billion classic photos (I hope). At the national park it was just the one ridge of the mountains, a big valley, and then another ridge to the west. Going south the ridges appeared more on both sides and the peaks got higher. It was true, as the mist and haze (pollution?) blurred out distant ridges they did look blue. After a hundred miles the road became the Blue Ridge Parkway [Oh. "Blue Ridge Mountains of Virginia..." yet another song], a 469 mile park. This 'park' was only the width of the road, so there were not many trails to walk, though we broke up the drive over four days by doing a few, taking full advantage of the picnic areas and overlooks as the weather was just perfect; clear skies and 70s.

Did a detour off the parkway to visit the 'Natural Bridge', which we didn't see ($7), but it was funny to see tour buses and a massive souvenir shop selling natural bridge T-shirts, dishcloths, everything. It's only a river-cut tunnel! George Washington carved his initials on it! Wow!

No, it was so good to get out into nature and fresh (nearly) air. The roads were quiet in the main until we reached the end of the parkway, where it became the Great Smoky Mountains on the North Carolina/Tennessee border. Views from peaks in the early morning showed brown mist polluting the area. Peaks here are over 6,000 ft. Nice views. The roads here in this fifty-mile park were crazy, not as well-organized as the previous parks. Drove through the Smokies in one day. Again more colourful trees, streams, and mountain viewpoints, including the highest in Tennessee at 6,643 ft, driving nearly all the way up. Did more walking trails, actually meeting a bear and two cubs. They seemed very tame, getting quite close. People were freaking out to get photos (including Mark).

Great week though; leisurely pace, nice weather, plenty of exercise, good food, and brilliant scenery. So lucky to hit the area at such a perfect fall colour time. Everywhere looked like something from a classic photo book, though parts of the Blue Ridge Parkway stretch had been destroyed by farming, being meadows. Glad the van made it up and down those mountains, too. So, again, imagine driving from Land's End to John o' Groats on one road and seeing nothing but mountains, trees, and valleys, mainly unspoilt. Well, that was it. I say unspoilt, but actually the first national park was reclaimed from farmers who'd devastated the forest.

This drive had taken us up to October 16th, being near Knoxville, Tennessee. Heading east towards Nashville we drove through Knoxville. The main attraction of this city is that three big interstates intersect here! It was that good. Instead, we stopped at Oak Ridge. It was here that they built a town in the war to do research into nuclear weapons and the nuclear process. There is now a big energy research centre there, employing 5,000. Remaining as a historical treasure is the graphite nuclear reactor they built in 1942 as part of the development of radioactive materials. A big wall full of plugs (bungs) is all that you can see of the reactor of graphite blocks. This was still running until 1962, when they shut it down. Also in the town was the Museum of Science and Energy, with practical displays. Interesting. Saw a lecture on 'atoms' and their makeup and splitting. The lecturer was very good and informative, also telling Mark that if all the space were removed from him he'd be the same weight, but microscopic. Now we know about neutrons, protons, electrons. Well, I was reminded of what I'd forgotten from physics classes.

Drove on to Nashville, with an overnight stop on the way, about 200 miles away. It was a Saturday, and a nice day too. We'd decided to splash out on a motel for a treat and have a night out to sample the country and western bars. Took a while to find a place that was cheap and not too far away. Got one three miles from the city centre, $30 (£17) for two double beds, a T.V, and a bathroom. The street it was on led to downtown so it was easy. The area had lots of tyre fitters, so we got new used tyres, or 'tires,' put on. Did the real American Saturday thing; crashed on the bed watching live college football (Tennessee vs Alabama), with a bottle of beer in one hand and tortillas in the other. What a life. In fact, we'd passed all the fans driving to Knoxville for the game as we approached Nashville. The game, a 'college' game, had a crowd of 98,000 and the good game lasted three hours, with cheerleaders and massive marching bands. This happens all over the country every weekend.

Had a soak in the bath before heading into town. Very quiet. We searched for a place to eat 'southern food' and sample the C&W, but were surprised to find none of that. The only C&W bar we found charged $5 to get in, but we didn't go in, even though they were playing "we'll have some fun on the bayou." Very few music bars. Instead of finding a southern restaurant we had a fast food meal in a cafe, but chatted to the owner for ages about world travel. First place we checked out had mellow bluesy music and sharply-dressed people, mainly older. No hats and boots!? Found a little bar next to that where a young lad, Bobby Beaver (his real name?), played country songs. That was good. Moved on to a bluegrass bar where a few old boys plucked banjos and guitars, but it was very dead in there. An alternative music bar next door was no good, so we went to a club near where we started. It was all on one small street. In here, I got in free as it's my birthday, and they had a great band playing normal stuff (Gloria Estefan, Pink Floyd, etc.). So, we'd sampled a load of different sounds in "Music City", but it was not what I'd expected to see.

Stayed in the motel til chuck-out time before driving down to the city centre. 'Music Row' had some souvenir shops (Jonny Cash, Hank Williams Jr., etc. all having their own) and Country Hall of Fame, etc. Very small area, not much there at all. Expected more. One thing Nashville is known for (though I didn't know it) is its replica of the Parthenon of Athens, in this "Athens of the South". Not really like the original, a brown concretey colour. A sunny day. In the park where this was was a music show in the bandstand. About ten acts came on and played a couple of their own songs, mainly acoustic guitar songs. All very good. A lot of talent here.

Also, Nashville was home of the 'Grand Ole Opry', the breeding ground for country stars of the past. Nowadays it's moved to "Opryland," a big and expensive amusement park. Even something as dull as country music can't escape capitalist exploitation to triviality (sounds good!). One amazing thing, though, is the big hotel at Opryland. Inside are two massive courtyards with a glass roof, full of palms and tropical plants, waterfalls, and a rotating restaurant. All the rooms have balconies that overlook all this. Very classy and well done. Not as good as our van though!

We wanted a real southern meal, but struggled to find one, so resorted to "Cracker Barrel," a chain of restaurants serving old country cooking. It was good though; wooden chairs and a log fire, but busy and had that hurried feel. Excellent food, sampling hickory smoked ham (hmmm), biscuits (like scones), grits (corn stuff like rice pudding), and apple strudel cake. Very nice. We'd had a motel room, a big meal out, another meal out, and a night out at a half dozen bars for $40 each (£25). Not bad.

Nashville wasn't quite what I'd expected. The city centre was very small and quiet. My hopes were matched, though, when we visited a small bar before leaving the city. A 'bluegrass' bar, where on a Sunday night the locals have a jam. A small, low-roofed, dark bar with posters and photos of old events and stars. Only a few people there, apart from the fifteen or so people who'd come with banjos, guitars, violins to play that bluegrass thing. Brilliant. Most of the guys were so cool as they played. Foot tapping, but after an hour it all sounds the same. This was what I'd wanted to see, though!

OK, so I've moved on to New Orleans on the 26th of October. Picked up the mail OK. Thanks. Some great letters. Lots of gossip! So, in between the above two lines we've 'done' Graceland (excellent and very interesting), Memphis, and a few other places on the way to New Orleans, seen plantations, swamps, and all the deep south stuff, and eaten (wait for this...) catfish... oysters (!!)... gumbo (a thick seafood soupy thing), jambalaya, pecan pie, red beans and rice. Real southern style! New Orleans is excellent, the French Quarter was "buzzing" when we went on Saturday. Jazz, blues, rock, all there. Nice wrought ironwork on balconies, etc. Off to Florida soon. Oh, and I won $85 at the races!!

Still, more of all this another day. As for now, glad all's well there. Apologies again for not writing before, but this drags out and I waited for your letters. I've just bought a real camera, so wait for the bill; I was going to get a cheap one, but got a decent one (manual) with all the lenses, etc., for $75, which is still very cheap really. This is my life camera now (investment!). I'm going to be into photography, so watch out.

Next. Souvenirs. I wanted to get something from Graceland, but it was expensive junk, and made in China, so not really genuine. So, I thought, if you want (I mean really want) or need anything then I'll fetch stuff back, because it's bound to be cheaper here. Anything, so long as it's a) easy to carry, b) easy to get hold of, c) less than £250, d) isn't a simple electrical item, as USA is 110 V, though I can get 240 V in more complex goods (TVs, videos, CDs... though I doubt you want that). This offer is valid til whenever and goes for y'all there. Better than wasting cash on junky souvenirs that don't really mean much. Try and decide so that when I phone later we can sort something out.

We'll be touring Florida for a while and get a flight just before we know we're finished, as we can't go til we sell the van. Disney World is the next biggy, I suppose. I'll maybe get something for the kids from there, as I know there'll be endless goodies there.

It was nice to get mail at last. The letter was from Vicky (Lufbra). She's back in the UK after touring Australia.

Take care and I'll phone soon.

Love

Dave

PS. Won't send films now, OK, so no need to expect them.

Somewhere hot and sunny,

Florida

Hello,

Just a brief letter (yes, I always start like this) to let you know all's well and a few other things.

Firstly, at the moment we're in Naples, southwest Florida. It's 86° or more, and we're lazing on the beach. I'll say something about what I've been up to later.

OK, changed my mind about the photos, as it'll be a few weeks before I return, so it'll give them a chance to be developed. We'll send a couple of packs of four I think, as we have eight films now. I've also had a film developed here from my new camera. Pretty good, though I used it as a test for a few things. Enclosed a couple of reprints they did by accident, which show wide and telephoto shots. A few bits on the negatives were done by the developing place, but they're generally good. Used 200 film, so they're not so sharp. Also, will send a few other leaflets and bits of info back with the films to take up the weight to the limit for that price.

Next, I enclosed a few postcards. Spending plenty of time browsing around shops and malls, of which there are endless ones. Seen so many bargains, or should I say, it seems so much cheaper. If you do want anything, like for Xmas or something, then let me know. What I thought is, we'll be returning to Orlando in a couple of weeks, as we have still days left for Disney World, and so you could write to me there. If you have any ideas, just note them down and the British price, and I'll check them out here and call you later on. That goes for camera stuff too. I've put in some prices for cameras, though Sears isn't the cheapest. Places like K-Mart and Walmart have very cheap goods; everything from clothes to electronics. For example, I bought myself a jacket (a winter ski-type one, nice and shiny) for $25 (£15). The Orlando address will be at the end of the letter.

I think I'll tell you details from Memphis onward when I send the films, but I'll say that Walt Disney World was just amazing. Endless things to do. High-tech rides, well organized, no waiting. Not too busy, so that helped. Also, World Showcase had buildings and restaurants of various countries, including Rose & Crown pub from somewhere (can't remember). We even saw the fireworks display (which they have nightly!) on November 5th, though no scarves or woolies needed for this one (even though it was at 9 p.m.). Still taking advantage of the 'free' stops for overnight. Not travelling very far now, taking it easy.

Watched Tampa Bay get humiliated by the Minnesota Vikings in American football; it was a poor game, but I got a feel for the American family sport, with everyone having barbeques in the car park before the game. Will check out the swamps of the Everglades soon, Miami (briefly), and then go up the east side back towards Orlando. Hopefully we can set ourselves up somewhere on the coast near Orlando to sell the van, etc., before we come back. I have a visa til the 23rd of Dec., so I'll be back by Xmas I suppose.

Oh, well, it's time to leave the beach after a dip in the warm Gulf Stream, as with everything in Florida you have to pay to park near the beach, when you can squeeze past the condos and motels that have 2 ft between them. No, this side's not bad, quite posh even. I think the Miami side is even more developed.

Enough for now, hope that's it. Hope you're better, Dad. Will be in touch again soon.

Love

David.

Orlando:

American Express Travel Service,
2 W Church St, Ste 1,
Sun Bank Centre
Orlando, Florida 32801